St. Louis Woman

Two facets of Helen
Traubel's career:
As Isolde in *Tristan und Isolde*
and with Jimmy Durante
in television.

NBC Photo

St. Louis Woman

by

HELEN TRAUBEL

IN COLLABORATION WITH RICHARD G. HUBLER

WITH AN INTRODUCTION BY VINCENT SHEEAN

Duell, Sloan and Pearce   New York

First Edition

Traubel, Helen. St. Louis woman. In collaboration with Richard G. Hubler.
With an introd. by Vincent Sheean. [1st ed.] New York, Duell, Sloan and
Pearce [1959] 296 p. 21 cm. Autobiography. 1. Musicians—Corre-
spondence, reminiscences, etc. 1. Title. ML420.T75A3 927.8 59-5557 ‡
Library of Congress

MANUFACTURED IN THE UNITED STATES OF AMERICA

VAN REES PRESS • NEW YORK

With love, to Bill

Contents

Introduction by Vincent Sheean   ix

1. *Brünnhilde in the Bushes*   3

2. *Chanteuse in Pigtails*   14

3. *Kid in the Front Row Center*   24

4. *Lulu in the Highest*   33

5. *Rubberneck with a Song*   43

6. *Damrosch and the "Man"*   56

7. *The Ego, Bill and I*   71

8. *First Concert and the Met*   88

9. *How It Feels to Sing*   106

10. *Behind the Met Scenery*   121

11. *Costumes and Critics*   133

12. *The Diva Settles Down*   146

13. *Olé, South America!*   159

14. *The Golden Chords*   169

15. *Wagner, I Love You!*   179

16. *A Blow for Liberty*   193

17. *L'Affaire Margaret*   203

18. *Bing, Bang, and Bangkok*   217

19. *The Last of the Met*   232

20. *Night Clubs, Movies, Television*   245

21. *The End of a Beginning*   261

      Appendix   275

Introduction

HELEN TRAUBEL is as American as Mark Twain. In some ways she even reminds me of him—not just because she hails from Missouri, but because the extraordinary range of her aesthetic being is akin to his. Mark Twain's gift was deep and high; his classical English was a kind of superstructure over the unlettered dialect, so spring pure and April fresh, of Huckleberry Finn. We think of him when Miss Traubel gets herself a "four-dollar hairdo" to go and sing her first New York recital at the Town Hall—a recital given over to Gluck, Beethoven, Schubert, and Wagner.

But Miss Traubel has an extra element that was not in Mark Twain, that of the German heritage. She describes herself as a "krautgirl" who had her own *Schimpflexikon,* and there are passages in her remarkable career which bear this out in full. Stubborn, determined on her own way, unwilling to sing until she felt herself fully prepared, she made a career which bears no resemblance to any other. At one end of her aesthetic scale there is the Immolation Scene from *Götterdämmerung,* which, as she did it with Toscanini in Carnegie Hall in 1941, was the most superb performance of Wagner's music I have ever heard anywhere. At the other there is the equally immortal but **unimagi-**

ix

nably different "St. Louis Blues," a folk song, as she says, from her native village.

The word "krautgirl," which I have learned for the first time from this book, supplies one of the reasons for Traubel's capacity to absorb and give forth Wagner's music without any training whatsoever in Europe. She had the language and the aptitude for its music from birth. She was therefore more privileged than the other American singers of our time, who have had to learn very laboriously indeed some things which to Traubel came by nature. This is not to contradict my original statement: she still is as American as it is possible to be, but for her own particular career she had an ancestral advantage. Her German mother was the greatest singer she ever heard in her life, she says.

She had many other advantages by nature, aside from that memorable voice. She came to opera with a constitution that was proof against the severest strains. There was one season during the 1940's when she sang twenty-five evenings at the Metropolitan in New York besides all her opera and concert performances elsewhere. Twenty-five opera evenings would not be startling in lesser music, but these were almost all Brünnhilde and Isolde, with Sieglinde now and then to relieve the stress. The physical power and stamina required for such work are at least equal to that demanded of the greatest athlete: voice and musicianship cannot, all alone, supply them.

Prowess, this is—phenomenal prowess. But the listeners of the past twenty years know that Traubel in Wagner's music was far more than a marathon runner. She had a very nearly ideal adaptation by nature, voice, musicianship, and physique to the superhuman demands of these works. Very nearly, I say, because of course Wagner did ask the impossible. No slim little Irish princess of sixteen would ever be able to sing the music he wrote for Isolde, and no heroic soprano could gallop around the stage on a horse while singing the war whoops of Brünnhilde. These things are impossible and never have been done. Granting that the music requires a noble voice, great musical maturity and command, it is obvious that a Brünnhilde or an Isolde is likely to be at her best around the age of forty or afterward, and will sustain the heroic line best if she has throat, lungs, and diaphragm heroically developed and protected. Traubel was never a sylph, but when we look at the photographs of those who sang these parts in Wagner's own time we see that even he (in spite of his impossible demands) realized that no sylph could deal with this music. Those who want sylphs can go to the ballet.

The career of an American singer is beset by many pitfalls, traps, and ambuscades. One of the worst is premature success, and Traubel seems to have had a dread of that: hence her constant plea, in her youth, of "I am not ready." Better this than its brief, flashing, and worthless opposite. When she did come to the stage for which she was born, that of the Metropolitan Opera in the music of Wagner, she was entering an arena which had been dominated for several years by Kirsten Flagstad, an idol of the populace. There were at that moment a number of heroic sopranos who alternated with Flagstad in the four or five principal Wagner soprano parts. Within a short time they had vanished (even Flagstad, who remained in Norway after 1941), so that Traubel alone was asked to assume the full burden, and did. It is a curious example of the way in which life arranges a destiny: the circumstances demanded this of the singer just when she was ready to undertake the task, not too soon and not too late. Thus she had to learn and perform (for the first time anywhere) these exhausting and exacting parts, as Flagstad had done before her, so that within two or three seasons she acquired and projected her concepts of all three Brünnhildes, Isolde, and Kundry. Traubel and her predecessor were both phenomenal, of course, and very different, but they were alike in this: that both of them learned and tried out their heavy assignments right on the Metropolitan stage. Like Flagstad, Traubel knew only one Wagner part—the same one, Sieglinde—when she entered the Metropolitan.

One cannot easily pronounce upon the polemic that arose when Traubel left the Metropolitan company to sing in night clubs (with television and musical comedy afterward). She gives her own story fully in the book. The opera company's point of view was that she should do one or the other but not both, and she chose. To my mind this is a matter of the individual personality; it is a decision from within, not to be judged by others. "The St. Louis Blues" may have been Traubel's Huckleberry Finn, native and basic as no cultural superstructure could be. Moreover, years of Wagner's heaviest music are a cruel ordeal for voice, spirit, and body; nobody could be surprised if any woman (even a Brünnhilde) prefers, after a while, much less work for vastly more pay. I do suggest, however, that it may be precisely *because* Traubel is so completely American, so ultra-American, that she was able to make this extraordinary transition and succeed in it. It is difficult to think of her European peers (Leider, Lehmann, or Flagstad) engaging in any such enterprise: they were all much too self-conscious. To their way of thinking—and I can hear them saying it—no "serious" artist belongs in a night club at all; and if such a situation should by necessity arise, the artist should sing only "serious" music.

This point of view, which I attribute without authority to those illustrious singers, implies among other things a disregard for the milieu, for the framework, in which "serious" music would be very much out of place. Traubel, as I understand it on her own showing, determined to do her best in these new surroundings in accordance with the standards and demands of those surroundings. If this involved all sorts of horseplay she was ready for it and indeed it found an echo in her own consciousness: was she not a "krautgirl" with a laugh which could make everybody within earshot (which is something) laugh, too? She always had that laugh; it was not developed for night clubs or television; I remember it well from times before she had ever heard of such things. And if she sang the "Toreador Song" at the Copacabana in New York, as she seems to have done, I am sure that there was nobody in the audience who appreciated the joke more than Traubel herself.

America is a country in which social categories shift and change with cloudlike rapidity—this is partly why Europeans take so long to understand us—and the same phenomenon applies to the professional fields. Mark Twain was a pilot on the Mississippi; somehow or other that made him into the towering, super-American writer, or helped to do so; if he had not been so lazy he might have written almost any kind of classical work, and did a good few; *Huckleberry Finn* and *The Prince and the Pauper* are deeply connected. In music we have seen persons of talent move from one category to another with an ease almost unknown in Europe: Rosa Ponselle was a primary example, stepping out of vaudeville to the stage of the Metropolitan. In the past, when vaudeville was in flower, artists of the high categories (Bernhardt, Calvé) graced its programs often, although rather in a condescending manner—that is, they bestowed half an hour of their art upon the vaudeville public, at vast fees, after they were no longer able to sustain an entire evening in their own fields.

Traubel is unlike all others in that she made her fame at the highest level possible to a singer and then—while her voice was still unequaled for power and beauty—flung herself wholeheartedly into the realms of popular entertainment. It was in her nature to do so because, as a St. Louis woman with diamond rings, she felt at home there: laughter, even the most robustious laughter, never seemed to her incompatible with dignity. In the considerable weight which she avows, there is not one ounce of condescension.

Let us, even so, those of us who do not frequent night clubs or look at television, let us recall the magical sonorities of Miss Traubel's voice in the first act of *Tristan* or the last act of *Götterdämmerung*, long moments unequaled in our time for the evocation of a master's intention. The voice was superb, yes, and only one other in the world could compare with it, but beyond voice itself there was also that other quality ("Ruhe, ruhe du Gott!" in *Götterdämmerung*) which comes of absorption in the meaning of the music. We who heard those things, and treasure them in our ears, will never doubt that Helen Traubel was a "serious" artist.

VINCENT SHEEAN

St. Louis Woman

1

Brünnhilde in the Bushes

IT was a crisp winter evening in New York—November 1949—
when I attended my first opening night at the Metropolitan
Opera.

I had been singing star operatic roles for ten years in the great
circle. I had seen many such nights, of course, but I was always on
the opposite side of the footlights.

On this particular occasion I wanted to see how grand opera
looked from another point of view. It would be fun to find out
just how people enjoyed great music, why they came to hear it.

I am not quite sure of the opera that night. If it had been a
Wagnerian work, I would have been up there on the stage to sing
it—it was probably *La Bohème* by Puccini. I was dressed—or
undressed—in the height of fashion. A black dress covered as
little of me as possible; no jewelry; my red hair piled on top of
my head.

I arrived in the amphitheater of the opera house, feeling like a
princess in a fairy tale. I was escorted down the aisle by an old
friend. We had seats on the aisle—third row from the front.

It was about ten minutes to eight. I was prepared to gawk at the newcomers like a rubberneck from the country. Singing with the spotlight in my eyes, I rarely saw this kind of high life.

I kept twisting about, staring at everyone. The first couple I saw mincing down the aisle in tight white gowns were a pair of twins. They looked exactly alike. They were identical from white hair to white shoes to enormous blue-white diamond chokers. I put their ages at perhaps thirty or forty. I admired the daring downward swoop of their décolleté.

"Punch me in the ribs," I whispered to my escort, "if any more big game comes down the aisle when I'm not peeking." He nodded. A moment later I got his signal. A well-known New York society woman was bearing down on us, foam breaking across her bows. She swept past, and my eyes nearly fell into my lap.

"I know what's holding her head on," I said. "It's those diamonds like robin's eggs. But what holds her ears up?"

"She has her earrings wired on," my friend whispered.

She was seating herself in front of us. So I dropped my program and bent over to pick it up, meanwhile inspecting her ears. My God, he was right! The woman had platinum diamond-specked wires curled over her ears to help hold up their massive load of emeralds and diamonds.

The next moment I was overwhelmed by a seat mate. She was a woman who wore gorgeous rubies with exactly the same abandon that a Ubangi chief wears copper collars. She clasped me in her arms—a difficult feat, even at that time—and cried out her grateful recognition. I bruised my nose on a hundred thousand dollars' worth of rubies and embraced her, too.

"We love having you down here," she told me archly, "but we'd love having you up there even more."

At the time I had no idea that this meant she would leave after the first act, so I thanked her. I mentioned her decorations.

"Oh, these," she said, glancing down complacently at the crimson glitter. "I am very fond of them. They are brand new."

Overhearing us, the two all-white women down in front¬

dazzling except for the pink on their lips—turned around and smiled broadly at me. They waved, I waved, and they turned about again, still smiling.

"They're so friendly," I said in an undertone. "So young, too."

"They have to be friendly," my friend said in his wry undertone. "They're mother and daughter. The mother is over eighty. She has had her face lifted so many times that if she does anything but smile she cracks it. The daughter is over sixty."

At the end of the first act almost every single one of the gorgeous front-row attendees left. They had come, been seen, admired, and fulfilled what was for them the purpose of grand opera. There was really no reason to stay longer.

I left at the end of the first act, too. I went into another part of the house—the gallery.

I sat there, looking down at the stage. Suddenly I was overcome with the feeling that I wanted to cry.

The whole magnificent performance—with its musty scenery, silly costumes, traditional gestures, stiff formality, and exquisite music—was pathetic.

I saw my friends on the stage, singing out their hearts, giving all their art. I knew that of the packed thirty-five-hundred-person house, much less than 10 per cent had any enjoyment at all in the performance.

The whole world was not listening, as we had so often believed. I realized then that not even all the people in the audience came to listen to the opera.

Nearly all of them—students, socialites, tourists, habitués—were fonder of Sherry's bar on the third floor than the performance.

Most of them were snobs.

I was convinced then that it was chiefly snobbery alone that supported the opera house. Opera opening nights wherever they existed in the United States—and it was only in the Metropolitan Opera in New York City that any genuinely complete company remained in America—were on a par with a glorified society sideshow. The rest of the season was an exhibition of cultural hoity-toity for the vast majority of subscribers. The sweeping music and drama on the stage were simply a background for chitchat and preening, entertainment for a club for those who felt superior to keep them feeling so. Oddly enough, even a lot of the standees were snobs in the highest.

It was a moment of personal revelation. I began to see that instead of being in the center of the real musical world, I had been on the edge of it. I was insulated from the heart of appreciation and instinctive knowledge.

I had been singing for my own pleasure and the vanity of wealthy and powerful dilettantes who were able to support such institutions as the Metropolitan and deduct their grants from their income tax as a charity grandly donated to art.

I felt fiercely that art should need no charity. It should be its own reason for being. Great music—and opera contains the greatest music ever written—should go straight to the soul of people. It should not be something endowed, controlled, and directed by social fiat.

For me the music in the grand operas of our time is one of the finest crystallizations of art that have ever existed. I would suffer terribly if I could never hear opera again. I feel a daily, vital need for such music.

But let me say that I also feel a need for music that is classified as rock and roll. I remember I was sitting on the beach with my husband, Bill Bass, at Laguna one day in 1955. He was fooling with the dial of our portable radio. Suddenly I heard the heavy, accented, whanging chords of the music and the indistinguishable words of a singer.

"Please leave that on," I said.

I got up and walked around, snapping my fingers to the beat. It was a wonderful experience, humming the tune, learning the rhythm. It was three days before I found out it was Elvis Presley who was singing.

I cannot say I exactly admire his art, but I am very much impressed with his instinctive technique. Perhaps such rhythm and beat can give me a new dimension, teach me something about getting music to the kind of people that need it and want it—even if they do not know it—and will support it by millions of dimes rather than a dime's worth of millions.

Appearing at Chicago in a night club once, I opened my program by singing a charming Viennese waltz. In the middle of it a man in the audience leaped up. He clapped his hands and shouted: "Get hot, Helen, get hot!"

I do not think I missed a beat. I shouted back at him: "Give me time, give me time!"

I did get hot—later on in the program. This is the sort of applause I enjoy as much as the *"Brava! Brava! Encore!"* of the opera addicts.

Opera has a long way to go to catch up to popular music. I have sung successfully for years in both media. I can criticize opera as an old friend and praise popular music as a new admirer.

Opera is an old maid of the 1890's, bewildered but still haughty in the whirl of a rock-and-roll ball. It is confused as to what is happening to it. If it does not emerge from this state it will be a tragedy.

Opera is too long, text and music. The language is incomprehensible; it needs real translation into colloquial English. It should eliminate repetition and tradition. The creaky plots should be cleaned up. The acting and scenery must be drastically revised. Conventions, taboos, costumes have to be literally thrown out the nearest window.

As far as the ear is concerned, there is no greater delight than an opera. As far as the eye is concerned, there is nothing more disenchanting.

The difference between it and popular music—both of them use the same eight notes, lest anyone forget it—is that what is popular has to survive in the open market place. It has to submit itself to a democratic sampling in order to exist. It lets in the air and the sunlight, the freshness that music needs. It blows the dust out of the files of those shaky scores sanctified by custom alone.

It reflects the instinctive—and excellent—American feelings and taste. Why else is the single greatest international ambassador of good will for this country the exportation of jazz and its artists— such as *Porgy and Bess,* done everywhere in the world except the Met?

Perhaps popular music is perishable, but that is the fate of a great many lovely things. Who will be the judge to say what will survive and what will not a few years from now in our turbulent, changing world?

Nor can I say that popular music is all the American ear needs. Opera is a necessary part of our life, though it is so largely disregarded. It can become basic to our music if only the ideas and the approach are changed. What a wonderful idea it was to popularize the song "Martha" from Flotow's opera *Martha!* How many wonderful melodies there are in Wagner, Beethoven, and the other immortals!

Times change; with the times, the understanding of music changes. Not the eternal greatness of the masters but the way they are used in the modern world.

We are not the fusty Germans of Richard Wagner's nineteenth century. We are not the religious devotees and (even then) snobbish patrons of the eighteenth-century Johann Sebastian Bach. Most of the music that is considered "classical" antedates the whole foundation of our country. Yet America has gone ahead, dynamically revising the constitutional concepts which created it.

Is there any reason why music should not do the same? Should not music such as opera have its own Declaration of Independence from the past?

Perhaps I feel this so strongly because I am fond of enjoying people—and being enjoyed by them. Opera always tended to isolate the artist from the audience. Some artists have enjoyed it. I did not.

During the New York opera season, Bill and I used to live at Sixty-first Street and Park Avenue. We did a great deal of walking, looking in the store windows, watching them redecorate once a week. On every walk a few people would come up to me and say: "Oh, Madame Traubel, how we adored you in *Tristan und Isolde!*"—or whatever was the current presentation at the Metropolitan.

After I was a guest on some of the Jimmy Durante television shows in 1951, we had scores of people during each stroll running up to us, pumping my hand, and crying: "Helen, you were swell! When are you going to be on again?"

This was what I needed. For my ego, for my art—I was never sure. It is impossible to separate ego from art in most cases. I have never tried. It simply made me happier to be the second-person intimate than the first-person singular.

Starting in 1941 I was a regular guest on the radio Telephone Hour. I always had to sing one of the B's—Bach, Beethoven, Brahms—or the big W—Wagner. I wanted to do some popular songs but the sponsors never would let me.

"They don't expect that of Traubel," they would say. "You can't let your audiences down. Think how you would be murdered by the snobs! You can't mix the classical and the *common!*"

But I remembered rehearsing for the radio, having a ball with the orchestra and technicians. I could ham it up as I liked—winking at the oboe player, holding a high note, laughing as loud as I wanted to at the jokes. Everyone seemed to have as much fun as I did. As a matter of fact, that was where the co-producer for Durante's show first found me. He came into the studio early and heard the guffawing. He slipped in to find out what was causing it. He discovered it was only me, cutting the stays on my operatic corset and letting my hair down for the audience that really mattered. Months after he remembered their reaction well enough to book me for five Durante comedy shows, more encores than any other similar guest up to then.

I do not mean I never had fun in grand opera. I always did, especially with that tremendous tenor—tremendous in weight as well as voice—Lauritz Melchior. He and I were both big—*this* big—and we should never have played the romantic lovers, Siegfried and Brünnhilde—at least visually.

But there we were on stage—I being in the midst of a ring of gas-jet fire with a shield laid over me for punishment by Wotan. Lauritz would struggle over the hill, according to the plot, see me, and start back in astonishment. According to the libretto, I was the first woman he had ever seen. Naturally, he commenced singing at the top of his voice:

"What is this? This is no man!"

Just as naturally, in every performance, this set me giggling. Whatever else I am not, I am clearly identifiable to everyone as a woman.

My giggling would set the shield to quivering, then to rocking dangerously. Lauritz would commence to choke up with hysteria. The wings would be hissing with warning whispers: "Helen, stop your laughing—this is serious! Quit!"

My turn came. I would sweep up my yards of costume, stand and sing for five or six minutes hailing the sun, the moon, blades of grass, and everything else. Lauritz stood by with egg on his face, holding up his arms and making comments out of the side of his mouth, paying me back for my whispers about his performance a moment before.

No one ever tampers with a Wagner performance but I did manage to get my way about the scenery. That is, the scenery underneath me. I persuaded the Metropolitan management to remodel the very uncomfortable papier-mâché rock on which I was lying to fit my comfortable contours. I have often wondered how many sopranos have lain there since, in the depression especially carved for my capacious po-po.

My widely varied experiences in the musical world have given me the impression that the best music can be both "cultural" and entertaining. This does not seem a difficult symbiosis to me, but perhaps it is. I recall that once in my highbrow days I dared to insist upon singing Jerome Kern's "All the Things You Are" upon my supposed purely classical program. Out of millions of listeners the sponsors got exactly four letters of dignified protest. On this basis I was called in by the sponsors and gently reproved:

"We must do the bigger—heavier—more dignified music. We don't engage Helen Traubel to do what any pop singer can do. We have a mission, if you like, to do the important music."

"Yes," I said. "You mean the things that practically no one wants to hear."

That was the reason I spent thousands of dollars to have the "St. Louis Blues" set into a full symphonic arrangement. I made it part of my personal repertoire. It was a jewel of a tune, as it always has been—but in that kind of setting it stood out and blazed like a comet.

That was why, in 1953, I insisted on doing not a whole staid program of Wagner in San Antonio, Texas, but one that was half classic and half night-club tunes. The response was tremendous: the six-thousand-seat hall was filled, thousands were turned away. The proceeds helped sweep the sponsors out of a ten-year doldrum of debt.

I have always seemed to possess a humble excitement toward all music—that it should be fun, that it should have a sense of humor, that it should adapt itself endlessly to the times in which it finds its expression. Possibly this was never so well illustrated as the time Ed Gardner fell on his knees before me in the Brown Derby at lunch. As the originator and leading character in that wonderful show, *Duffy's Tavern,* he took this method of pleading with me to appear.

I was delighted to. As I told him, I was one of his original fans. I was going to ask him to let me appear anyway. My only condition was that he could kid opera all he wanted to, but that I would never be forced to say anything against it as a form of music.

Before I was through, I had appeared three times on the program. I think my chief asset to the show was as an unrehearsed audience. I am considered by my friends as the most uninhibited listener in the world: any joke, any act, any kind of talent pleases me. I have been told that my laugh—which can be heard booming for blocks—is worth its weight in gold to any comedy turn.

I was especially glad of that on *Duffy's Tavern*. Ed and I kept each other in gales of laughter. He continued ad-libbing to the howls of the audience and myself until the show ran three minutes overtime. Ed was still going at the top of his bent and I was anemic with laughter. Neither of us saw the frantic signals from the control room—nor did anyone in the audience.

Finally they got through to him with the cutthroat gesture that indicates that a show is off the air. Ed clutched his hair and cried tragically:

"We didn't get in the commercial! I've lost my sponsor! It's all your fault!"

Luckily, I was not responsible for that. The sponsor had enjoyed the show as much as anyone. He never complained about his dropped blurb.

This is the kind of thing I enjoy, and opera I also enjoy, in its own way. Yet it *is* difficult to captivate a modern audience by swooping in singing "Blow, Blow, Thou Winter Wind" (pronounced "wynd")—and it is so easy to catch their hearts with something like "Oh, What a Beautiful Morning!"

Possibly I was wrong, cutting down the traditional number of twenty-four waves of my scarf offstage (to the departing Tristan) to three different gestures. Tradition or not, it simply wore me out to flag him down that much. Especially when Lauritz was making faces at me in the wings dressed like an ironmonger on vacation.

Let me escape for a moment from this blessed jungle of reminiscence and start at the beginning.

How did I get to be this confused—and determined—in doing what I wanted to do in music and in life?

I think it started when I was quite small—when I used to comfort myself every night, falling asleep, dreaming I was a famous singer and that thousands of people loved me just for hearing me.

2

Chanteuse in Pigtails

I HAVE had a lot of fun singing my way through life, and it must have started just after I was born in South St. Louis on June 16, 1903.

It was a wonderful place to grow up: wide asphalt streets, big overarching poplar trees, long, green-shaved lawns, houses of brick or clapboard with wide porches, and the smell of cooking coming out under the fretwork along the eaves.

It was the part of the town that was made up mostly of Germans in those days—everyone spoke German when they met. There were singing societies, *turnverein,* the Liederkranz clubs, and any number of festivals and places where the beer (my father told me) was wonderful.

Helen Francesca Traubel. I got my middle name from a friend of my grandmother who became my godmother, Francesca Latta, a redheaded, kindly woman who spoiled me all of my life. Perhaps she cannot be blamed more than any other. I was a skinny, light-chestnut-headed, hazel-eyed spoiled brat from the beginning—"Queenie" or "Skinny," they called me—who got such a kick out of just being alive that they let me get away with it.

There were four in our family. Otto Ferdinand Traubel,

14

my father; Clara Stuhr Traubel, my mother; Walter Leonard Traubel, my brother, and myself. It always seemed as if there were a lot more: what with relatives and friends we never sat down to a meal alone and the only time the house was silent was at night when we were all asleep and even then our two dogs would be gently snoring.

I have no recollection of the time when sound—the outstanding sensation in the world for me—did not surround me. The singing, the clang of the streetcars, the clop-clop of the horses, the hiss of carbonated water into a soda, the tinkle of a piano or a guitar, the strong sound of a baritone voice singing in the distance—the list is endless.

Even today my favorite sound comes every evening about eleven. I quit whatever I may be doing and step outside the front door. The coolness makes me shiver, and I hear the endless chanting of the tree frogs and the crickets and feel the wet smell of life falling asleep. Those are the best five minutes of the day: when I pull up to my own personal gas station and fill up again.

Sounds that many people hate I have a fondness for. Traffic: the sound of it has movement, diminuendo and crescendo, color and depth. It is never the same, a symphony of infinite variations always going on and never repeated. The bass shriek of a jet ripping open the sky is very exciting to me, and a ride on the subway in New York is a genuine thrill. After all, music itself is no more than modulated noise, and some modern compositions are not even modulated.

Such sounds I can absorb and interpret for myself. I cannot stand a dissonance in an orchestra or a grating voice—I suppose it is the shocking noise that I dislike, the unexpected lack of harmony.

I think this comes from my earliest memories. I used to wake up in the morning to the sound of my father's deep, resonant voice. He would come into my bedroom quietly before I was awake and put his head on the pillow and whisper softly into my ear. He had a voice under perfect control, and its tone was the first thing that came into my head in the morning. He did it every morning to Walter as well, and as a result we all woke up laughing.

Ours was always a joyous household. I think most of it came from my father. He had a classic, handsome face with sharp features and a Roman nose, yet his eyes were as soft and melting as those of a woman. Clean-shaven, of medium height, he had a fine round stomach that showed his addiction to good food and drink. He always smoked cigars, and his slight cough was a continuous reminder of his presence.

He was a highly jovial and very active man. Five minutes after he came in the house in the afternoon he would be loading Mother and the rest of us into his big black Reo touring car. He would have planned a jaunt to the country that always ended, as he wanted, at a newly discovered restaurant. "Come on, kids, let's go!" he would shout. We would drop anything we were doing and follow him. Mama would always be prepared, hat on, and veil ready to be drawn down.

My father was a druggist and ran a store at the corner of Jefferson and Chouteau avenues. He owned the small property and the two-story brick building. The store occupied the front; a general surgeon had the three rear rooms. We had the six-room flat above—parlor, second sitting room, dining room, kitchen, two bedrooms, and bath. Papa had come from East St. Louis originally where my *grosspapa* and *grossmama* lived with five kids. *Grossmama* Traubel, after my grandfather's death, raised the children and dabbled in real estate, dying worth more than fifty thousand dollars—quite a sum in those days. At one point she actually helped start a bank.

I always knew that on my father's side the family made money and kept what they made; on my mother's, they always lost everything they had. I am sure that I became something of each:

I can detect the same failings and virtues that I knew in those days about my father and mother.

Mother was the daughter of a German baker who made delicious things out of dough, but who could never bear to collect a bill. At his death they found he was carrying perhaps a dozen families free—and had been doing so for twenty years—at the rate of about four hundred dollars a month. My mother, one of four daughters, was tall, dignified, and wore her light-brown hair high on her head. She had an immense air of reserve. When she wanted to show her disapproval of something she would simply withdraw in spirit. (I have been accused of doing it myself: simply drifting away on an inner cloud.) She never had to punish either of her children—so fearful were we that she might stay away from us altogether.

We always really knew she would not do anything so cruel. She loved us too much, and it is her love and my father's assurance that I still treasure as my finest memory of those days. They gave us a glowing security that kept us warm. We could not be afraid or doubting or reluctant to challenge life on its own terms. We were too sure of our welcome within our family. My father and mother may have quarreled, but Walter and I never knew about it. A little stiffness, a little withdrawal, we noticed occasionally, but it soon vanished. They both had plenty of time to talk things out, and they would never go to sleep without making sure all was well.

Walter, my brother, was two years older than I. He was a very gentle person, a trait which clashed with the vehement way in which he played football. He loved sports and hated to go to pharmacy school, which he did only to please Papa. He finally graduated and joined a textile firm. He became a salesman, settled down in Dallas, Texas, and spent the rest of his life there. He died in 1955, a loss to me of someone that I dearly loved.

The drugstore, of course, was the hub of all our activities as children. Next to sounds I can recall smells most vividly: the

high smell of spices, the low rolling smell of bitter drugs, and
the heady tickle of soda water. There were spice factories in St.
Louis and we used to visit them just to sniff. Right out in back
of the house we had an immense flower garden but I cannot
remember any one scent, only that the nasturtiums used to bloom
everywhere. My recollection is of an overpowering green smell,
the odor of everything growing.

My father kept his drugstore for more than twenty years, pre-
scribing for his friends and acting as an amateur doctor and
adviser on the side. But for us the whole affair was built around
his imposing nickel-marble-ebony soda fountain. It was a real
fountain of life for us. We made it work every minute of the day.

Walter and I were allowed only two sodas a day, but, if it was
warm, we could have three. We were given permission to mix one
of these ourselves, and of course I always said: "Walter, three big
scoops of ice cream—and just a couple of drops of soda." I went
into the biggest debt of my life in ice cream. I believe that by the
time I was ten I was devouring sodas that belonged to the weeks
in my late forties.

My father also decreed that we could give a soda apiece to our
friends. The tide of tumultuous youngsters so overwhelmed him
after a few weeks that he cut this down to six sodas apiece daily
for our friends. This was because there were only six of the wire
chairs in the fountain. More youthful customers than that, swill-
ing free sodas, got in the way of the prescription department. I
can still hear one of the two clerks crying out in agony: "Mister
Traubel, you'll have to do something about these kids, they're
driving me crazy!" He might have said "nuts," but I doubt it; in
those days nuts were merely something to sprinkle on top of
the marshmallow.

My father died when I was twelve years old. It seemed impossible that we buried such a person, full of so much life and energy.
He stepped on a nail in a board from an opened crate in the
back of the shop and failed to care for the puncture. He got

gangrene that lasted fifteen weeks, and it was complicated by diabetes. His septicemia was impossible to stop in those days without the drugs that science has recently discovered. I was so sure, after his burial, that he was still alive that I followed a man that looked like him for a dozen blocks because he had a little cough like that of my father. It was a cruel disillusion when the man turned around and proved to be a stranger.

Those years were full of gaiety and time went by so quickly I could not even snap my fingers at it. My father and mother left the flat over the drugstore for another house that had ten rooms and a big porch and an enormous attic. It was two streetcar rides (both for a nickel) away from the drugstore but only across the street from the school. "We all like to get up late," said my father, "so why shouldn't we get as close to the school as we can?" He liked to live in the easiest possible way, but he never shirked doing the hard things. His life centered about Mama, me, and Walter. He tore out all the partitions of the attic, laid a hardwood floor, and put benches around the sides. We had frolics up there with our friends, roller skating and riding our bikes.

School was just a long interruption in our round of fun. At mealtimes we would sit down at a crowded table and devour the rich German food together with liqueurs and wines. My *grossmama* had a table that could sit thirty easily—each chair having arms—but we were not quite so grand. We contented ourselves with a dozen or so. In the parlor we had a couple of pianos and two phonographs—a Victrola and an Edison with the thick black records. There were also more than two hundred books of songs, and we sang every time we got together.

I suppose now, looking back, that it was music which formed the indissoluble bond of our family. Music was everywhere. Stray musicians were always visiting our house and staying awhile even though we never knew some of their names. All of us could sing: Father in a pleasant baritone nothing, Walter in a growling bass, Mother and myself with full dramatic soprano voices. My mother

especially loved to sit at the piano and regale us with her favorites:
"The Rosary," "Die Lorelei," and "The Sweetest Story Ever
Told." We must have heard them hundreds of times, laughing
and giggling on the floor with our elbows on cushions; my mother
sang them again and again.

I was a tomboyish little girl who laughed continually, who ate
too much, who fell in love with everything and everyone around
her—and who wanted to sing all the time. It was a natural instinct,
but I suppose it sometimes made me a little pushy in the St. Louis
social life. I was always in the midst of any song fest. The most
strategic spot, of course, was on the piano bench. I always managed to sit there, eager to let loose a high C. Every song I heard
I learned by heart; and I usually insisted that the company and
my family listen to me sing all of them. My father and mother
liked to hear me—my voice was good and strong even in those days
—but too much was what I wanted and what I seldom got. The
only thing that made me pout momentarily was losing a solo part,
even if it was only a few bars. I can still remember singing lustily
while sitting at a table and playing hearts or rummy. The older
people sat in the next room and harmonized while they played
pinochle.

Even though I might have been a nuisance in wanting to sing,
I was never treated cruelly; and I have often wondered whether
it is better to spoil a child or to bring him up short. Perhaps my
love for singing might have been stopped as a youngster if anyone
had criticized me too severely or forbade me to sing. As it was, I
never sought any kind of a career except singing; I never wanted
to do anything or thought of anything other than singing for
as many people as would listen to me at any hour of the day and
night. In those days my voice seemed to spring inexhaustibly from
inside me, as though it would never cease pouring out. Every
song I sang was an experience that thrilled me, transported me
miles above my audience, floating along on the notes. Childish

ego, yes: it was also an assurance of a talent that was given to me at birth and of which I have always been confident.

As a matter of fact, I was so fond of music itself that I learned to play the piano. For four years, three times a week, I bedeviled the teacher—a long-suffering gray-haired, fat little lady named Mrs. Tatum. I loved to hear the cello and wanted to learn how to make those mysterious low sounds, but I never got round to it. I drove my teacher crazy on the piano by listening to a tune by ear and instantly memorizing the first couple of pages. These I could rattle off and the end was usually just as easy to remember. But it was the middle, the damned middle, that used to frustrate me! I do not believe I ever learned the middle of any piano selection.

Most of this happened in the Big House—the one we moved into from the flat over the drugstore—in 1909, when I was six years old. We lived a great, wild musical life in those echoing ten rooms of the $10,500 structure. My mother sold it when I was thirteen, after the death of my father. "*Ach,* Helena," she said sadly, "what do I want with so much room now that Otto is gone? It only reminds me of what used to be"—but always when I remember my home the vision of that house comes back to me.

During those years of growing up, when everything outside seemed helterskelter, everything inside my head was very steady and still, as if I had some personal telescope focused on the far future. I knew what I was; I knew what I wanted to be; and I knew what I hoped to become and what I would work myself to death to become. I was to be a singer. Not particularly a great singer, perhaps, but one to whom everyone would be glad to listen and from whom the world could draw some happiness.

Happiness! I have always felt that was the commodity I could sell. Not soap or underwear or automobiles or possibly rocket ships, but the feeling of security and love, lapped round in music, that I myself experienced when I was young. This is the most wonderful sensation I know—and I have always wanted to share it.

I liked St. Louis tremendously. I thought there was nowhere else in the world I would like to live and grow up. At the same time I was very aware of the fact that there was a world outside my own home, outside the city, outside the state and country. My father took the family to Chicago to hear opera, three or four times a year. For three months of the year, he was forced to travel on the road to buy drugs and staples, but he took us all with him to New York every two or three years.

The first time I went to that city was when I was six. The pictures it evoked in my mind—it is my favorite city—remain with me today. I remember the ferryboats; the two or three horse-drawn streetcars that still remained; the goat cart in Central Park; the concerts on the Mall with the summer breeze stirring my hair and the stars overhead dimmed by the lights of the towering buildings around; Coney Island with its din and color; and the old Holland House with its wide porches and prim smells where we always stayed—all these and more remain with me today and form a kind of background against which modern New York rushes through its daily life like a pantomime before a curtain.

The first opera I saw was in Chicago when I could not have been more than seven. It was called *The Love of Three Kings.* I was fascinated by the rich costumes and the fact that in the middle of the piece the heroine—still bravely singing high notes—was choked to death by someone. (The opera might have been *Otello,* I cannot tell at this distance.) What I recall is my own amazement and envy that the prima donna could hit those notes while she was being throttled. When I got home, I tried to sing while strangling myself, but I never could get the full, round clarity of that woman. The singing was lovely. It held me nailed to my seat—and I was the type of obnoxious little girl who would even run up and down the aisle during the most frenetic vaudeville bill. You can imagine how much I loved music if I stayed in my seat during a whole opera, even refusing to go to the little girls' room! I was so entranced at one point that my mother leaned over to me and smiled indulgently. She whispered: "Helena, it's only make-believe!" To which I hissed indignantly: "Sure, but *I* believe it, Mama!"

Before I was twelve I can make a modest estimate of the operas I had heard—and it would be more than thirty. Father and Mother were always absorbed but they did not have their critical faculties atrophied as I did when I listened. Walter never cared very much for opera or even for singing, but he was interested in the mere sound. He could get much more out of the nuances of singing without even wanting to understand the words. He could shut his eyes and tell what was going on to the smallest detail without having any idea of the plot.

In New York I saw the opera three times. When I was nine, my father managed to get us tickets to the Metropolitan Opera. I always liked crowds of people, and they were certainly there to hear Geraldine Farrar sing the pathetic leading role in *Madama Butterfly*. The music enchanted me as usual, and I never saw the awful sets that I was to complain so bitterly about when I grew up. I liked the gilt, the hushed attention, the feeling of living right in the middle of all the music that poured out around me. Again, this was my second security; the cocoon that great composers, conductors, and artists can weave around anyone who will remain willing to listen. I took a lot of time, for example, to understand Wagner—I had to go back to his music again and again for years to discover it. At last I learned his language, what he was telling me—and I entered into a new world.

3

Kid in the Front Row Center

THE most fortunate part of my life has been that I have never had to do anything I considered to be work. Not that I did not work: becoming a singer is harder on the nerves and physique, more taxing for the soul and body than almost any other occupation. What I mean is—I loved every moment of it. I had the luxury of doing what I wanted, not what others told me to do.

It is true there have been many things in my life that I did not care for. I learned a trick early in my childhood: I made them all a series of games. If I did not do the distasteful things well, I lost the game. I hate to lose, so I worked at winning this kind of "game."

So most of what I recall of the past is rose-colored. I can still see the hazy night of the first time I really sang in public—for a fee—in St. Louis. It was in the Washington University hall on some occasion to raise money for a good cause. I sang Gounod's "Ave Maria" and something about spring, perhaps Mendelssohn's perennial chirping. I was on stage for about twenty minutes and I received one hundred dollars.

The five hundred-odd people who heard me knew me, most of them. I smiled as I sang and nodded at friends in the audience.

I wore a plain white chiffon dress decorated with Alençon lace, my hair was done up on the top of my head like Mama's (I had been waiting years to do it), and I had no make-up. I looked five or six years older than my almost-thirteen, and I was as tall as I am now though a good deal thinner. The concertmaster of the symphony orchestra played the violin with me and we had a piano accompanist: *"Schön, schön,"* he kept whispering to himself, "beautiful, beautiful!"

Not that I had not sung in public before. From the third grade on up, whenever the teacher of my class had an extra five minutes to fill, she called on me. I was delighted to respond with numbers taken from vaudeville to opera. I was also a habitual party singer. In general, I was as willing to burst into song as any bird you might find on a bush.

When I sang for my hundred dollars I had already commenced taking music lessons six months before. I had wanted to start off as soon as I could—I had no illusions about the training it would take to make me what I wanted. I went to the Roman Catholic church in our neighborhood and offered to sing in the four-voiced choir. After two Sundays they awarded me all the solos.

Not that I was Catholic. Our family was thoroughly mixed up in a religious way. My mother was Catholic; my father was a Mason, a Knight Templar; my grandmother was Lutheran; and Walter and I fell somewhere between. Actually, denomination never has made any difference to me. What I wanted was some place to sing and the churches provided it. The middle-aged, quick-tongued organist who was the Catholic choir leader always called me "Jujee." She was in despair when I came in late for the services. I sang high mass and an assortment of religious numbers, but I always had trouble with my giggling in the choir and singing too loud for the others. I remember that one or two of the uneasy parishioners spoke privately to the priest about the possible buckling of the stained-glass windows. In those days I was

considered a "light dramatic soprano"; now, I am sure, I am one
of the heaviest there is.

Competing with the roar of the organ and the other voices,
I got volume and strength. But after fourteen months I deserted
the choir and started to keep my mouth shut. Not because anything went wrong but because my new singing teacher told me
to. My days of simply opening up wide and letting go were over.
"You should study, not sing," she told me. "This free-and-easy
style of yours is all very well but it interferes with your musical
line of thought. You have to stop it if you want to be a real
singer." There was nothing I wanted more to be—and I quit
public appearances (except for perhaps two or three a year that
I could not resist) for five years. I want to talk more about my
teacher, Louise Meyerson Vetta-Karst, but it will take another
place to explain how she was at once my closest friend and my
most overbearing tyrant and female Svengali.

All I can say, then, is that I vanished from the platforms of
St. Louis for those years because I was so terribly curious about
what it took to study. Nor did I wholly find out in that time. I
was able only to discipline myself and come back at the age of
seventeen to some sort of controlled soprano outbreak—this time
at the Congregational church for one hundred dollars a month.
I sang there every Sunday for the next twelve years.

Two years later, for the next ten years, I doubled in soprano
by singing at the local synagogue, the United Hebrew Temple. As
anyone can see, I was obviously impartial when it came to matters
of religion. If I had a soul, it was in my voice. My rule was invariable: I would rehearse for the synagogue on Thursday and sing
in the services on Friday night and Saturday morning; I would
rehearse for the Congregational church on Saturday afternoon
and sing for the services on Sunday morning.

Everything went on swimmingly. Of course I came late for
rehearsals but I was on time for the services. Each choir consisted
of four people including myself, and I had all the solos. In the

Congregational services they were anthems such as "Save Me, O God," "Come Unto Me," "I Will Lift Up Mine Eyes unto the Hills," and so on. For the synagogue, they were the magnificent old songs such as "Kol Nidre" and any number of the traditional chants. (The Jewish religious music is among the best in the world, I think.)

I had my difficulties at times. I remember that the Congregational minister came to me and said: "Helen, I know you can't listen to what I say every Sunday; I probably don't have that many new ideas. But I do wish you would stop whispering and giggling for just one Sunday!" I did my best, but I have no idea how good it was. One of my duties came to be that of assistant farewell sayer: I used to go to the door with the minister after the service and say good-by to the congregation, to the people who loved me and were my friends—and whom I still love.

In the synagogue the choir loft was overhead, mostly hidden from the sight of the audience. If our fun became too obvious, the rabbi would bear down hard on his concealed buzzer to the choir from the lectern. I loved to listen to what he said. Not the words; they never had any attraction for me, no matter what pulpit. I adored his voice: a deep, almost singing tone that was like listening to a bass solo. On one winter's service the baritone of the Jewish choir could not get to the temple because his car stalled. So, without notice, I took his place, singing his part and my own. It was difficult to do, but I got through it. The congregation was buzzing and the rabbi was so astounded at my daring that he missed part of the services. But he thanked me afterward even though it was an unheard-of act for a mere woman to do.

In some ways, I suppose, I was a trouble to the Congregationalists. Once they suggested—via a new minister—that the choir march around the aisles singing. I put my foot down on that. I was in favor of as little ecclesiastical exercise as possible. I finally won the battle: the children's choir paraded and the adults sat still.

All of the church people were such good friends to me. They used to send up to the choir loft gifts of handkerchiefs they had made, jellies, tidbits of food they knew I loved. In those days I never tried to invent my own pleasures; they came ready made, tailored to my size.

At the same time I was becoming mildly famous in St. Louis for an entirely different talent. My laugh was making my voice one of the most noticeable things in town. I have always been a trifle on the uninhibited side when it comes to something humorous. Anyone who knows me knows that the simplest joke will really start a hurricane inside: I laugh so hard that it can be heard over acres, my knees get weak, and the tears come. I think it is simply because I enjoy all that is enjoyable so thoroughly.

At any rate, I used to love the early nickelodeons. I would sneak away to them on every occasion that I could get loose from my commitments at home, at church, or at my teacher's. I would sit entranced at the sight of Pearl White hanging over a cliff, of the flickering Westerns of the Flying A, at the sight of Charlie Chaplin. This often kept me out well past my normal bedtime hour of nine o'clock.

Though it happened again and again, my mother never believed that I was really at the nickelodeon. She called everywhere except at the theater. My friends would tell her.

"Have you seen Helena?" my mother would ask distractedly. "She should be home long ago and I'm so worried."

"Don't worry, Clara," the neighbors would say. "She's all right."

"But how do you know?"

"We know where she is. She'll be home soon."

"But where is she?"

"She's at the nickelodeon, in the front row," they would say reluctantly.

"How can you say that?" my mother would demand. "She never would go there at this hour. She promised me she wouldn't. You must be making a mistake, eh?"

"No mistake," the neighbors would assure her. "We heard her laugh."

My mother never reproached me about these late nights. She would merely look sadly at me when I came home and murmur: "They heard you laughing at the nickelodeon again tonight, Helena."

Whatever musical standing I may or may not have enjoyed in St. Louis during those years I was always considered an outstanding asset by the local vaudeville houses. Until the death of my father, he and my mother always had four—not two—seats reserved weekly in the theater. They never wanted to miss a new act or fail in seeing an old one—and they were expansively built enough to be able to overflow onto the next seat. I would go, too, mostly on the cuff—I was always running up debts for pleasure—and sit bug-eyed at what was going on. Bug-eyed and guffawing. I became so notorious that the manager used to be asked by the acts if "that little girl with the big laugh is still coming to the show." When assured that I was, they would heave a deep sigh of relief: I was considered the fuse that set off the laughter of the entire house. I could have gotten in free just on that but I never took advantage of the opportunity.

My laugh affected people differently. It always embarrassed my brother so thoroughly that whenever he sat next to me and I commenced to throw my head back and enjoy myself, he slipped down and hid under his seat. He missed some very funny things that way, in my opinion. The conductor of the orchestra, Morris Spier, just in front of me, used to hold out for a while and then commence to laugh himself. He would laugh until he cried. The tears would slick up his big nose so that his glasses fell off and he had to fumble for them in the pit two or three times a performance. I would usually climb over and find them for him, while the orchestra blared away on its own. Other members of the group, particularly the brass section, used to claim they could not pucker up when I was laughing. Years later, as I have said, it was my booming amusement penetrating through the so-called soundproof doors of a national radio studio that brought me onto radio and television.

I must confess that my voice was developing a certain arresting quality at about that time. I learned that from the incident of the strawberry man and our police dogs.

As far back as I can remember in my childhood, we had dogs—usually hunting dogs, though after Papa died they became watchdogs. At this particular time we had two tan-and-black German police dogs called Hans and Fritz. We always called our animals by such Katzenjammer names. We even had a pair of parakeets that we called Hans and Fritz though I believe both of them were female. These dogs were large and curious, and we had to erect an eight-foot wire fence (which they could leap though they were beaten if they did) to keep them in the yard. They were perfectly willing to let any stranger in, but somewhat reluctant to let him out. So we posted our signs: BEWARE OF DOGS.

An alley ran in the back of our house and during the languorous summer months of St. Louis it used to be infested with fruit peddlers. We were visited by watermelon men, cherry men, peach men, apple men, and berry men. We used to buy ten watermelons (we loved those green cigars of fruit) at a time and line them up for consumption on the back porch.

On this particular morning I was dressing upstairs. I heard a strawberry man crying his wares in the alley in a rather unmusical voice, then silence; then the unmistakable click of the gate. I looked out my window.

The strawberry man had ignored our sign, entered, and was making for the back porch, when suddenly Hans and Fritz appeared from their runway under the porch and silently commenced to escort him. He lost his nerve, whirled, and started for the gate. The dogs started for his trousers. I poked my head out of the window and let loose: "HANS! FRITZ!"

My shout froze the dogs like statues. It also froze the passers-by,

I guess. No one moved in the neighborhood for moments—except the unfortunate strawberry man. My stentorian tones—that I later used with much the same effect in opera—startled him so much that he fell face forward, sprawling in the midst of his own crate of strawberries. The next moment he was up and out of the gate, streaming with the gore of the crushed fruit and screaming for legal vengeance. We pacified him while the dogs devoured the remains of the crate, bought berries from him every year afterward—and it became a reasonably good joke for the family.

Looking back, only now do I realize what a wonderful childhood I had. The whole world was amazing to me; it seemed so filled with delight, just for my use. I turned everything I saw into something that was mine alone—that made me happy.

It was not really much effort. When I was not singing, studying at school was the most difficult thing I had to do. And often, in the midst of a lesson, my father would come and persuade the teacher to let me out—he never told her why but I knew: hunting and fishing.

My father loved to roam the countryside around St. Louis in search of rabbits and quail. He liked to go dove hunting, to blast away at the great flocks that fluttered out of the tops of the tallest trees. There was not nearly so much restriction on game shooting in those days as there is now. It was delightful. We went north in the summer to Michigan, Wisconsin, and Minnesota. In the winter we prowled through the Ozarks. I was angular and active, making my father puff to keep up with me. Perhaps I enjoyed it more than he did.

Our especial delight was his private duck blind on the Illinois River. In the marshes, silently waiting in the shivering cold of early morning ("Sh-h-h, Helena!"), seeing the glorious colors of the sunrise and the ducks coming in, I was happy for some of the few times in my life by myself. I have always liked company but on those occasions I felt that my smiling, waiting father, who would from time to time give me a paternal pat, and the rising flames of the sun in the east, and the bite of the weather were quite enough—almost overwhelming—company for me.

My father assigned me one duty: to blow the duck call. I was overjoyed at this opportunity to make another kind of noise. I spent hours each day at the advent of the duck-hunting season blowing the thing. It seemed to be very effective indeed in attracting ducks at the blind, but it was even more persuasive in attracting the neighbors to our door.

It was often too difficult for me to go down to the blind and blow the duck call in solitude. Besides, I liked company. So I used to lie in my warm bed at night and practice blowing calls of mating ducks—angry, soothing, indifferent, loving—all the gamut of duckdom.

The neighbors did not appreciate it. They usually threw off their covers, slammed down the windows, and eventually stamped over to our house.

"Otto!" they would cry. "Otto! Tell that girl of yours to stop blowing that damned duck call! Let us get some sleep!"

At last I sadly gave up duck calling. I still am convinced that it was the beginning of my own practicing in the low register, give and take a few flat notes.

4

Lulu in the Highest

MRS. LOUISE MEYERSON VETTA-KARST was a small-boned, very pretty, and dominating woman. She had long, blue-green eyes, heavy red-brown hair piled on top of her head, and a complexion of pure cream—with exclamation points of black eyebrows. She loved singing more than anything else and, I think, she loved me next to singing. I know I felt that way toward her.

Lulu—as her friends called her—was closely related to Chouteau, a fur trapper in the early days, one of the first settlers of the trading post of St. Louis. When she was very young, she traveled to Europe and lived there for a time, then came back and married the French consul in St. Louis. Six or seven years later she was divorced, went back to France, and entered the Sorbonne for seventeen years of studying music. She knew everything about it; and she was determined to pass it along to the future. I was selected as the vessel in which this was to be conveyed.

She was composed of opposites, and the one which I most often encountered was the fact that she had an explosive temper and yet the most tremendous patience I have ever seen in one person. She was a close friend of my family, and it was my mother who told me she would be my teacher when I informed the family that

I wanted to study. "I want to be a real singer," I said grandly, "and I don't care how hard I have to work."

If I had known then just what those words meant, I might never have gone to Lulu. I could not have imagined that I would be her pupil for just exactly the same time—seventeen years—as she had studied abroad. It would have terrified me. Today I would not exchange all the treasures of the world for those priceless years of training.

Priceless is exactly what they were—without price. Lulu never charged me a cent for all the time, effort, and knowledge she put into my keeping. At the end of the second month of my working with her—at the rate of three dollars an hour—I gave her a check for thirty-six dollars. She refused to take it and sent it back home with me. My mother was thunderstruck and instantly rushed to the phone. I can still hear the sharp voice of Lulu coming out of the receiver over my mother's protests.

"Clara," she said stridently, as if she wanted me to hear, "I want to control Helen. I want a hold over her. If she feels she is obligated to me, I can hold her better. As you know, she is sometimes a stubborn and self-willed child and she may weaken. It will be a very long pull before she can sing—I mean, before she can sing the way I want her to."

For nearly eighteen years I never sang anywhere in the world that Lulu did not permit me to sing.

How she came to be my teacher is a story that has always impressed me with the idea of fate. In my life, at least, the happenings of my career have come about with a kind of fatalistic quality that sometimes makes me feel as if I were a beloved puppet of some stronger force.

I had been singing with the choir of the Roman Catholic church for a few months and I had some Italian friends who were impressed with my untrained voice. They used to urge me to take lessons and I always refused. "At least, then," they said, "why don't you visit someone who can really tell you what a treasure you have in your throat?"

Their daughter, Florencia Bettini, had been taking piano lessons from one of the foremost teachers in the city—a tall, dignified, handsome man who was highly respected by the Midwest society of the day. He spent five or six months yearly in Europe, he was music critic for the now-defunct St. Louis *Times,* and in every way was the leading musical arbiter. I was impressed by his reputation and finally he agreed to hear me and I agreed to go.

I was not too happy about it. I kept mumbling that his studio was the place where "the kids with lots of money went." The size and rich decorations made me unhappy; so did his brusque greeting and the fact that he ordered me up on the small stage with an accompanist and sat down and commenced to open his mail. I determined that I would show him. My accompanist was my Catholic organist—her first name was Ave Maria (she came from a *very* Catholic family)—and she nervously began playing. "What bad manners he has!" I whispered resentfully to her and opened my mouth for the first note.

The song I had selected started on a very high sustained note. I hit it and held it—and watched my audience of one like a hawk.

As soon as that note hit his eardrums, he jerked as if someone had stabbed him. But he kept on ripping open the envelope. As I went into the song, he took out the letter and opened it, but I do not think that to this day he ever finished it. He sat nailed to his chair, and I, like any young singer proud of her voice, was satisfied.

He did not wait for me to finish. He bounded up in the middle of the song and cried: "My God, what's your name?" I told him what it was and that I was almost thirteen. He shook his head. "I know I'm not wrong," he told me, "but in something as important as this we must make sure." He dragged me out of the studio and beat on the door of the next studio. I waited outside as he rushed in and I could hear the argument: "I don't care who you're teaching, Lulu, you have to stop and listen to this angel! I tell you, I don't care! Put it off, throw her out, do anything!"

Finally he came out again, disheveled and breathing hard, and took me inside. That was the first time I ever saw Madame Vetta-Karst with her eternal cigarette in her mouth and ashes over the front of her dress—a woman of real beauty, about sixty years old, staring at me as if she wanted to drill holes in my head.

"Sing!" she said in her gravel voice. I repeated the song I had done for the piano teacher. Lulu seemed unimpressed. She got up and peered at me.

"What's your name?" she asked.

"How old?"

"Where do you live?"

Then she was silent. Finally she said: "I want to teach you, my girl."

"I'm sorry," I said firmly.

"What do you mean?" she flung at me. "That is a great compliment. I haven't talked about money. You have a healthy voice— a voice to be, to be. You don't know how to sing yet!"

"My mother doesn't want me to take lessons from anyone except a woman she knew as a child," I told her. "I'm very sorry."

Lulu puffed away fiercely on her cigarette. "Who is this woman?" she jerked out. "Maybe I know her."

"My mother sang but not professionally," I said doubtfully. "I can't—"

"Nonsense!" she snapped. "What's her name? Oh, never mind that, what's your mother's name?"

"Mrs. Traubel," I said. Lulu shook her head impatiently. "What's the name of this wonderful teacher she wants you to have?" she sneered.

"A woman named Lulu Meyerson," I said defiantly.

A change came over Madame Vetta-Karst's face. The hard lines in it melted and changed. She did not smile, but somehow it seemed as if she had relaxed inwardly and were enjoying the moment.

"Tell me, child," she said. "What was your mother's maiden name?" I was surprised at the gentleness of the question.

"Clara Stuhr," I said.

"I see," Lulu said thoughtfully. "I see." She marched to a telephone and, turning, demanded our home number. "It's no use," I said, "because—"

"The number, child!"

I gave it to her and she told the operator and waited. Suddenly she rasped: "Clara! This is Lulu—Lulu Meyerson!"

From then on, for seventeen years, she was my second mother. Probably I spent more time in her company, in that old studio, than I did with my family if the hours of sleep are not counted. And the first lesson I ever took with her was the same as the last: scales and more scales, up and down the scales until I felt as if I were climbing endless mountains of notes.

Perhaps the hardest lesson for me to learn in starting with Lulu was obedience. I had been used to having my own way; my voice was the magic wand that opened most doors for me in St. Louis. Now, with the whip of her gravelly tones cutting through my weary ascending and descending of notes, it was different. Yet I loved it. It was wonderful because it was, I knew, the object of my whole life. This was a person who really knew singing—who knew what a throat was capable of. Anything that I ever proved later in life by my singing was something that Lulu dreamed of first.

Starting with a half-hour each day of scales and increasing steadily from then on, Lulu listened to me and corrected me, closing her eyes against the cigarette smoke, leaning back almost with her ears cocked to hear the slightest deviation from what she had commanded. It was as if some famous baseball coach had picked a kid off the sand lots and was trying to teach him to swing

and hit like Babe Ruth. When I despaired, she assured me that
I was capable of it; when I was supremely confident, she deflated
me expertly. Four, eight, twelve notes up and down, trying to
make each one as perfect as possible.

That is what I always started to do, what I never finished
doing: simply to sing an absolutely perfect set of scales. I would
take the middle of my voice and work down five notes, then up
five notes. I would try for fundamental tone production. What I
was interested in was not volume or holding a note, or hitting a
high or a low. I only wanted balance and control to be achieved
and held to their utmost limit. I wanted perfect clarity, perfect
tone, perfect levels. "You don't want any *holes* in your voice,"
grated Lulu. "That's why you have to work." She knew that most
singers of the "easygoing" type were breathy glottis gulpers—she
tried to get me to develop my diaphragm and my rib cage so that
my voice would have the power of sustaining anything I wanted
to sing.

I would practice scales for a month and then, possibly, as a
particular reward, she would allow me to learn a song. Another
six weeks of scales, then another song—nothing popular, only the
classic literature of music. I got so I could hit and hold high C's
and get down to B flat below middle C—with a range of about
two and a half octaves—but I never considered this as an ac-
complishment in itself. My training with Lulu added three
notes on top and three or four below what I had naturally, but its
great and incomparable contribution to whatever nature had
given me was simply the purity and sustaining of notes in flight.
"Your goal must always be a beautiful sound," snapped Lulu,
whose voice was anything but, yet who had all the wisdom of the
ages in her aristocratic head about the art. "Never forget that!"
I hope I never have.

I learned not to stab at a note but to take it in stride, as an
automatic matter of musical principle—a habit rather than an
inspiration. So many singers hit high C: the rest of their voice

sounds like a cackling hen but they have high C—and what have they got when they hit it? They generally hit it so hard they destroy its sound.

I mean beautiful sounds. There are tones in Richard Strauss, for example, that are dissonant—when Electra is demented—but even these can be given a weird beauty of their own. I simply do not believe in dissonance for its own sake unless it can undergo a transformation in voice. I can honestly say I have never found anyone who would tell me anything except that my singing was a beautiful sound—though God knows what they might have said behind my back. Singing for its own sake—simply using the voice as a gymnast might use a trapeze—is a usual trick. Melchior used to amuse himself by doing it just to prove his point. In the Wagner *Ring* at the Metropolitan, he drove the conductors of the operas crazy by holding notes thirty or forty seconds long, then drawing a breath and starting all over again—and filling the whole of that monstrous auditorium with the sound. The orchestra might start to play or they might start a bowling game in the pit—Lauritz would go right on piercing through the din. We used to keep a stop watch on his holds backstage and make bets on how long, O Lauritz, how long?

This is simply having acrobatic fun. Serious study or serious singing is always concerned with the beauty of sound. I have listened for hours to Pablo Casals on the cello to achieve one tone with my voice; to Fritz Kreisler or Jascha Heifitz on the violin to get another. I must say with Lulu, the ultimate truth: "My voice is an instrument, an instrument only. Anyone who thinks of it as anything else is not a singer—but an exhibitionist."

Just as a player has to take care of his instrument, so I have learned to take care of my voice—the way a violinist might cuddle with a Stradivarius. When I had to sing up to eighty performances a year including a couple of dozen operas in addition, I was forced to coddle my voice. I went to movies and sat on the aisle wearing a white surgeon's mask. Little children sometimes mis-

took me for a zombie left over from a horror movie the week before and fled out screaming. I had to keep away from all crowds—
something I despised because I am so fond of being with people
at all times. Invitations to friends went out worded as follows:
IF YOU HAVE A COLD, PLEASE STAY HOME.

Every day I was forced to practice for an hour or more—and
then sing my heart out at work. This went on from five to seven
days a week. My husband still talks of my morning exercises as
"my warm up," as if I were a pitcher in a bull pen in Yankee
Stadium. Indeed, sometimes I feel that I am pitching the notes
at my audience, trying to win my own personal game. I have been
lucky because my voice, unlike a fiddle, has not had mechanical
difficulties, though occasionally I have suffered physically.

Lulu taught me all these things from the first. From the moment I was assigned to her until the moment we parted, there
was no monkey business. I was never given my own way for a
second—me, lazy little Helen who had got her own way for so
many years by wheedling and singing!

"You've got away with murder in your life," Lulu would rasp,
"just because you can sing. Well, that's over!"

"You're lazy, stupid, and idiotic! You can't learn a thing—
you'll never be great!"

"You big cow! Can't you do better than that?"

They were insults that I dearly wanted to repay—and that
Lulu wanted me to repay. I did, eventually, and she admitted
it—by becoming the singer she hoped I would become.

About once a year Lulu would say in a hoarse whisper: "You
have the most beautiful voice I've ever heard," and I could see
the tears in her eyes. Then she would break out with a denuncia-
tion of my inattentiveness: "I'm going crazy, beating my brains
out, trying to get your undivided attention—and here you are,
paying attention to your own voice as if I didn't exist! Pay attention to me, I'll pay attention to your voice!"

Because of those years today I never think of singing as "hard" or "easy." I love to sing songs where I can use my voice in expanding—in long-sustained phrases. If a song is wordy, I sometimes have difficulty breaking up my own sound in order to get the words in the right order. I recall that in 1947 in Chicago—which has some very perceptive music critics—one of them wrote that my singing some light, familiar songs in a recital was "like sending a dreadnought to do a rowboat's job." I enjoyed the truth of that, and the counter-claim that I have kept in my memory was one made during a tour with the Philadelphia Philharmonic Orchestra in Michigan in 1950. I was singing excerpts from the role of Brünnhilde in Wagner. The audience was entranced and I was satisfied. I rarely read reviews, I take my cues as to a good or bad performance from what I feel coming over the footlights in waves from the audience. If they like me, I can feel it; if they don't, it is like throwing one vast mattress over me, smothering me to death. But this line from a review was read to me and I have always remembered it with pleasure: "The wonderful Traubel hoisted a few tones over the audience that you could chin yourself on."

With such recollections always comes the vision of Lulu Vetta-Karst. I can hear her harshness, warning, admonishing, denouncing—and very rarely, praising—over all the din of the past years.

"You're too soft, too soft—you're like mush!"

"You're a tomboy! You'll never be a lady! I can kill myself but you'll never be fit for society!"

"You have to learn how to grow up! How can you have lived this long and stayed so naïve?"

Once I stopped in the middle of a tone. Lulu whirled on me, her dark eyes flashing. "Why did you stop?" she demanded. "Did I tell you to?"

"I—I didn't think that tone was very good," I stammered.

"You! *You* didn't think it was good!" exclaimed my outraged teacher. "I'll be the judge of what's good or bad, you little snot nose!" All that afternoon she used a whip of verbal scorpions across my back.

She never let herself get soft toward me even at the end. When, in 1944, I returned to St. Louis in the midst of my triumphs, I was the guest of honor at a women's club reception. I had been in town for twenty-four hours and I had not called Lulu—something I had never done before and which I knew was unforgivable. To her I was still her pupil and no one else.

I had not seen Lulu for three or four years and she was not invited to the party. But she came: she came in late, dressed in a beautiful gown, smoking the inevitable cigarette, the cynosure of all eyes. She went to the middle of the room, planted herself there, cocked her head, and put her arms akimbo. She stared at me in the receiving line—and I, of course, went directly to her and caught her to my heart.

"I was wondering if you would come," she said to me. "I was wondering if you had got too big for your pants."

"My God!" I said, genuinely shocked. "How could you think so, Lulu?"

She regarded me a moment through her slitted lids, then threw away the cigarette and hugged me in return.

"I know, I know," she said in her growling voice. "Dear Helena, I was a dog to doubt you, a bitch!"

She was old, very old—in her late eighties—when she died in 1948. I was not able to get back to see her in time but we had kept in touch and she still loved me, for which I am eternally grateful.

5

Rubberneck with a Song

IT was 1916 when I started to study with Lulu. That year, too, commenced the feeling against the Germans—even in St. Louis—that brought the first unhappiness into my life.

The German community in St. Louis had always been such a close-knit, *gemütlich* group that I thought nothing could be changed about it. Its love of life was as permanent as the stars to me. World War I proved that I was wrong. I recall two incidents which proved that certain emotions can shatter even the tightest ties.

My *grossmama* and *grosspapa* used to entertain some of the first families of the city—wealthy, social, with pronounced German points of view. When war broke out and our country entered it, my grandmother made a point of announcing at each party that hers was "an American household." She wanted no discussion at all that would be in any way derogatory to the United States. On one occasion a male member of one of the most prominent families—during the after-dinner session of liqueurs, coffee, and chocolate, pipes and cigars—made what my grandmother thought was a slurring remark about Americans. She bristled and interrupted. She asked him to repeat what he had said and explain it.

43

He had his own courage: he did just that. "I thought so," said my grandmother coldly. "You are criticizing my country, the country of my family. We are not German here, we are American. I would be very happy, sir, if you would do me the favor to leave my house and never come back." He did. From that day until the day she died, my grandmother never spoke to that family.

As children, we always spoke German at home. We spoke it at the social gatherings, at the song fests, at every intimate group in which we participated. But such a language was not for my grandmother once the conflict began. She forbade any of us to speak German in her presence. That was the first time I learned how well she spoke English. I remember making a mistake and lapsing into German once in a while. My mother would lean over to me and whisper: "English, Helena, only English!"

My grandmother was an extraordinary and dominating figure in our life. She taught me the real rules of living: that no one really has a grudge against the world or against a person, only against himself. In our family it often happened that one of us offended another: "Mama, you should hear what Helen just said!" In such cases my grandmother would make a sweeping gesture. "Come to my house! We will all have supper!" she commanded. "After supper we will hear the complaints and adjust things." Most of the time we found we were ashamed to bring up what had made us angry. If we had a real injustice, my grandmother would sit in judgment and issue her decrees that one should apologize or make amends. We did what she said. No one ever went away from her table with a bad feeling.

In those days I was accused rightly of being "more of a ruffian than my brother" and I had no thoughts of anything but music. I should have been thinking of college but I never did—and I never went. If I had, I am sure I should have flunked instantly. My concentration was entirely in another direction. I should have had no time to study the bare elements of a curriculum.

By 1924 the emotions of World War I had been largely forgotten as a way of hating and judging. My voice had not changed in my eight years of studying with Lulu: it had only increased in depth and timbre, in its control and focus. Those years had given me—sharp and clear in my mind—the image of the artist I wanted to be. Perhaps it is an ideal which I never achieved but which I have always kept in front of me from that day to this, a personal shrine.

It is not enough to have what is designated as a beautiful voice. Though mine has rarely been described as anything else, I am not always happy with what I can make it do. There must be the vision and the ability to take sheer, unadulterated work as your portion, day after day, month after month. "Who is a good voice teacher?" someone once asked Giulio Gatti-Casazza, the czar of the Metropolitan Opera in those days. "That is an easy question," the great operatic director answered instantly. "It is that teacher who is lucky enough to have an exceptional pupil." I was exceptional in my gifts, possibly, but what gave Lulu and my other teachers pride in me was my ability to concentrate on my voice and to be willing to work like a slavey to perfect it. To some this may sound like vanity, but if I had pride in my voice, I was forced to be humble about myself. I had to consider my singing and myself as separate entities.

I have often been advised not to put all my eggs in one basket —and that may be right. The load of eggs I carry around consists of my ability to be a human being rather than a mere vehicle for sound: and I put eggs into every basket available. All of them in each basket. I have been lucky enough never to have to ask anything of anyone and I have managed never to owe anything to anyone—except the most valuable things, love and companionship. God knows how many voices have been beautiful in this world. God knows how very few of those so blessed have labored on their scales and exercises until they were developed, the one idea my mind fastened onto very early and never lost hold of.

It is difficult for me to make up my mind about things beyond music. There are so many good things in life to choose from, I feel I have to give or burst. Every morning when I wake up I feel I must contribute to the world some part of me. A friend once said to me: "It's a great responsibility to be your friend; you're the easiest person in the world to take advantage of. People like you spoil others—they demand more and more and if you don't give it—because you started it—you're to blame."

That is the basic defect in my character: it is hard for me to expect something in return from others and everyone must. I cannot, as I once believed, simply flow outward—something must flow back in to me, to replenish. Art supplies some of this; people supply much more. I consider my deepest failing to be the fact that I am a very poor judge of people. I like everyone—until they disappoint me. Then something inside me closes like stone gates. I cannot help it; I feel like the child in a fairy tale, picking daisies in the fields and running up to the castle gates only to have them slam shut. It is this bitter disappointment that gives me firmness in a crisis. After I make up my mind, there is nothing left for me except to go forward and remember with gladness.

I draw a great deal of my strength simply from cities and the people of cities. I have never liked small towns too much because they seem to hoard their energies. In the great hives of cities I find a high spirit, a flow that I can leap into and share and perhaps contribute to. San Francisco, the city of broad vistas, amiable people, and individual ideas with its great civic pride; New Orleans, with its languid atmosphere, half-awakened from the past; Chicago, homey, friendly, wholesome; Paris, a perfume of a city—heady, gay, and light—with a subtle indirectness; London, a man's city with its impersonal frankness and its disciplines that come from its history; Hong Kong, with its color and drastic rawness of simply fighting for existence, a day-to-day city—but above all, New York, the great impersonal "I-Am-City," which needs nothing because it *is*. It reaches into every fiber of you and analyzes you until there is nothing left except a breathless emotion.

It was in New York that I found a match for what I thought was my talent. It was not conceit that made me think so but a kind of wild expectation or hope—it was what I felt in my voice, something so far in the heights that perhaps I never achieved it. The soaring buildings, the bustle of life, the brisk clarity of the weather, the feeling of being alive—all these I could anticipate when I sang. Singing was so much of my life that it could take me out of myself; I could be proud of what I did and yet stand aside and criticize myself mercilessly, night after night, note by note.

In those days I never quite did what I wanted to do in song. When I did, I was transformed. I literally felt that, supported by the orchestra, I could walk out over the heads of the audience. I was drunk on sounds in those days: there was no noise so loud that I could not stand it and rejoice in it; there was none so soft that I couldn't hear it and be ravished by it.

Another in my assortment of faults is that I like to be comfortable. Not that this is a sin in itself. It just tends to make anyone fond of his possessions. When I was young I saw three of my dearest relatives—my mother, uncle, and aunt—cajoled one by one out of their fortunes. Furniture, apartment houses, even personal belongings went. They must have lost well over two hundred thousand dollars. Perhaps this has had some influence over my own thinking: I am wary of holding anything too tightly and too long.

I recall putting ten dollars every week under the cover on my uncle's dresser so that he would not be embarrassed about asking me for spending money. I recall my mother and aunt saying, in their most distressed accents, "But I can't let that go; I have to keep that; don't you remember what a nice time we had when we got *that?*" It cluttered up their attics—and their thinking.

Yet I have possessions galore that I have collected over the

years. In clothing alone I have a full storeroom packed with
hangers. I know I have a dozen very expensive brocade robes
from the Orient, but I could let them go and use a three-dollar
bathrobe just as easily. I must have thirty evening gowns, forty
street dresses, a couple of dozen suits, trunks of unused underclothing, more than a dozen pajamas. All this truly frightens me
to think of—though this is not a great deal of clothing, personal
and professional, for a woman whose dresses are part of her
necessary wardrobe to earn a living. I have thousands of dollars'
worth of jewelry which I love to wear when the occasion per-
mits. Now, for the first time, after a lifetime of apartments, Bill
and I have a small eight-room house in Beverly Hills.

Out of all these physical possessions I have not gotten one item
of spiritual benefit. I could live without lace on panties and
enough underclothing to guarantee a clean change; I could use
no more than a robe, a couple of suits, three or four dresses. Like
a meal, you can use only one at a time. The pride of possession
has become meaningless.

What do I really value? My husband, my singing, my health,
and my friends. Of these, the singing—which for such a long time
was my whole dedicated life—is now the least. Of the three, I
would choose my husband as my most precious possession, that
and the understanding we have between us on life. If he would
die or be taken from me? Then I would have the memory of
twenty-three years of superb and happy living. That would have
to be sufficient.

I say this: "When you were born, in the beginning of life, who
promised you anything?" I am steadily growing more and more
into a state of amazement that so many people need so many
things—that ultimately control their way of life and their thinking. I am trying to do away with just that in my own life. A piano
used to be one of the most important single possessions to me.
Today I do not own a single one: I rent them.

Not that I regret what I have. I have a sort of shamelessness about it. My voice has trapped me in a special kind of life. I love to spend, to live up to the grand tradition of the opera prima donna. But what I am ashamed of is that so many people have less than I, have so many fewer blessings.

My God, does all this mean I'm getting old and sentimental? Maybe I am moving over the hill and don't know it. What I enjoy these days is talking and sitting around in the morning or evening over coffee, laughing and reminiscing. The future is wonderful but it is never so bright as the past or the present to me.

My friends in St. Louis used to ask me, when I was young, "When are you going to New York, Helena?" I would say: "I'm perfectly happy right here in St. Louis. I'm following my own dream. I have the best teacher I can get. I want to sing as beautifully as possible. Until I'm sure I can do it, until I'm ready to leave—I'm satisfied right here, thank you."

That is my attitude toward this world and heaven. Until I am satisfied that I have done the best I can with the talents I have right here, I am satisfied, thank you. Heaven can wait.

My first public singing, after I was taken on as a pupil by Lulu, was singing concerts (eight years later) with the St. Louis Symphony Orchestra. In 1924 it was an excellent, very responsive organization of perhaps eighty-five men. It was and is one of the three oldest such symphonies in the United States. Rudolph Ganz was its conductor. He was a great pianist in his own right, a tall, gentle man who performed miracles with his musicians. The first time I sang with them was in the old Odeon Theatre. Right after the concert, the building burned down. Rudy winked at me at our next rehearsal in a rented hall and whispered: "Who knows, Helen, how many places like that you will burn down?"

Afterward we gave our recitals at the Municipal Auditorium, a fine, fireproof building, and I am happy to say it is still there. I went out on two tours with the orchestra—one of ten and the other of seven weeks. We covered the Middle West, from New Orleans to Chicago.

Rudy always played beautifully for me. He often accompanied me himself on the piano. He even composed and sometimes orchestrated for me because, as he said, "a beautiful sound should have a beautiful setting." I was paid eight hundred dollars a week and sang seven times a week on tour. I was not very well acquainted with concert life—my mother was always with me so I always felt at home. When my turn came to sing they just turned me around and pointed me toward the stage. I went out and opened my mouth at the right time. Audiences never bothered me. I could feel their friendliness and their warmth for me, and as soon as I commenced to sing all feelings of stage fright or anything like it fell away and I floated upward. In those days musical audiences were always enthusiastic and of a remarkably high level of cultural consciousness. One knew what to expect on every occasion in every city because no one except those who loved music ever came to hear it. Music throughout the country was not yet a society exercise in mink and gabble.

My billing was always in comfortably large letters beneath that of Ganz. The first number I ever sang with the orchestra was an aria from Puccini; the last was a Wagnerian number. I usually indulged myself in excerpts from *Tannhäuser,* or *Carmen,* or *Louise* by Charpentier. I must have calmed down a little in my estimate of myself in those hard-working days because my family stopped calling me "Queenie." Mother handled the money—after those years I was the earning mainstay of the Traubel family— and I had little to do except tour the various cities, admire them, and do my chore of singing each night. Romance never entered my head: I used to see one of the cellists—a real krauthead right out of a St. Louis barrel—perform as a ladies' man very successfully with a line of damsels at the stage door every night. I wondered at his charm with the hand kissing and bowing. Later in life I found out what it can do for the female ego.

In 1926 Ganz went to New York. He gave a concert in the Lewisohn Stadium there. I sang the "Liebestod" of Isolde from *Tristan und Isolde*. The dressing rooms were open, under the stage. During the performance I noticed a man walking back and forth, back and forth, before mine. Finally, I demanded nervously: "Who is that man?" No one knew. At the end of the performance, I found out. He was a guard posted there by Arthur Judson, one of the most successful music agents in the business.

Judson, I think, was one of the handsomest males I ever saw. He was tall, with perfect features, erect carriage, and perfect aplomb. He came right in and said: "You have the greatest voice I have ever heard."

"Thank you," I said.

"Come to my office," he said, "I would like to talk to you."

"I'm sorry," I said obstinately; "I'm very busy."

I was not being shy or coy or impudent—I was simply wary and a little scared. Judson must have sensed it. He laughed. "All right," he said. "Where are you staying?"

"At the Algonquin Hotel."

"May I call you in the next few days?"

"All right," I said.

Mother and I lived in the Algonquin Hotel near Times Square because it was a busy place, full of coming and going. We loved it, though we did not know many of the famous people that inhabited it. We paid a solid price for a living room and two bedrooms—fourteen dollars a day in those times—and were unhappy about it. A tenor living there with his wife felt much the same way. One day he reported excitedly to us that he had found a fine new residential hotel—the White Hotel—at Lexington and Thirty-sixth Street. It had been just built and it had what seemed reasonable rates. We moved in.

From the first the manager loved my mother; the pastry chef loved me. Two or three times a week he used to send up baskets of *petits fours*—the basket being made of fine peppermint candy.

We got to be very fond of this gift and kept expecting it; we even shared it sometimes with our friends when our consciences and weigh-ins commenced to bother us. The manager's only complaint was: "Mrs. Traubel, there's no service in the kitchen when the chef is getting something for you!"

Both of us loved food. We ate everything we could get our hands on. We especially liked sampling something new. My mother used to go out to Times Square and buy large bags of roasted chestnuts and devour them; so did I. I can still taste the smoky sweet savor of those chestnuts—and I suppose we may have eaten as much as a bushel a day between us. The vendors got to know us. We used to sit and gossip with them while we crunched.

"You shouldn't do this, Clara," I would say to my mother. "It isn't dignified."

"Oh, Helena, I know," she would say, her eyes shining and her mouth stuffed like a goose, "but I don't care what I look like when I'm eating, I can't help loving these chestnuts." Even the people at the restaurants and hamburger stands called her by her first name and gave her extra helpings of whatever she wanted. There is no bond greater than that between people who love food. I succumbed; I was never happier than when I did.

I have always been grateful that in my profession a stylish stout is considered an asset to the production of rich tones. You have to have the space to make the noise and you have to have the weight to surround the space. Eating and talking have always gone on in me and around me as far back as I can remember. At our family table I got the habit of pointing for something to eat rather than interrupting some long-winded relative. Today my conversation suffers because of it. "Keep the hand down and use the head and say what you want," my husband has to admonish me.

That first trip in 1926 proved to me that New York had all I wanted as a place to live. With rides on the subway, the ferries to Staten Island, the walks in Central Park, the museums, concerts, zoos, and theaters, I felt with all my heart a part of its electric way of existence. I wanted to stay. But I knew I was not yet ready to meet what the city had to offer. I would have to learn much, much more. As it was, it was ten years before I came back prepared to do what I wanted to.

Meanwhile, I was looking desperately for a singing teacher. I knew Lulu would not mind. She was always confident that however far I roamed I would always come back to her. Not because of sentimentality but because she was sure of her own talent dovetailing with what my voice needed and my own good judgment about her. I used to go to her studio when I returned to St. Louis and say: "I couldn't find what I wanted anywhere else, Lulu." She would give her harsh bark of a laugh and say: "Why not?"

"They couldn't produce the tones I wanted; they couldn't show me the way to sing beautifully."

"All right," Lulu would say grudgingly. "It shows you have a good pair of ears anyway."

The Ganzes—Mary and Rudy—took me to visit a voice teacher whom they knew and endorsed. She was one of the most famous in the world, having taught for years in Europe and had lately opened a studio on Fifty-seventh Street. I sang the familiar aria from *Louise* while she listened. At the end, she rose—a tall, austere woman—and moved around the piano toward me. Her eyes were moist.

"This is a great, great voice," she said emotionally. "I must teach this girl."

"Do you hear her?" demanded Mary. "Aren't you flattered?"

"Oh, yes," I said doubtfully. "I don't want to seem impertinent, but tell me—what is your theory, madame?"

"Theory?" she said, amazed. Rudy, sitting in the corner, smothered a smile with his hand.

"I mean," I said, "how do you teach what you want me to learn?"

"Helen!" cried the scandalized Mary.

"I have to know," I said stubbornly.

"Of course she does," said the teacher. She launched into a long dissertation on her ideas about singing. Mary listened in ecstasy; Rudy kept grinning and looking at my reactions from his corner.

I had heard the same vague lecture a dozen times. I was not looking for a teacher to show me how to produce tone: Lulu was doing exactly what I wanted in that direction. I needed someone to show me how to sing a song—how to convince an audience. My prospective tutor, out of breath, paused. I nodded. "I really meant what you want me to do in practice," I said politely.

"I can show you in France," she said. "I conduct a school at Fontainebleau every summer. I take perhaps ten or a dozen pupils —the daughters of the rich who feel complimented and want to get rid of them—for four thousand dollars apiece. You will go with me for nothing! I shall pay all expenses and teach you, too!"

"Thank you very much," I said stubbornly. "But tell me, can you give me the name of someone who follows your teaching and who has become successful?" Mary stared at me in stupefaction. I heard a snort from Rudy. The teacher, a little stunned, rose and pointed to a picture on the wall. It was of a Metropolitan Opera singer who was famous at the time but who, in my heart of hearts, I had always considered a hack. She sang any role at any time on short notice—from contralto to soprano. She did a competent job, surely, but it was nothing of which I thought I would be proud.

"I'm sorry," I said promptly. "I don't care for her singing at all."

After that there seemed little to be said. We murmured our good-bys and went down to the sidewalk. Mary was furious with me; Rudy was laughing so hard that he was bumping into people as he walked.

"Good heavens!" said Mary indignantly. "How can you be so gauche, Helen? This is the greatest singing teacher alive today!"

"I know," I said contritely. "She may be, and I'm sure she will mean everything to some people, but she has nothing for me."

"You can't expect to push Helen," interposed Rudy, still chuckling. "There has to be some sort of rapport between teacher and pupil." He laughed all that evening.

I imagine I was brash and impudent in those days. It is hard to think of a girl in her twenties who has such fixed and immovable convictions. But I believed then that I was right; I still believe it. I had no desire to be any person but the one I had dreamed of as a little girl; it was the rock-solid quality of this dream that kept me going. I recall that I was supposed to be taught by a great tenor who also taught in Europe. I refused when I heard his name. "Why?" demanded my exasperated listener, who happened to be Walter Damrosch. "Because his picture is on Lulu's wall," I said, "and the inscription reads: 'To Madame Vetta-Karst, who teaches what I try to do.' That's not the teacher I want."

Perhaps I can say it this way: I was only nibbling at the edges of great music. I wanted to be able to eat a full meal, a royal repast of the greatest music known in the world. To do that, I knew instinctively, there must be no compromise whatever. Nothing must be held back, either in my larynx or my heart.

6

Damrosch and the "Man"

IT must have been some time in 1926 or 1927 that I had my head scraped as clean as a billiard ball.

The idea came to me when I used to pass a magnificent hair shop on Forty-fourth Street between Broadway and Sixth Avenue. It was a dream of an establishment. It had the most tasteful *décor* with a window full of all kinds and colors of wigs. A big sign in the window—day and night—proclaimed HAIR TREATMENTS for all who would come and be shaved.

It seemed like a suggestion well worth taking. Perhaps there was a hypnotic quality about my going back and forth in front of that shiny plate glass with its eternal capitalized admonition. Whatever it was it affected me strongly. Something dreadful was happening to my fine-fibered chestnut topping. It was getting very thin. I felt I should do something drastic, especially when it itched as I gazed at the sign.

One day I abruptly turned off the street and went into the shop. They examined my scalp. They clucked alarmingly over what they found. They never did tell me what it was but they advised me solemnly that they had detected a "very bad condition." They would have to go right down to the roots.

"Shave it?" I queried.

"Ah, *oui,* madame," they said sadly.

"You mean I can have one of those beautiful red wigs in the window?" I cried. I commenced to laugh. "Go ahead!" I told them. "Go right ahead!"

I think they were shocked at such an offhand decision but they took the measurements of my head for a wig and let me have my own hair for seven days more. The next week they shaved me as neat as a baby's bottom. I saw the shape of me on top for the first time—a good deal like an oddly turned breadfruit, I must say. They massaged my head furiously and rubbed in a burning salve, washing and rubbing—and finally let me go. I tried on my hat. It fell over my ears. I realized then that I needed that glorious red wig.

It was bobbed. Something I had always been too young to dare to do to myself but for which I had always longed. I went home swinging my auburn tresses against my neck and glorying in the new feeling of them. If I may say so, there is something about shaving off her crowning glory that gives a woman a great feeling of freedom. It is altogether equal if not superior to getting the vote.

I strode into our apartment like a conqueror. My mother looked up. Her face screwed itself up into astonishment.

"Helena!" she said. "You've cut your hair short!"

"Yes," I said, chuckling, "yes, I *have* cut it short." I took off my hat, careful not to knock the wig sideways. "Do you like it?"

"It looks rather nice," said my mother cautiously. "It doesn't look too bad."

"I like it," I said. "It's easier to keep this way."

"Oh, yes," my mother agreed. "Very definitely."

We said nothing else about it. As was our custom, we went to the theater that night. When we came home I went to the bathroom first and got ready for bed. I came out without my wig. I walked over to my mother, planted my feet, and spread my arms, a big smile on my face.

My mother stared. She stared and stared, as if she were paralyzed. She had an expression of horror on her sweet face. At last she got her vocal cords to function.

"*Mein Gott,* Helena!" she whispered. "What did you do to yourself?" You would have thought I had cut my throat in the bathroom.

"Nothing," I said.

"Nothing!"

"I just had my hair shaved off and a wig clapped on top."

"But why? Why?"

"I was losing all my hair anyway. I thought I might as well do it fast as slow."

Suddenly my mother burst into laughter. She laughed until the tears poured down her face. She became nearly hysterical and sank into a chair. This alarmed me, but before I could get the smelling salts she managed to blurt out: "Oh, Helena, if you could only see you as I do!"

It was to take six months before my hair came back to any length at all. I had it mowed several times before my cure of the scalp whatzis was complete. I had only a soft stubble on my head when we went home to St. Louis for Christmas.

Naturally, for our folks the occasion was a big one. Everyone swarmed into our apartment house, friends and relatives, neighbors and well-wishers. The place was bedlam incarnate. I did nothing about it until twelve o'clock midnight, Christmas Eve. Then I went into the bedroom, tossed my wig on the bed, rubbed my crew cut for luck, and went into the crowded parlor.

Everyone was kissing each other, laughing, yelling, having the time of their lives; singing and dancing, telling stories at the top of their voices. When I entered, an instant hush fell over the room. I put my arms on my hips and winked at them.

That did it. The howling and shouting that broke loose fairly rocked the house. I was grabbed and spun about, kissed around the room, bombarded with questions, and poured full of champagne. The worst of it all was that someone sneaked into the bedroom and got my wig. Everyone in the parlor tried it on. It paraded around endlessly—they almost ruined a two-hundred-dollar confection. I looked perfectly dreadful for the rest of the evening. No one noticed anything but the wig—on someone else.

That first year in New York for work and study was a blessing. It built up my self-confidence; it gave me a goal for my blind instinct of singing. I studied with a woman named Renée Criticos for six months, with the idea of putting more thought into my songs, of giving them more emotional content. It was then I commenced to learn that music was more than tone. I signed no contracts but I did some half-vast recitals at the urging of Judson.

Judson was always trying to get me to try my wings of song before I was satisfied they would support me. I was not coy or bashful with him—I was simply certain of the point in my career that I had attained. If I was going to go further, I had to take my own route. Judson wanted me to go to Europe. "I've spoken to a *great* conductor," he said mysteriously. "I have you all lined up for ten concerts next spring."

"I'm sorry," I said promptly. "I can't go."

The strained notes of overpublicized Marion Talley were ringing in my head—a girl who had so much promise and had made her debut that year at eighteen at the Metropolitan. She vanished from the musical world three years after. I had thrilled to the great sound made by another singer who had just appeared on the American opera stage, Lauritz Melchior—but I had not the slightest idea that he would be my future partner. At that moment I only realized my trip to the top was much longer than I thought as a girl.

"Why not? Why can't you go? It's a great op—"

"I'm not ready," I said automatically.

Judson was exasperated. He plumped his hands on his desk. "And when will you be ready?" he demanded.

"I don't know. I just know I'm not now."

"Why not?"

My voice rose a notch. "I'm not satisfied with my sound and my handling of songs," I said.

Judson shook his head and looked ceilingward. "What do you have in mind?" he asked after a while.

"Nothing except studying." My curiosity was piqued. "What would I get for the concerts?" I asked.

Judson glared at me. "Nothing, my dear," he said. "As a matter of fact, you would have to pay ten thousand dollars."

I laughed my loudest. "Where would I get money like that?" I demanded. Judson measured me expertly.

"I should say," he said slowly, "that a person with your looks and talent should have no trouble in securing it from some amiable music patron."

I was pleased at the compliment. I stood up. "If I'm good now, I'll be better when I'm ready," I said. I could not resist adding: "Why don't you give me the money, Mr. Judson?"

He grinned and said: "I might just do that." But we never came to any agreement.

I went out on tour for him for four months on those half-concerts. I appeared with great artists such as Wanda Landowska, that genius of the harpsichord, and Hans Kindler, great on the cello, the instrument I have always admired most because of its marvelous tone production. I would dress myself in a red velvet gown, go out and do my songs, and come off more than a little dissatisfied with myself despite the applause. Wanda and I always got along wonderfully. I recall once, waiting in the wings, that her music stopped. A ripple of laughter ran through the audience. I peeked out. Wanda was on her hands and knees among the pedals of her ancient instrument.

I thought she was sick. I stage-whispered: "Wanda, what's the matter? Are you all right?"

She turned her lovely, ageless face toward me and said in perfect simplicity: "But, Helen, the pedal has fallen off. There is no one to fix it." She had a screw driver in her hand which she probably carried in her bosom. She screwed on the pedal and calmly got up on the seat and went on with her program. The management and I were rolling in a fit of hysterics backstage.

I came back to New York and saw Judson once more. He informed me that he had more concerts for me (I was getting five hundred dollars every time I sang). I put up my hand. "No more singing for me!" I cried. "I can't stand hearing myself. I'm getting worse and worse!"

"I have a contract with you," Judson said sternly. "You are going to honor it."

"No contract," I informed him. "You sent it to me but I never signed it." Judson turned white, emitted a groan, and buzzed for his secretary. She confirmed what I had said. Judson reluctantly let me go.

Back I went to my womb of St. Louis. I had been more than a little unhappy with my abortive birth into the concert world. I was to stay there for the next eight years—singing, as usual, at the Pilgrim Congregational Church and the United Hebrew Temple, earning about thirty-six hundred dollars a year from both jobs and occasionally getting one hundred dollars for a funeral of any denomination. The money went to my mother. I went to Lulu regularly—up and down the scales, learning a new tune, up and up and down and down the scales again. It was to be 1934 before my life was to take a really significant change.

In New York I had sung for Walter Damrosch. He had not let me finish my selection before bounding up and inquiring what I was going to do with my voice. I gave him my stock answer: go back to St. Louis. He appeared disgruntled but he said no more about it. He evidently forgot completely about the girl from the

country because the next time we met he was convinced I was
a stranger.

It was eight years later, at the St. Louis *Saengerfest* in 1934. I
was happily studying with Lulu, giving joint recitals at the
Ethical Culture Society, and once in a while singing with the
St. Louis Symphony. That year the town commenced to buzz: it
had been chosen as the headquarters of harmony for that year.
It was a huge honor for a city. More than fifty—sometimes nearly
one hundred—German singing societies would attend, selecting
one metropolis in the spring for a week of lung straining and
beer drinking.

I heard about it and thought no more of it. I was busy fishing,
my favorite participation sport. I have always loved to go after
anything that shakes a fin. I have tried all ways. My favorite
still remains a worm on the hook and a cork on the water. There
is something infinitely quieting to me about sitting by a stream
and dreamily waiting for the cork and line to jiggle. I have
caught all kinds of fish in all sorts of streams, from sunfish to
bass, while softly inviting them with a lied or a piscatorial
"Liebestod."

One day I returned home to find an invitation to be the featured solo singer at the *Saengerfest*. I discovered that Walter
Damrosch had been invited to be the guest conductor. This offered as much of a challenge to me as a bobbing cork. I accepted
on the spot.

In those days Damrosch was a tall, handsome man with an
aquiline nose, good figure, bushy white brows, and white sleek
hair. He talked as if he were the Pope of Music—which indeed,
to most of the United States, he was. He had a magniloquent,
sonorous way of making pontifical (and sometimes pixie) utter-
ances. Everyone listened when he spoke. He had started his
famous Music Appreciation Hour on radio. His voice was piped
into practically every school. Previous to that he had been conductor at the Metropolitan and had led the New York Symphony

which later merged with the Philharmonic. He was still one of the great powers of music in the land. His name was on most of the vital committees and social bunds that took care of such matters.

I asked about the program. I saw the selections: all Wagner. That suited me down to the ground.

It did not suit Damrosch. I learned (long afterward) that my acceptance of the offer to be the soloist had enraged the old man beyond belief. "Who," he demanded resonantly over the telephone to the apologetic committee head in St. Louis, "is this Helen— Helen What's-her-name?"

"Traubel."

"Traubel! I don't know her, I've never heard of her, I don't want to hear of her! If you think you can foist some squeaky little local-talent girl onto me, you are very badly mistaken, my man!"

I imagine that the committee might have thrown in the towel, paid me off, and got some other, more reputable singer but for the fact that their civic pride had been roused. Telegrams and telephone calls raged between Damrosch and St. Louis. He demanded I quit; they refused. I went on serenely practicing my numbers with Lulu, unaware of the storm that was blowing in the stratosphere.

"All right," said the St. Louis delegation finally, "we'll meet your demand, Mr. Damrosch. All we ask is that you rehearse with her. We will stand on your judgment. If she does not measure up to your standards, we will hire whomever you say." His pride mollified, Damrosch agreed.

Completely ignorant of all this, I came down to the Arena Auditorium that morning at eleven thirty, humming a tune, ready to go to work. Damrosch was on the stage. He nodded and spoke to me very politely without the slightest sign of recognition.

"What would you like to sing?" he asked. I said mischievously: "Anything, as long as it is the aria from *Tannhäuser* and the 'Liebestod' of Isolde," the two selections he had programmed.

Damrosch's lips tightened. "We'll start with the 'Liebestod,' "
he said. As he told me afterward, "I said to myself: 'We'll blow
her off this platform right now.' " He had one of the best pieces
in the world to blast a budding soprano: the voice had to come
in exactly on the note of a bassoon. It is very difficult to hit it
correctly. But I had sung it enough so that I did not care if the
bassoonist dropped dead. I could hit the note in my sleep.

"My dear," said Damrosch in his best pontifical tones, "we'll
try it right now if you don't mind."

"I don't mind," I said. He looked at me once and turned to the
orchestra. With one hand on his hip and the other condescend-
ingly waggling over the heads of his men, he coughed and ges-
tured me to begin.

Three kettledrum notes introduce the "Liebestod." I took my
three and let loose. I kept going and watching Damrosch out of
the corner of my eye. His head jerked around, his beat became
slower and slower. I finished the number and he sprang upon me.
He kissed me on both cheeks.

"My dear, I must see you after rehearsal!" he boomed excitedly.
He turned to the orchestra, all of whom were St. Louisans and
my closest adherents. "Why," shouted Damrosch to them, "why
have you buried a voice like this in this miserable city and done
nothing about it?"

The first cellist—the same romantic krauthead that used to
go out with us on tour and make the women swoon—moved diffi-
dently. He said: "We thought you *might* like her, Herr Doktor,
yah?"

After the rehearsal I met Margaret Damrosch, who was always
one of my best friends. "You have one of the great voices of
the world," she said instantly.

"I wish I could think so, too," I said. Damrosch came bustling
in.

"This is insanity, hiding yourself in this out-of-the-way city!"
he cried. "You must come to New York!"

"Thank you very much."

"You will come, then?"

"No."

"Why not?"

"I don't think I'm ready, Dr. Damrosch."

He was amazed. "You will sing under my sponsorship. You will be the hit of the Metropolitan! You *will* sing at the Metropolitan?"

"I don't feel so inside myself yet," I said seriously. "I want to, of course. But not yet, not yet."

Damrosch dropped down on a chair. "I found Johanna Gadski," he said in a low voice. "I found her in a remote German city many years ago. I trained her, brought her to this country." He stopped. I knew what he was thinking. Gadski was one of the really great singers of all time in the era from 1895 to 1917. I had heard her, and though she was then on her decline, she was one singer I truly admired.

"I have wanted all these years to find another voice and when I find it, she tells me she is not ready," finished the seventy-two-year-old Damrosch sadly.

"I'm sorry," I stammered. "It's the way I feel. I must go on with my training."

Damrosch sighed and shook his head. He looked at Margaret, who looked down at her hands.

"Well," Damrosch said heavily, "I'm composing an opera, *The Man Without a Country*. It is written for men only. It has no female voices in it—I did not know there was such a voice as yours in the world. Now I shall go back to New York and rewrite the whole work—if you will only consent to sing the lead in it."

"No," I said.

"You can sing it at the Met or at my home!"

I shook my head. My eyes felt wet. "We've met before, Dr. Damrosch," I said. "You thought I was good then but you never even bothered to remember me!" I left the room.

During the next week that Damrosch was in St. Louis he and his wife invited me to have lunch with them often. He asked me again and again to take the role in his proposed opera. Just as often I refused. He was not used to having someone as stubborn as himself—I think he died still thinking I was crazy in trying to perfect a beautiful sound. But at length he yielded.

"What do you want me to do?" he asked me on his last day.

I relented a little. "Why don't you send me the opera when you have it finished and we will see," I said. I had no thought that he would rewrite it with such a vague and conditional reply. I was wrong.

Meanwhile, I went back to one of my hobbies: singing for a women's group. It was called the Piano Club, an organization of wealthy girls who gathered round to try out their voices and compositions. One of them was my special friend. I always sang the songs she wrote. I disliked them and told her so: they were invariably about tombs and death and vague philosophic topics. To me it is difficult to write such philosophy into a song—the singer is usually dead before she starts.

"I write for the sake of writing," she said, "instead of buying a new hat."

"Why don't you just try some new words?" I asked. "The tunes are so nice."

"They don't suit my mood."

"If you want to sell them, you have to be a little more cheerful at least."

"I can't compromise my talent, Helen, I'm very sorry," she would say.

Finally, in the fall of 1935, she asked me to give an invitational recital of her songs in New York. I agreed. We put on a whole program of her compositions. I thought it went off very well—but she did not. "Helen," she said, "you sang so damn beautifully that no one, no one at all, listened to the words of my songs!" It was at this concert that Giorgio Polacco, the sprightly little Met conductor, heard me for the first time and became an instant friend.

I assume that the recital came at just the wrong moment in my life for her—and the right one for me. That year I commenced at last to hear a little of what I wanted to hear in my voice. I was convinced what I was working for was right. That was the year Damrosch took me up on my promise to appear in *The Man Without a Country*.

He had called me in 1935, saying that the music was finished. I had later read the score, which was fairly good though far from great. He asked me if I would help him audition his score for a Met production. I reluctantly agreed, saying I would sing it only if it were performed in his house.

In 1936 I arrived in New York alone. I wanted to travel that way, to sop up all the electricity and massiveness that it could contribute to my feelings. I wanted to renew my affair with the big city. I went to the American Woman's Club and set up housekeeping. The Damrosches welcomed me and we commenced rehearsing the opera at breakneck speed for two weeks. At the end of that time the performance was given with a cast of eight and a chorus of eight—before the most select musical audience possible in America. Every notable figure who was a cog in the intricate mechanism of music in the country put in an appearance at the behest of Damrosch.

It was a wonderful setting near Fifth Avenue in the fifties. Damrosch had bought two houses instead of one and had knocked out the adjoining walls of each so as to make one immense mansion. I have had many of my happiest musical intervals there, just sitting with Damrosch and hearing him play and improvise melodies or burst into arias on the spur of the moment. In those days we really had jam sessions of the voice, something that is rarely seen today, with the notes and their arrangement being composed on the spur of the moment.

I must say all eight of us in *The Man Without a Country* sang our little hearts out for that top-drawer audience. After it was over and the congratulations—polite and sincere—had died down, we had supper. I was sandwiched in between Edward Johnson, the former tenor and manager of the Metropolitan Opera, and John Royal, vice-president of the National Broadcasting Company. This craggy-faced, abrupt Irishman and I struck up a friendship—good enough for me to call him Finnegan for the rest of his natural life.

It was Johnson who got in the first licks. "Why don't you sing the part of Aïda at the Metropolitan?" he asked.

"I'm not ready," I said.

"If you got the part you would be," he riposted.

Royal broke in from the other side: "My God, where have you and that voice been?" he demanded.

"In St. Louis," I said.

"We have to have you at NBC," he barked.

"What could I do?" I asked innocently.

"Sing! Sing!" he cried.

"No," I said.

"Why not?"

I gave him my usual answer and he roared like a wounded lion as Johnson listened with both ears. "Set your own time!" he told me.

That night Damrosch kept me up until two in the morning, having me, as his protégée, tell him all that had been poured into my rose-pink ears. "Why don't you do Aïda?" he said amazed.

"Because she's a downbeat slave girl," I said. (I have never learned the part to this day.)

He was stunned. He walked around the room as I told him about Royal. Damrosch nodded. "At least go to see Royal," he said. I promised I would. I got up to leave and he clasped my hand and looked soulfully into my eyes.

"I may be in my seventies," he said in a stage whisper, with Margaret smiling just behind him, "but I have ideas—ideas about you. A beautiful woman with a magnificent voice and I—where we could go, what we could do together, eh?"

"Calm down, Walter, calm down," Margaret said. I left them, a very happy girl.

Before I went to see Royal I agreed to appear on Damrosch's Music Appreciation radio program. I went down to the studio and sang a few songs by Brahms, and as I left, I was met at the door by Royal. He had heard me in his office over the radio intercom and recognized the tone.

"I heard it," he said with a grin. "Now I know we have to get you. We don't have this kind of singing anywhere in the United States today."

We went into his office. He sat me down and said: "We'll give you your own program. Anything you want. You name, we'll get."

"I have to earn my living," I said naïvely.

"How much do you make in St. Louis?" he asked.

"Five thousand a year," I said.

"How much do you want here?"

"It would take at least ten thousand for me to live in New York," I replied.

Royal jerked around, punched (he never pressed) a button, and hollered for his secretary.

"Not so fast!" I cried, alarmed. "What's going on?"

"You said, you did say, ten thousand dollars, and ten thousand it is," Royal returned.

"You're using blarney or something on me," I told him wildly.

"I know, 'You're not ready,' " he mimicked me.

"No, I'm not. I have to go back to St. Louis!"

"All right," Royal said abruptly. "Take the contract with you— but don't keep us waiting too long."

Nor did he give up his campaign there. He hammered at me luncheon after luncheon: sign, sign, sign. He tried to romance me, flatter me, and flatten me—all difficult feats at that time.

Damrosch was having more success. He blandly overrode the pledge he had given me and wheedled me into saying I would sing *The Man Without a Country* in the Metropolitan.

A year later I did, appearing for the first time in that six-tiered, rococo opera house. The opera was given three times that spring, I remember, and twice in the fall. It was not much of a success, I am sorry to say, for Damrosch. My reviews were acceptable. He was very disappointed at its reception though most of the reviewers were quite kind to him. All I recall is that my tenor was a man much smaller than I. In one scene I had to teeter across a gangplank, arms out, singing lustily to him. It was a rough few seconds for everyone in the house. If I had slipped and fallen on that fellow, *The Man Without a Country* would have been *The Country Without a Man*.

But before doing the opera—and after a few more programs with Damrosch on the radio in 1936—I fled back to St. Louis. I did not want to leave but it was imperative: infected tonsils were poisoning me. I was unable to sing.

Before I left one incident happened to me that changed the whole course of my life.

7

The Ego, Bill and I

AFTER my fourth or fifth television program a few years back, a man from Newark, New Jersey, wrote in. He said irritably that he was tired of hearing so much laughter from me. He said it seemed that every time he turned on his video machine he heard me laughing. It was driving him out of his mind.

At the same time the network was getting thousands of letters from people who were writing to me simply to say: "Thank you for laughing. It makes things easier, brighter."

If that lone man buried in Newark had only known, my laughter was not always bubbling at the top of my nature. There were times in my life when I felt the cold shadow of the only emotion I ever dreaded: the bleakness of unhappiness. I learned it took tears to create laughter.

I remember that winter night in 1936 when I opened the door of the house of a friend in Greenwich Village in New York. I went inside, into a big living room. There I saw, for the first time in my life, a husky, well-mannered man with slicked brown hair and the most beautiful and useless hands I ever saw on a human being—"feathers," I called them. He was, as I discovered, wise and witty. He was forever gay and gentle. I sat down with him and

71

our mutual friend that night. We talked—from eleven at night until seven o'clock the next morning—about anything and everything.

Going home in the gray, chill, delightful dawn of New York— with the streets hosed down, the early risers hurrying along the sidewalks—I leaned back in the corner of my taxi. I thought: "I would like to be married to a man like that."

It was impossible. I was already married. I had been married since I was nineteen years old.

It happened in the apartment house that Mother bought and moved into after the death of my father. The year was 1922. I was young, eager for any kind of adventure, in love with life. As we always had, we were having a gathering of friends one evening with the resultant hubbub and pleasant eating and drinking that always went on. I noticed a silent young man in a corner. He looked to me like a romantic combination of John Gilbert and Ronald Colman, who were my idols in the movies. I went over to him and introduced myself. He shyly told me his name: Louis Franklin Carpenter.

That was how I met my first husband. We dated each other for a year. I suppose we fell in love in a romantic way. I never even met his family who lived in a small town in Indiana. He was reserved, a man full of aloneness; he was moody, gentle, and aloof. I was eager and outgoing, ready for the wave of the next moment to break, to dive through it into the unknown beyond. I was restless about my whole life, full of the knowledge of what I wanted to be. He was satisfied—life was altogether acceptable to him as it was.

I do not know the exact moment when he asked me to marry him but I impulsively agreed. Perhaps it was my own energy that drove him to propose. I told my mother about it. She shook her head gravely. "You have to make up your own mind, Helena," she said. "I'm not going to say anything but I am not sympathetic. You could make that young man unhappy, you know."

"Nonsense, Mama!" I said.

The next day we were off to Minneapolis. There my fiancé, a car salesman, had a new job. We had eloped and we let our small social world think what it wanted to about it. I was delighted. Lou, in his own reserved way, shared my pleasure.

I stayed in Minneapolis only two months. It was a fine, bustling city—though a little chilly—yet I had the most miserable sixty days of my life. I felt as if I had taken a plunge into some sort of limbo where I was very slowly freezing to death in a self-made hell. I was not only away from my family and my friends—that had formed so tight and protective a ring around me all of my life— but I was away from my music. Lou cared nothing for music of any kind; he never could know what it meant to me in those days. Without it, I was naked. I had a tremendous yearning to do anything musical, to get back to that plateau where I could soar and float in that magic atmosphere. I was incomplete, away from something I had loved more dearly than anything else in life. For the first time I can remember I was frightened to death.

I begged Lou to go back to St. Louis. He heard me out, nodded solemnly, and said: "We'll do whatever you want to do, Helen."

We went back to my mother's apartment in our house. Lou got back his former job. I went back to my studies with Lulu. We all lived together in the boisterous, vital surroundings of our previous existence. Nothing was changed except that my husband had been added to my mother, aunt, and uncle. I do not believe Lou and I were alone for one moment of the years following. I cannot blame him for whatever frustrations he felt. As I said to a friend years later, with the reminiscent regret one feels about a youthful experiment that did not succeed: "Our marriage never had a chance."

Dozens of times my friends and my family—though never my mother—asked my why I had married Lou. I was driven to the point of angrily defending us when we really needed no defending. At last I came to the point where I asked the question of myself—and then went to ask it of him. I got no answer except that he loved me.

Perhaps this would and should have been enough. But for a girl as insatiable about the world as I, who wanted to surround it with her arms and squeeze it to death with delight, it was not enough. "We have nothing in common except chemistry," I said to Lou one night. I was being deliberately frank. My words never stirred him. I must have been developing what Bill calls today my "glacier attitude." I was overwhelming him, crushing him in spite of all obstacles—perhaps with coldness.

Going back to St. Louis, I knew I had not come home. I had left home when I left New York. My home town was the sky-scraper city on the Hudson; the beat of its streets matched the beat of my own needs. I knew it was high time for me to leave St. Louis, the place where I had been born and lived and learned so much. It was one of those grieving premonitions that had to be obeyed.

Lou and I had grown apart. In my years of leaving and return-ing, of going and coming in and out of St. Louis, in the flux of life that was rapidly becoming part of me, he was meaning less and less to my nature. He went his way, I mine; he was quiet and industrious, while I was impulsive, outreaching. I had met Bill, and this man, a year older than I at thirty-three, attracted me strongly. Sex, yes: but it was much more. The keenness of his mind, his high spirits that gurgled over like champagne out of a glass, the wide interests he had, and the roster of friends that matched my temperament so well—all these stirred me deeply.

But Bill had his own impossible situation. He, too, was married —unhappily and firmly married. His wife was a girl from a Boston Brahmin family, beautiful and high-strung. She was highly talented as a decorator. I met her. We became good friends. I knew, and she knew that I knew, that their marriage was on the verge of divorce.

The first night I got back to St. Louis, I asked Lou for a

divorce. He seemed surprised, though I had been away from him and St. Louis for nearly two and a half years. "Do you really mean it?" he asked. I nodded. "Is there someone else?" he asked. I nodded vigorously. Lou sighed and slowly stood up. "It's still the way it's always been," he said. "If that's what you want, it's what I want. I wish you'd think it over—and give us another chance." I shook my head.

On Bill's end of the line almost the same scene was being repeated, except that he was requesting her to divorce him. She first replied as Lou had to me. Bill said quietly: "I *do* want to give you a chance. But this time I want a chance for myself, too." After that crisis it worked out without a hitch. We were granted our divorces and, as Bill said, by that time our determination had hardened "so that we would have left the country and lived in sin the rest of our lives," if it had not worked out. Luckily, all four of us in this offbeat drama found happiness. Both our former spouses married again and have their own families.

I happened to meet Lou on the street in St. Louis long afterward. He was still his handsome, affable, quiet self. We chatted a little while and, just before we parted, he suddenly asked the first pointblank question I had ever heard from his lips: "What do you remember of our marriage, Helen?"

"I have a very pleasant memory of being married to a wonderful young man," I said truthfully.

He smiled. "Yes," he said slowly, "but we're all older now, aren't we?" We shook hands and said good-by. I have never seen him since.

I had arrived in New York originally on March 17, 1936, St. Patrick's Day. I saw the picturesque parading of the green up Fifth Avenue; I thrilled as always to the sharp, keen winds that whistle around the skyscrapers, to the great unceasing sound of life and ambition and activity in the city. I had stayed there studying until the end of May and only went back to St. Louis for the very definite purpose of having those tonsils snipped out.

I had no fear of my vocal cords being injured. I had supreme faith in my doctor—Dr. I. D. Kelley, a tall man with a booming voice who had himself studied with Lulu and took care of my nose, throat, and ear troubles. I was secretly in love with him as a child—and he must have been sympathetic because (he said, on principle) he charged me no more than three dollars a visit. "One singer to another," he put it. He charged a hundred dollars for the whole operation which came off perfectly. My tonsils had been so infected that their swollen bulk would almost strangle me at times. After the operation was over, Dr. Kelley visited me. Wiping the sweat of recollection from his brow, he told me what a difficult operation it had been because of his fears. I told him I supposed it must be something special: all he had given me was a local anesthetic. "The operation was quite a trial for me, too," I said.

Tonsils out, able to sing again, I accepted a spot as soloist on the Magic Key program for NBC in New York. Finnegan and Walter Damrosch had both phoned, urging me to return and embark on my career. I took counsel with my mother. She said sweetly: "Why don't you go, Helena?" I shook my head. "You can always come back again," she added. "I will *always* be here, waiting for you."

It was not true, but I wanted to believe it. I knew the inexorable doors were at last swinging open. I myself was at last assured enough of my talent to be ready to step across the threshold. I took a leave of absence for a year from my church singing and local concerts. I left, not knowing I would never come back to St. Louis as home.

I had to find out more about myself and my capabilities. Partly to do this and mostly to earn more money to support myself in my studies, I went back to New York and to Finnegan. I said I would be delighted to face his black oyster of a microphone and sing my heart out for NBC.

Finnegan said he, too, was delighted. I went right to work,

earning my money, salting away as much of it as I could. I sang weekly for months—and then abruptly decided I had had enough of what I was doing. Not because of NBC: I received nothing but the most gentle treatment at their hands, considering that I was something of a radio unknown. My reason for leaving in the fall of 1937 was much more elemental: I loathed the way I sounded.

To me, to my perhaps super-critical ear, I sounded strange to myself. I was someone else, acquiring bad singing habits. Perhaps it was just selecting songs and singing them and not caring much about any one of them. On the radio I simply did not have time for rehearsal. Nor for understanding, for digging into the guts of any bar of notes that was presented to me. I simply picked up a sheet and let go.

I went upstairs to Finnegan one Tuesday and told him I was leaving. He grinned at me.

"Yes, I understand," he said. "I can see it's been coming. I wondered how long you would go on like this." This statement puzzled me. I asked him why. He said: "You seemed so dissatisfied every time I heard you."

I never knew until long afterward that Royal had heard all of my rehearsals. All my candid comments and criticism came direct from the studio upstairs, via the personal radio on his desk.

I went upstairs to get back my contract with NBC. Actually, there was no need for this. I had never signed a contract with NBC. They had sent one to St. Louis and I had left it there without bothering to sign it. Nor had I signed the second copy which was supposedly in the files at NBC. But up I went to the contract department and asked for it. "I'm very sorry, Miss Traubel," said the head of the department, "but we must keep the contract for our records. Don't worry: Mr. Royal has canceled it."

"I don't care about that. I want the contract."

"I'm terribly sorry. We can't give it to you," he said.

I plumped myself down in a chair. I declared: "I'm staying right here until I get that contract."

After an hour and a half he broke down and brought me the contract. He was amazed that it was unsigned. He asked me weakly why I had wanted it. "I just thought it was the best thing to do," I replied.

Back to work I went to learn to use my voice better. My head-quarters were in my apartment at Fifty-seventh Street and Seventh Avenue. I made arrangements to learn to sing almost all over again.

This came about because of a concert I attended where Marian Anderson, the great contralto, was featured. She has one of the most exciting voices in existence. Anderson had always seemed to me too tight in the larynx to let herself go completely, but her songs were totally, wonderfully expressive.

During one of the concert breaks I stook in the lobby talking to a friend from NBC. I said how much I wished I could "deliver" a song like Miss Anderson.

"Her teacher is here," said my friend. "Would you like to meet him?"

"I would like nothing better."

He took me over and introduced me to a little roly-poly man— brown hair, blue eyes, a man who looked almost exactly like Santa Claus without the white beard. His name was Giuseppe Boghetti. I told him what I wanted. He cocked his head to one side and said: "So you want to sing like Marian Anderson?"

"No," I said. "I want to sing like myself. I want to learn to sing a song with the same finish that she does."

"There's no problem to that. My studio's right across from Carnegie Hall. You must come and see me."

"There's no problem indeed," I told him. "I live catty-cornered from Carnegie Hall."

Previous to this I had acquired an accompanist called Eva Zayde, a tiny, four-foot-ten-inch White Russian girl who was one of the loveliest little persons I have ever seen. She was with me for twelve years, starting in the fall of 1936. We never addressed each other at any time except as Miss Traubel and Miss Zayde. She worked with me every day five and six days a week, from early in the morning to late in the evening. She came to every performance to satisfy her own vanity, as she put it.

It was she who accompanied me to Boghetti's studio. I found him a very aggressive little man—from whom I learned more about song interpretation than I have from anyone before or since except Lulu. He asked me again whether I enjoyed the concert. I told him I had.

"Would you like to sing like her?"

"No."

"What do you mean?" he asked. "Do you want to talk theory?"

"I would say if you talk about feeling or theories, we could go on all day about it."

Boghetti bristled. "Are you challenging me?" he asked.

"No," I said, "I am going to spend some money on you. I want to find out why I'm going to spend it. I'm satisfied with the way I *sound,* but I want to sing."

"What's the difference?" he asked.

"I want you to take what I have in sound and apply it to songs. I'm ready for it now."

"Really," he said musingly. "Well, I will be honored to do it."

"Why did you want me to bring an accompanist?" I demanded.

"I wanted to see how you would sing," he said. "As you say, we could talk all day about theory and feelings."

He had won the final round. He was very happy. So was I. We quarreled violently but never seriously. I worked with him for four years, at twenty dollars an hour, two or three hours a day. At the end of that time, because I refused to take money from anyone, I owed him a thousand dollars. It was one of the first debts I paid when I had enough money to do it. With him I was

able to "expose" myself, to be corrected, to sing songs, to find
what color and expression really meant.

I would sing a Richard Strauss song, a prelude obbligato. He
would show me how to pick up the phrases and make it a full
coherent piece of music rather than a series of broken expressions.
He showed me that every song should be one grand arc of melody
from the beginning to the end.

I learned a tremendous amount from him; it was a complete
musical experience within the framework of emotional expression.
I enjoyed it so much that I budgeted myself sometimes on food—
but I was extravagant with Boghetti.

The days when I was not working with him I worked alone an
hour; then three hours with Zayde; then sang in the bathtub. I
had put aside four thousand dollars from my NBC work. I was
spending this as well as keeping up the St. Louis home—sending
Mother a hundred dollars a month, some of which she saved and
even sent back to me. By this time my aunt and uncle had died.
I had no financial responsibility any longer beyond Mama.

In March 1938 I managed to join the ranks of major opera
artists. I was selected by NBC to sing the Wagnerian role of
Sieglinde from *Die Walküre* in concert form with the Minneapolis
Symphony directed by Dimitri Mitropoulos, together with
Emanuel List, the great German basso, and Melchior, who was
ebulliently sweeping all before him at that moment. Our com-
bined talents were a decided success. The critics wanted more.
But other chores than music were piling up, no more than just
plain living.

Bill and I had got our divorces some time in the middle of
1938. We were married in October. Our troubles and delights
had begun. From October 1938 to October 8, 1939—when I gave
my first recital at Town Hall—we lived by the skin of our teeth.
It was the worst and the best time of our lives.

Worst because we scrounged to eat and walked always on the
knife edge of a budget; best because we learned to rise above it

and find ourselves in happiness with each other. Bill and I will never forget those months in the heart of New York. If we thought ourselves tough before, that year tempered us to do what we had to do—the event that came to a climax that next fall.

Bill and I married without money. His family's silver firm had gone *kaputt* in 1929. He had entered into a gentleman's business agreement for the promotion of an optical process. It had succeeded but Bill had no written contract. He signed away his stock and salary in the enterprise for less than four thousand dollars. I had just about that much in the bank. We decided to pool our funds and our future in my voice.

Bill tried to get any kind of work—from a trucker's helper to soda jerk. He failed at all of them, to his immense humiliation. Meanwhile, I was slaving at my lessons from dawn until long after the necklace of green and red lights went on along Park Avenue. We set so much money in our account aside for food, rent, and music, entertainment, and other essentials. Most of it went for my lessons. As a sample of what we spent, we allowed ourselves fifty cents twice a week to go downtown to attend the movies on Forty-second Street. We would walk from our apartment—still on Fifty-seventh Street at Seventh Avenue—down fifteen blocks after ten o'clock when the prices dropped to a dime. After the show, we would spend what we had left for hamburgers and popcorn.

Our only luxury in all those months was a rented piano at a cost of six dollars a month. My teacher lived in the same building. Anyone who wanted to see us had to come over—and bring his own food and liquor. I cooked all our meals in the big two-story living room, wedging myself into a tiny pullman kitchen. I must say that the odors I made were delicious and the food was good. Our friends came in during the evening: we sang, played cards, joked, and had a grand time, much as we did back in St. Louis when my father was alive. I used to go to the window and look out on the endless stream of traffic moving to nowhere across

Fifty-seventh Street; I would think how much he would have enjoyed such a night.

Bill and I always ate the things that went furthest. They were stew, potatoes, spaghetti, cereals. In a depression time, when top sirloin steak was only twenty-nine cents a pound, a steak dinner was an enormous celebration for the two of us. It was then that Bill and I both started to round out a bit—in philosophy and flesh.

In those days in New York we never borrowed or fell behind in our rent or paid for anything that either bodies or souls did not really need. We refused to be discouraged by the present. Our method of getting around it was to talk and think only about the future.

We had no new clothes. We could not afford them. I became expert at turning Bill's cuffs—trousers and shirts. Today, I think I could get a job at any tailor's. Both of us soon felt so shabby that we stayed indoors most of the time, only venturing out after night when the darkness hid the frayed edges of our clothes. Clean but shabby—that would describe us—clean but shabby.

"You have to say one thing for us," Bill remarked ruefully one night, contemplating the shirt I was mending for the sixteenth time. "Our tempers are the only things about us that aren't short."

It was true: we have never had a quarrel from that day to this in which there has been any tincture of bitterness. Bill often has ideas that are different from mine; many times he can make me change my mind just by remaining patient. He showed me this quality of understanding so many times during that year; I have never seen him lack it since.

I did indulge myself in one extravagance. I took a trip to St. Louis in June 1938, to spend my birthday with my mother. A friend drove me out there and I shared the car expense for a total of sixteen dollars. I took a train back for about forty-two dollars. I got the money by selling a thousand-dollar insurance policy I had kept up for years on my mother. I got only three hundred sixty-two dollars. I gave the rest of the money to her.

It was not a happy reunion for me. My mother was lying helpless in the hospital.

It had happened in the spring of 1938. I had visited St. Louis to fulfill an engagement by singing on one of the famous Magic Key radio programs—those I felt I could do adequately awhile after I had quit Finnegan and NBC. As usual I stayed at the house of friends. My mother had been induced to sell her apartment and was living with friends as well. She and I had been shopping that day and I looked at my watch. "I'll have to hurry," I told her. "Would you get the rest of these things for me?" She took the list and smiled; she loved to shop. "Of course I will, Helena," she told me. We kissed and parted.

Back at the house, getting ready for the program, I did not hear from my mother. This was not unusual. It was not until I was backstage at the studio just before my appearance that I was called to the telephone.

"Miss Traubel," said an unknown voice, "we have a woman here named Clara. We think it is your mother."

"Who is this?"

"I am calling from the city hospital."

It was my moment to go on. "Please send her to St. Luke's Hospital," I said rapidly. "I will be there as soon as I can." I was rushed onto the stage. I finished my numbers, ignored the curtain calls, and was on my way.

It *was* my mother. She was lying in the receiving room, her face gray-green with pain. She had started shopping and had fallen off a stool in the store, fracturing her hip. She would let no one touch her for the hours before I came, something I had never expected. She looked up at me as I ran in. The faint, pain-tortured ghost of the smile I loved crossed her face. "I'm all right now, Helena," she managed to whisper. "You will tell them what to do, please." She was sixty-eight years old and a strong woman,

but her injury was terrible: her jagged hip bone protruded
through the flesh.

I fell on my knees besides her as the doctors hurriedly gave
her a hypodermic injection. My mother was still conscious as
they moved her inside. She was to stay in the hospital for fifteen
months. She was never to hear me sing, as she had hoped, in my
first recital; just as my father had died a few weeks before my public singing debut at the Wyman School commencement.

I stayed in the city a week, despite concerts and appointments,
mostly beside my mother. It was she who dismissed me when she
heard I was canceling a concert. "Helena," she said tenderly, "I
am so well taken care of here. You have waited so long for your
success, you must not fail now. God bless you, go, my dear." I did
as she told me, writing her twice a week. I spent what money Bill
and I could scrape up to come back and spend my birthday with
her. Even then she pushed me out of the nest once more: "Go,
Helena, don't come back. Keep studying. I will come to hear you
when you are ready."

So she wanted it. She was regaining her spirits and her vitality
in the hospital. She was adored by the other patients. She held
tea parties in her room, she was visited by the people that had
been sent home, she wrote gaily of people sending her "cookies
and fried chicken, all the most delicious things to eat." She finally
left to live with my brother in Dallas, and one day soon after I
got a wire saying that she was very ill; in two hours, another,
saying she was dead. It was three months before my Town Hall
recital.

I had talked to my mother about my marriage to Bill just before
her accident. She must have seen the inner glow in me. I can still
hear her saying: "This is right, Helena, this is so very right." I
had introduced Vetta-Karst to Bill on one of our visits to St.
Louis and she had dug into him with a stare from those penetrating eyes. I never knew what she thought of him until years later

when I said good-by to Lulu at the station. Suddenly she kissed me and murmured hoarsely:

"Be good to Bill, Helen. It's love, not music, that counts in the end. If I'd been able to choose somebody for you—and nobody's ever been able to do that—I'd have chosen that one. Even Lulu couldn't have done any better for you."

Mother died in July 1939. I had no money to go to her funeral, though I paid for it, together with the thirty-five-hundred-dollar hospital bill. I felt no need to go because I had said good-by to her ten days before. In those heartfelt, secret moments we had said all that was needed between us. I had intended to send to Texas as soon as I could, to have her come to live with Bill and myself, but it was one of many things that never happened.

She said to me that night: "Helena, if I could only hear you sing again." I told her: "You will, you will"—but I never fulfilled the promise I wanted so much to keep.

In those days Bill and I used to go to concerts a great deal. We sat up in the peanut gallery or sometimes downstairs, using the free tickets that our friends gave us. I would listen to the voices of the women who were singing opera—for huge amounts and with great acclaim—and come out of the hall with a feeling that was as near the bottom as I ever allowed myself to get.

"I'm listening to them and I'm not hearing anything," I told Bill. "They have wonderful technique and experience but the voice—the production of just plain, pure, outright sound—it isn't there. I can't be the only one in the world that's right, everyone else wrong. Someone else must see that."

"What can you do about it now?" demanded Bill.

"We'll wait and see the reviews," I said. The reviews duly came out. They ricocheted me even further down into my personal pit. They raved about the singers and told the public of a performance that, as far as I was concerned, never existed except in their imagination.

"Maybe I'm crazy," I would tell Bill dully on such Monday

mornings. "I *must* be. They're at the top of the heap, after all. The critics and the public like them. All these singers either have great voices and don't sing well or they sing well and don't have the voice."

"Maybe you have both," Bill said wryly.

I glared at him. "Well, what do you think?" I challenged him.

He laughed. "I'll tell you after your first concert," he told me. His face became serious. "I don't see what you have to complain about," he said. "After all, you did just tear up a ten-thousand-dollar contract with NBC, didn't you?"

"Yes," I said, a little taken aback.

"And didn't Erno Rapée just call you up the other day and offer you fifteen thousand dollars for fifteen weeks?" Bill demanded.

My thoughts flew back. It was true. The swarthy, curly-headed little director of the Radio City Music Hall—the one who established its original and deserved reputation as a temple of popular music—had got me down to his plush office. He had asked me directly if I would sing fifteen Sundays a year for the Radio City performances. It was a lot of money at the end of 1938—at a time when most people did not make half that sum in a year.

"I'm not interested," I said.

"Why not?" Rapée queried. "You could do worse."

"I don't want to start my singing career at the Music Hall," I said stubbornly.

I looked at Bill across the breakfast table—we were devouring oatmeal and prunes. "You agreed with me that I shouldn't start there," I accused him. "You said the exposure wasn't right."

"I know," he agreed, "but these decisions are your own." Suddenly we laughed together.

We both knew what we had thrown away. Rapée tried time and again to induce me to sing there. It would have been all right if I had been launched in the world where I wanted to be established, but not before. After being quiet so long, I had to have a recital on the top level.

"Don't forget," Bill said softly, "you can't get much sympathy for yourself as a poor, downtrodden woman who has just tossed away twenty-five thousand dollars."

8

First Concert and the Met

IN the fall of 1939 I carefully bought myself a dress. It was a very plain, untrimmed, Nile-green affair of soft wool. It had a low, square neck high in the back, with long sleeves that would conceal the longshoreman's sweat that always drowns me after a really tough recital. It cost me sixteen dollars; I knew the dressmaker.

I bought a new pair of green shoes for three dollars. I selected a four-dollar hairdo that clumped my auburn locks in machicolations on the top of my head. I carefully selected songs from Beethoven, an aria from Gluck's *Alceste,* and other parts of Schubert and Richard Strauss. I then picked some Wagner arias, a group of five songs by contemporary composers, and a selection from Damrosch's *The Man Without a Country.*

I was getting ready for my first stratospheric recital at Town Hall, the proving ground for so many neophytes in music. It was to be either the end of a long drought for me and Bill—or the beginning of an even longer one.

In the spring of 1939 I had gone to see Coenraad Bos. I wanted him, no other, to play for my first so-important 1939 recital.

Bos was the dean of all accompanists. As a child, I had promised myself that he would accompany me for my first recital. I could not have been more than fifteen years old when I went to a concert with Lulu and first heard Bos play. I recognized even then that he was all any singer could ask, next to her, playing the piano. In music he was always just where he should have been at the right time. His playing was exquisite, of the highest concert caliber. The volume and quality and feeling which he imparted to piano keys enhanced every singer's voice, a beautiful frame for a voice. I listened entranced to this ageless Dutchman, as bald as a mountain peak, as stern and changeless. He reminded me then and later of Jan Sibelius, the Finnish composer. In the middle of the concert I turned to Lulu and whispered: "If I ever sing on the concert platform, I *do* want this man to accompany me!" He had agreed to accompany me for a minimum fee of seventy-five dollars.

The rental of the Town Hall cost three hundred dollars; I had to pay the woman who arranged it all three hundred dollars more. The only person who appeared free on my program was the one who could have demanded the highest price: Walter Damrosch. Because he considered me his protégée, he would take nothing for appearing with me on the platform. Even this generous gesture alarmed nervous me. Damrosch was such a darling with musical people everywhere, he had such an easy manner from the platform, that I feared it would turn out to be one of his own perennial debuts. As it happened, he was wonderful. He accompanied me for the whole second half of the program without a single indication of his pre-eminence in the musical circles of that time.

What happened before the occasion, behind scenes at that recital, however, was quite different from this kind of professional generosity. It was to me a revelation of the most sordid side of the art I had chosen.

A friend of ours, knowing we were looking for some sort of prestige break-in to the musical world, gave us the name of a

woman who managed concerts. She had come to hear me one
summer afternoon—and had pronounced my voice adequate. She
offered to give me her contracted date on October 8 at the Town
Hall. (At that time, perhaps now, recognized managers "bought"
dates and promised to fill them with acceptable artists.)

Lest anyone think that singers attain their stature on the basis
of a free-for-all, it should be made clear that these things are all
sedulously arranged beforehand. Money is the key that unlocks
all doors to any kind of talent. I had seen too many build-ups,
too much cumshaw passed from hand to hand, not to know this.
I inquired the price and got the bid of three hundred dollars. I
thought that ended it. I was thoroughly mistaken.

The Friday afternoon before my Sunday recital, the "manager"
called me up. She demanded that I drop all my hustle of preparations for the concert and come to her office. I demurred. She
insisted, saying it was "terribly important." I yielded and walked
to her office two blocks away. She ushered me inside and came
to the point.

"I have great faith in you," she said.

"Thank you," I told her, wondering if this was all she had
summoned me for at this critical moment.

"I know you have a wonderful voice. Your appearance will be
a success," she said.

"Thank you," I said. "May I go now?"

She leaned toward me and made her point with a finger. "If it
is a success, as I know it will be, I must ask you to sign a contract
with me for your exclusive services," she told me.

I jumped to my feet. "No!" I cried. She wagged her head at me.
"Think it over," she said calmly. "It's now two in the afternoon.
Your program is exactly forty-eight hours away. You do not have
the contract with Town Hall for an artist to appear. *I* do. If you
do not wish to sign, I can cancel your appearance and substitute
another singer at a few moments' notice."

I hesitated. I could see she was not bluffing. "I want to telephone Bill," I said at last. She graciously nodded permission. With my head in a despairing whirl, I rushed into the next room and dialed our apartment. I explained to Bill what had happened. I told him I had, of course, made up my mind to refuse this kind of gentle blackmail.

He listened without saying a word. Finally my outburst had subsided. Then he said: "Helen, we've come so far and prepared for so much. You can't lose this chance. Psychologically, you are ready. Ready in every way. You can't let this moment upset the chance you've waited for." His quiet voice sounded like my mother urging me as she had so many times. The tears were flowing but I managed to gulp agreement with him. I went back to my "manager." I said I would sign. She handed me the contract. I read it: it was for *three* years, not one.

Again I passionately refused. She told me: "I have the date, *you* don't. I have an agreement with you to put on a recital by you. There is no date specified. It could be ten years from now, my dear—and I intend to hold you to it."

Again I called Bill. Again he listened. Once more he said: "Helen, this is your chance. No matter what is in the fine print, sign the contract."

I stumbled away from the telephone, unable to see for tears and misery. I kept thinking—after so many years of study and waiting, after so much trouble and worry—why should I have to endure another delay? What I had to do almost literally broke my heart. I signed the contract without reading another word.

It was the first contract I had ever signed in my life. For the next three years, this woman held Bill and myself to the contract, letter by letter: for all that time we paid her 5 per cent of our earnings. She never managed another concert of mine. Instead, we paid the Columbia Concerts Bureau an additional percentage.

To this day, my thrifty German blood can still boil at the remembrance of such polite bludgeoning. I must confess at the same time that Bill had been right. I finished my preparations for that Town Hall appearance with fierce determination, and floated out on the stage on a cloud of mingled fury and ecstasy —fury at the conditions under which I had to sing and ecstasy at the thought that I was at last making my real debut in the most professional atmosphere possible. Thus began what I like to call my "Saga of the Three Sundays."

At this point it is time for me to stop talking about myself and what happened. I was not entirely satisfied with my recital—I have never achieved that point in my singing career and I hope I never do. But I did not really expect the flood of superlatives that descended on me.

After that first appearance—October 8—the New York *Times* reviewer wrote:

"A voice of remarkable beauty and eloquence was disclosed." It went on: "Miss Traubel's voice is dramatic and opulent, produced with the ease of a solid technical foundation in poise and maturity. Its range in power and essential quality are truly Wagnerian though it can be modulated to the demands of phrase and color. The intonation was beyond cavil. Miss Traubel appreciates a good round vowel through which she can pour tone with thrilling prodigality. She knows the expressive value of a sharp consonant, articulated cleanly and pointed to the musical meaning."

Of the same Town Hall recital the *Herald Tribune* declared that I "displayed one of the finest voices to be heard anywhere today. Miss Traubel's voice is exceptional not only for its enormous size but for the sheer loveliness of its texture. Throughout its wide range it is projected with consummate artistry. This is a beautifully equalized expressive medium. There are no weak portions in its scale. The low tones are rich and warm; the middle register, full and satisfying. . . . Miss Traubel has achieved a technical perfection which few singers can match. Such tonal gorgeousness is in itself rare enough, but Miss Traubel in addition is a musician of rare perceptive powers. It is to be devoutly hoped that New York audiences will have more frequent opportunity in the future to enjoy the superb interpretations of this soprano."

This was a hint of what was to come as Bill and I sat over coffee late that evening, gloating over the early editions. He wore a grin as wide as his face. I, for the first time in my life, failed to notice anything of the food of that dinner that I put into my mouth.

The New York *Sun* said: "When Helen Traubel came from St. Louis in the spring of 1937 to sing the role of Mary Rutledge in Walter Damrosch's opera *The Man Without a Country,* some of our Metropolitan habitués wondered why a dramatic soprano so richly endowed should not have inherited the opera before. Yesterday afternoon there was a concert audience in Town Hall that had a similar surprise in the high quality of Miss Traubel's singing. Whether heard in opera or concert, the voice is a notable one. There were times in Miss Traubel's singing of lieder yesterday afternoon when the fastidious could have wished for less power of utterance and more variety of tone color. Her interpretations ran prevailingly to the heroic when she not only produced her voice in a manner to emphasize its richness and strength but revealed convincing gifts of interpretation."

The New York *World-Telegram* declared: "Miss Traubel, a singer possessing the voice and presence for the heroic roles of Wagner, who has been heard here before in the Damrosch opera, sang to a marked advantage. When her voice had warmed it rang out with thrilling power and intensity."

"If it were not that Miss Traubel's voice is lacking in support in soft passages," wrote the New York *Post* critic, "it could justly be branded magnificent. She had splendid ringing up of register and a low voice worthy of a genuine mezzo-soprano. Her too frequent use of her voice fortissimo yesterday indicated that her vocal shortcoming is the result of too much singing at the limit of her dynamic range. Her voice is essentially of operatic caliber. The addition of her name to the list of Metropolitan Opera prima donnas would be an asset to the Met and its subscribers in a not unexpected development in Miss Traubel's career."

The now-defunct Brooklyn *Eagle* said of the same concert: "She completely convinced the listener of her musical integrity as well as her attainments as a singer. We shall hear more of Helen Traubel." The article added pointedly that "not only has she the requisites of a first-class soprano, but her talent has been possibly overlooked by operatic impresarios. Yesterday she established her right to greater recognition."

I could not read much more. My eyes were swimming. The world was a bright haze. Across the table Bill finished his reading of the last notice. "Well, sweetheart," he said. "They sound pretty good."

After that tremendously crucial first recital, after those wonderful reviews appeared on Monday, I received a call at eleven that same morning. I cannot say that I was not expecting it: I was. The critics had been too unanimous in their blunt advice to the Metropolitan Opera. It was from one of the secretaries at the Metropolitan. She said that Edward Johnson would like to see me. I assented, of course. I went in my best bib and tucker, full of expectations, downtown to this Valhalla of music.

I was not too nervous as I waited outside in the office. My nervousness had largely gone with the recital the day before. In the face of such a set of phenomenal reviews as were tucked inside my purse I had little fear. My ever-present feeling of confidence had soared. I remembered turning to Bill that night, grabbing him, swinging him around, and saying, "Bill, if they think that's good, wait until next year! If they say they've never heard anything like that in twenty years—next time they'll say they never heard anything like it in *forty* years!"

But as I waited in the outer sanctum of the Metropolitan and the minutes went by, my confidence began to turn into anger.

Johnson, who very probably had a press of business, kept me waiting more than a half-hour. When I was finally ushered in, he was completely charming—and, I hope, so was I. I was seething inside. The little, very dapper Canadian with his bouncing gait, immaculate clothes, and probing eyes, who had once been a top tenor for the Metropolitan, talked to me for more than fifteen minutes about any number of subjects, none of them related to opera. It was I who finally brought the subject—tactfully, I think —back to what I supposed I was there for.

"My dear," said Johnson tenderly, "we would like very much to have you as Venus in *Tannhäuser*."

I stiffened. I knew very well the part of Venus in *Tannhäuser* was not for me. This conviction has persisted through twenty years. Although I have sung nearly all the great female roles in Wagner in my time, I have never sung that of Venus. If it was not for me then, it is not for me now. The woman must wear diaphanous clothes; she should have an unearthly beauty; she must be a siren of sirens; and she must be supremely aware of her power over men. I do not feel and did not feel at that time I was any of these.

"No," I said shortly.

Johnson's blue eyes sprang wide open. He commenced to argue with me. I listened. When he was through, I said three more words which concluded the interview. "No, thank you," I said, and left.

Next Sunday I went to Detroit. I had been engaged to sing on the Ford program. In those days the Ford Sunday program was the one great classical program on the radio. It was conducted by Fritz Reiner who was and is, today, one of the finest living conductors. It regularly gave a very fine classical program every Sunday night. I selected as my contribution the lovely "Liebestod" from *Tristan and Isolde* and a few cornier numbers such as "I Dreamt I Dwelt in Marble Halls," "Stars of the Summer Night," and one by a St. Louis composer named Ilgenfritz called "Blow,

Blow, Thou Winter Wind"—a selection I have since grown to dislike thoroughly.

I thought it went off well. Fritz congratulated me warmly; the audience was extremely happy; and I was re-engaged on the spot to sing the next January—the final proof of appreciation.

I flew back to New York on the night plane, happily dozing and humming to myself. In the back of my head I suppose I half-expected a call the next day from the Metropolitan Opera offices saying Johnson would like to see me again. Nothing of the sort happened. The telephone was blackly silent. I went on into rehearsal for my next appearance.

The very next Saturday a kindly music observer wrote about me in the *Sun:*

"By chance I was in Carnegie Hall last Wednesday afternoon just as a rehearsal of tomorrow's concert was beginning, and I dropped into a back seat of the huge auditorium to listen for a moment. I forgot two appointments and stayed until the end of rehearsal. The reason was the singing of a statuesque young woman with red-blond hair named Helen Traubel. When she had delivered Brünnhilde's last soaring phrase in the Immolation scene of *Götterdämmerung,* a gentleman of the Philharmonic Symphony and a little group of Carnegie Hall attachés broke into spontaneous applause. I was not, to my regret, one of those present at Miss Traubel's recent Town Hall recital and I was not therefore prepared for the breathtaking performance I heard, despite my colleagues' high praise of her work in that recital. Her voice has always seemed to me of unusual quality, but since I last heard her sing it has become richer and more flexible, and she has learned how to use it with magnificent artistry."

The following day—October 22—I sang for the first time in Carnegie Hall with the New York Philharmonic-Symphony. My name appeared on the famous ocher programs wedged in between a notice for Rudy Ganz and one for "The Hour-Glass is the figure this fall!" Barbirolli was conducting, and I think that he and the audience and the orchestra were as happy as I was with the performance. I appeared in a new black dress which I adored. It had no train, and long sleeves, and I was totally without jewelry. I stood completely still during my solo, which again was Brünnhilde's Immolation scene, which is the greatest aria of all opera. I did not move a muscle during the whole sixteen minutes and then walked off stage to a storm of applause. I believe I took eight curtain calls. This performance, in memory of the music critic, Lawrence Gilman, was also broadcast on the radio Sunday-afternoon program. It was my own immolation scene in a sense. It proved that at last I could handle anything in the whole catalogue of music as a *hoch* dramatic soprano—something which I had never *proved* to myself until that moment. The next morning the notices were kind indeed. The storm of demands from all the critics that I should appear in a Wagnerian opera became almost a hurricane. (It may be remembered that this kind of campaign had started voluntarily among the critics themselves, as far back as 1937, when I first sang in *The Man Without a Country*.)

The Brooklyn *Eagle* said: "The fact is she sang magnificently. Her voice rang true and clear. It had the essential qualities of production, of forcefulness, and of emotion. It conveyed the proper embodiment of the character. Here was not only singing of the first order but artistry as well. What she could do with the role on the operatic stage is a matter of speculation, but she gave every indication yesterday that vocally she may belong to a special group of sopranos who have sung Brünnhilde notably." Again the critical pressure on the Met.

The New York *Sun* said: "It seems preposterous that there should not be a more important place for so notable a voice and so good a vocal technique than America seems to have found so far for this singer, who it would appear has been before the public in the Midwest for a good many years." The critic went on to say that only Flagstad had sung the role with the "beauty of tone and conviction of utterance" that I brought to it. He added: "This is not to say that tone by tone and phrase by phrase it was quite all it might have been if the singer could have had the benefit of years of training and actual singing in the theaters, but Wagner singing is at once a specialty and a tradition. There is still room for improvement in her highest tones, which tend to take on a knife-like edge, though brilliantly employed, but to dwell upon such details would be to falsify the general effect of singing which, in the reviewer's opinion, was little short of magnificent. Evidently the hunt for great voices should begin at home."

This particular reviewer was quite right about the sharp edges of my high notes. It was something that I worked on for a long while afterward to correct permanently.

The next morning I again expected a call. This time, I was not disappointed. At precisely eleven o'clock on Monday, there was a ring from the Metropolitan Opera. Johnson would like to see me. Somewhat cautiously, I said once more that I was honored; that, of course, I would come down. I did so. This time he kept me waiting only fifteen minutes in the outer office. Once more I was ushered into the big stately office with its photos and paintings, heavy desks and furniture—where everything was full of stability, consequence, and tradition. Johnson leaped from behind the desk and escorted me to my chair. He sat down and after only a short dissertation on various other subjects told me that he was very happy to offer me the part of Venus with even greater enthusiasm.

I could feel the hackles of my short hair rise on the back of my neck. I swallowed and said, "Mr. Johnson, you are confusing me. You have offered me this role several times. I have refused it each time."

"I can't think you mean it," he said archly.

"I do," I snapped. He commenced to argue once more. Again

I cut him short. "No," I said, "that role is entirely out of the question."

"You can't mean this at all!" said Johnson. "It's a wonderful part. You would be wonderful in it!" He reached over and pressed a button. As if he had popped up through a trap door, Edward Ziegler, the sturdy, businesslike second-in-command in the Metropolitan Opera House, came in. He came directly to me. He said, "Hello, how are you, Helen? I'm so glad to see you," and he left.

This confused me even more. I turned to Johnson, who commenced talking about Venus once more. "No," I said determinedly. "This is a waste of time. I don't want it."

"What would you sing for us?" asked Johnson.

This was a question to which I had a ready answer. I knew precisely what I wanted to sing for my debut in the Metropolitan.

"I would want to sing the part of Sieglinde in *Die Walküre.*"

This is a part in the Wagnerian cycle which is not so spectacular as Brünnhilde but it is very moving. It is the part of a woman who is very sympathetic to the audience, a fine heartwarming character. Sieglinde has marvelous music to sing. In the plot she is married to an older man and in love with a younger. She is not a siren or an enchantress. She is a simple woman with a great deal of appeal—a part I thought I could dramatize with my voice.

Johnson seemed to relax. He leaned back and put his fingers together. "You don't seem to understand, Helen," he told me. "All I have to do is ring bells and I would have six Sieglindes in here in a moment. Why should you be the seventh? It is one thing, my dear, to sing an aria and another to sustain a whole opera."

"All I would need would be the opportunity," I said calmly. "I would like, if I may, to watch rehearsals. Then I could find out whether I could sustain the role or not."

"No, no, no, no!" said Johnson. "We cannot allow everyone in the public to come in and see Metropolitan Opera rehearsals."

"I'm not just one of the public," I said.

"What do you—why do you want to come to the rehearsals?" he said.

"I want to find out what not to do," I told him.

"No, it's impossible! We couldn't fling open the door even to everyone who sings," said Johnson. "Only to the members of the company." I could see his face getting red. He turned back to the old familiar subject. "Now, about Venus," he said. "Venus is—"

"It's impossible, totally impossible," said I, mimicking him. He bounded up from his chair. He commenced pounding the table.

"You're getting me hot under the collar!" he said. "I have some Irish in me, too!" He began pacing his office.

"Well, I have some German," I said. I began to laugh.

He glared at me. "Don't you think for a moment you can tell me how to run the opera!" he cried. I, who had been a little amused up until that time, saw that he was playing for keeps. I stopped laughing.

"Don't you tell me how to run my career," I said. "You or Ziegler, or anyone else!" I was sitting in the chair as he came and stood over me. I rose, towering above him, and pointed my finger at him, almost touching his nose.

"Mr. Edward Johnson," I said loudly, in furious and level tones, "you can take the Metropolitan Opera House apart brick by brick and—!" I told him what to do with the Metropolitan Opera House.

I received other calls from the Metropolitan saying that Johnson would like me to come down and see him. I said again and again I was not in. One afternoon the call was repeated two or three times. I gave the same answer. The next day the Metropolitan sent a wire, asking me to come down to talk, but I sent no answer. I went back to work.

In those days I was working with Coenraad Bos and with two other teachers, still and always learning how to sing. I got up at seven o'clock, went to work at eight, and ended my working at five thirty. I was cramming into myself everything I could possibly learn. I was sure that I had an instrument with which I could do musically anything in the world that I wanted. All I had to do was learn the parts and the songs. I had a solid satisfaction in the achievements I had created so far. I felt whatever disappointments I had now would be compensated for in the future.

My first recital outside New York came at the end of November. It was at Wellesley College. Once more it was a tremendous success. The Philharmonic-Symphony's first appearance had been so successful that three more appearances were scheduled for me in December, in New York and Philadelphia, on the tenth, eleventh, and twelfth. I was very happy to appear. It would prove to the opera connoisseurs that I had been no flash in the pan, that my twenty-six years of working and training and studying had at last paid off. One thing I could do at these three concerts—and I did it —and that was to let all stops out. I really sang *bravura* and *fortissimo*. By the time the cluster of concerts was over, the applause was louder than ever. Some critics actually said I was the greatest Wagnerian singer ever to appear.

In my first debut in Carnegie Hall, with a hundred-piece orchestra, the New York *Times* reported: "Hers is a voice that, far from being overwhelmed by an orchestra of a hundred men, is best revealed by just such a musical complement. And more to the point, by just such a score as the Immolation scene, for this voice is most potent in its heroic utterance." Of the same concert the *Herald Tribune* said: "She sustained the mood of the tragically transfigured spouse of Siegfried unswervingly, imparting to every facet of text and music the meaning intended by the composer. The plenitude of her vocal resources met every requirement of the composer." It added, "When Miss Traubel was heard in the recital in Town Hall recently, the magnificence of her vocal endowment, the depth of her musical understanding, and her regal presence seemed attributes which fitted her peculiarly for the delineation of the Wagnerian heroines. That impression was fortified by her superb interpretation of the overwhelming finale of *Götterdämmerung* on this occasion." My picture had even appeared on the cover of the *Musical Courier,* the sixty-year-old review of the world's music, one of the important publications of the time.

The New York *Post* said, on my second appearance with the New York Philharmonic-Symphony, that "it was again apparent not only that Miss Traubel has a splendid voice and that she is a fairly accomplished singer, but that she is a Wagnerian soprano not by virtue of temperament, birth, or experience, but simply because of the dimension and quality of her voice itself.

"Except for one conspicuous fumble with a high note, the Immolation was sung in a way that leaves little doubt as to the singer's potential excellence as a full-time Brünnhilde."

I wonder what the fellow could have meant about a "fumble" —in those days if I collided with a note, it had to be a touchback, at the least.

Even the staid *Christian Science Monitor* had gone on record as far back as the middle of October:

"Wagner immediately comes to mind when there is a question to Miss Traubel. She is cast in the heroic mold physically and vocally, a natural evocation of Brünnhilde. Again, she seems a likely new Metropolitan Opera principal. The vocal progress of this talented singer in a year is very marked." As far away as from Akron, Ohio: "The prediction is that she will be a regular member of the Metropolitan Opera very soon."

The New Yorker said I had sung Immolation scene "in imperial style [whatever that means], opulent voice, and with rare discernment." The *Christian Science Monitor* wrote: "Memorable in its excellence. Miss Traubel, majestic of voice and of presence, delivered Brünnhilde's mighty monologue with a richness and splendor of tone and nobility of style seldom to be met with." The New York *World-Telegram* declared: "Seldom is it one's privilege to witness so eminent an achievement. Miss Traubel, of course, made no attempt to act, but the majesty of her presence in her simple black robe and the single flawless gesture of her arms after her last note produced an effect comparable to the right dramatic action in a stage performance. Of paramount importance, however, were Miss Traubel's voice and singing. The evenness, strength, and splendor of color that characterized the former had their counterpart in the grand design of her declamation and the appropriately wrought detail with which its outlines were stored."

Whew! The Hartford, Connecticut, *Courant* said: "A voice of heroic caliber, yet with mellow warmth and susceptible of a wide range of expressiveness in color, it is admirably used and even in scale. The top is now brilliant and true in pitches. Miss Traubel sang with a musicianly understanding and deep appreciation of the text. Now for the Metropolitan and a high place among Wagnerian singers who have made deserved names for themselves."

In all the mass of complimentary words that poured out after that grand finale of mid-December, nothing could have been more down the line that Bill and I had hoped and planned on. The final comment of the *Courant* was the straw to break the camel's back, the goad we needed to prick the Metropolitan into action. It was a gleaming spur available to us in a couple of dozen newspaper reviews, glowing with the same enthusiasm.

On the Monday after the last Carnegie Hall concerts with the Philharmonic-Symphony in December, I received, as I had expected, my call from the Metropolitan, as usual, on Monday at eleven o'clock. They wanted me to come down and talk. I said I would not come down. I hung up.

The whole situation was getting a little ridiculous. The Met was under the guns of the critics; I certainly had no objection to singing there. But we were both standing like mad on the formalities. And Bill and I, as babes in the wood in the musical world, did not know quite how to find our way home.

At this juncture the Met got hold of a mediator. He was actually a friend of Bill's as well, William Matheus Sullivan, a big, husky, jolly lawyer who was internationally famous in the legal end of art and a Met director. He had been an opera buff for years and was, we found out, opposed to Johnson's policies. But he did know the intricate ins and outs of the politics of music as he knew the palm of his hand. He called us and we agreed to meet him for tea. I told him the whole story in one rush of words. He laughed heartily. Suddenly he became very serious. He said, "What can I do to help you? Call on me for anything!"

"Well," Bill said, "we can't ignore the Metropolitan. We don't want to. Helen is perfectly willing to sing there, but it should be something mutually agreeable."

"There's no reason why not," said Sullivan. "The critics have been asking the Metropolitan why she hasn't sung there. They want to know what's the matter with the management. The public wants Traubel. I would like to hear her myself in the Metropolitan. Let's see what we can do."

After some more discussion it was agreed that Bill Sullivan would write a letter in my name, saying that I would be, now and always, glad to sing at the Metropolitan Opera. He specified that I must have a contract flatly stating that I would debut in the part of Sieglinde in Wagner.

This was done. The letter was sent. There was an immediate reply—this time from Edward Ziegler, then the true power behind the Met thrones. He agreed to all the terms specified in the letter. He said he was calling a special rehearsal. I should bring down my score and be prepared to sing on the following Monday.

Such a prompt reply scared me. I called Billy Sullivan. He instructed me very carefully:

"When you go to rehearsal, remember, don't sing a note until you have a signed contract. Find any excuse to keep from singing."

With this advice under my belt, I went down to the Metropolitan Opera offices once more. They were ready to see me instantly. They ushered me in and Johnson only made the comment: "You're early." He started to lead the way up to the rehearsal. I halted him.

I said, "Yes, I am. I came down here to get the contract for the Sieglinde role."

"What do you mean?" asked Johnson. "You want the promise that you are going to sing Sieglinde put into the contract itself?"

"Yes," I said firmly.

"But that's impossible," Johnson expostulated. "We'd never put that into a contract. It's never done."

I had not noticed until that moment that Ziegler had been sitting quietly in the background. He came forward. "We'll do it this time," he said. "Please get the contract and see that she signs it, Mr. Johnson." Even at that moment Johnson boggled a little, but he left. In less than five minutes he came back with the contract.

I read it all, fine print, up and down, sideways. Then I signed all five copies. I watched Ziegler and Johnson sign them. I tucked my copy away in my purse. On Ziegler's arm I went up in the elevator to the rehearsal hall on the roof of the Met. As I entered, the musicians—more than a hundred of them, all of whom I had sung with either on the radio, or in the Philharmonic-Symphony —rose and applauded.

I had won my battle. I was to sing Sieglinde in *Die Walküre* as my debut at the Metropolitan.

9

How It Feels to Sing

TWO men—my father, Otto, and my husband, Bill—have strongly influenced me. My father prepared me for life; Bill got me ready for my career that is next to life for me. Perhaps in neither case did I really understand what they were doing for me.

As a girl I always hated to go to school. I kept very little of what I learned in my square little head because I did not care about any study with the passion I had for music. I believe I always had tutors at some time during every semester of my school terms. My father would sigh, call one of the local brains in to see me, and announce: "I want you to stuff this little goose." The cramming would begin.

In spite of his despair over my learning, my father was willing to admit he was responsible for my *dumkopf*ness. My mother used to tell him so, in gently reproving tones. She explained to him that he was taking me away from my studies too often. Hunting, fishing, baseball, circus, and song fests—it was just too much. It outbalanced school terribly in every way: in glamor, drama, excitement, and experience. My mother once said: "Otto, you must think if you might be ruining her life."

My father gave her one of those long, luminous looks that they shared and said, quite softly:

"Clara, it is very important that I spend as much time as possible with my family. Don't you realize it? This is my life, this is my life!"

I think he knew he was going to die. Whether or not he had this sort of premonition, I cannot know. I do remember that, years later, on a reminiscent evening before the fire, my mother told me that he had said to her on his deathbed:

"How glad I am, Clara—how glad I am that I spent as much time as I did with Helena."

He was with me so much; we shared so much—and he is still with me and sharing whatever I do. In those first days of my success at the Metropolitan Opera I felt him keenly—a benign and approving presence in the wings. For the presence of my father is much more than a ghost in my mind.

However, it was my mother whom I resembled in my physical structure—the build that made it possible for me to realize my ambition of singing. It may seem strange to anyone who does not know me for me to say I was actually the peewee of the family. The doctors of St. Louis considered the bone structure of the female Stuhrs something extraordinary. I recall a doctor in St. Louis, now dead—a friendly man named Graves—requested my mother that she have X rays of her bone structure. He especially wanted those of the rib cage and shoulders taken and turned over to him. He wanted them, he said, to publish with a special article in the *American Medical Journal*. He said it was "very unusual for a woman to have such tremendous shoulders and chest."

Much the same is true of myself, I suppose. Although the years have made me comfortably plump, I can still say my shoulders are a mass of solid muscle. I learned early to sing as Lulu taught me: wandering around the room, waving and flailing my arms, always keeping my diaphragm steady. I was taught to sing on my

knees; lying flat on the floor; leaning on my elbows; all with
Lulu's admonition in my ears: "Keep your breath in a vise!" My
clothes, even today, cannot be tight. If I take a deep breath and
lock it, it might blow up all my fine feathers like an atomic explosion. I can sing a tone in an opera aria quite as long as any
trained person can merely hold his breath—at least approaching
a minute. I recall Melchior and I used to compete with each
other occasionally, for fun on the stage, holding our notes as long
as possible. He always beat me because he actually enjoyed turning purple. My customary greeting to him on our nights at the
opera was a jovial: "How long tonight, Lauritz?"

When I signed my Metropolitan Opera contract, Bill automatically became my official business manager. Otherwise, it
would have been no deal.

It has always been a minor miracle to me that Bill and I ever
met. The one responsible for it was Robert Hanna, a friend from
St. Louis whom I had known years before. He had gone to New
York to become a writer. He had had a play produced and had
made motion pictures. Hanna had talked to Bill about me in
1934 in what, Bill told me later, were very enthusiastic terms. Bill
always maintained he never wanted to meet me. To him I was
simply a voice with a woman attached to it. He did not care for
that and he did not like St. Louis either.

I felt much the same way about Bill. I had avoided meeting
him even when Hanna described him in the most glowing terms.
I thought Bill would talk about himself; he thought I would talk
about me. We were two people straining at opposite ends of the
same rope. He had no use for the arty crowd; nor did I, but he
did not know that. I had little use for the business world; he had
even less, but I did not know that.

Hanna phoned me on that strange and lucky night in New
York. He asked if I would come over to his house. I said, "I
don't want to meet anyone there." Hanna was in the habit of

having me barge into a whole assortment of characters. "I just want to talk to you," I said.

"All right," he said. I had a strange hunch that there was someone with him from the way he talked. I said, "Robert, if there's someone there, promise me you'll get rid of him."

He said, "Yes, there is someone here. But I'll get rid of him in fifteen or twenty minutes."

As Bill told me later, he was there. He quizzed Robert after his phone call and learned that I was coming over. He was on the verge of leaving as Robert said, "Not until you have had a drink for the road." According to Bill: "He sounded so unsubtle, as if he wanted to get us together at any cost, that I said to myself, 'By God, I'll sit this one out and get it over with!'"

I arrived at the house, came in the hall, and said in an intuitive panic to Robert: "There's someone here!"

"Don't worry," said Robert. "He's just leaving." In the living room Bill made no move to go. I drew myself up, prepared to be really nasty. But when I saw this particular person, suddenly all my tension became ridiculous. I knew then what he was: gay, wise, with a good brain box, a man who could not only understand business but also happiness—one of the greatest talents in the world.

Bill never formally proposed. All we had was a deep understanding between us. He became tremendously interested in my career—I had no manager at the time—and we developed a specific relationship both intimate and professional. Bill could ferret out all the facts of a situation, then present them so well that the solution was immediately obvious. From the moment we met he knew quite well what I needed and wanted, even when I said no. He had handled all the intricacies of my Town Hall debut, of the Philharmonic-Symphony concerts, and the final signing by the Metropolitan Opera Association. It was inevitable that he would assume the full load of my contractual commitments and leave me free to do the only thing I wanted: sing.

When I joined the Metropolitan—signing my contract in the last few days of December 1939—I knew only one role. It was Sieglinde in *Die Walküre*. I was learning Elisabeth in *Tannhäuser*. During all that next year of 1940–41 I kept myself busy learning two of the heaviest roles in opera to be ready for the following season—the two Brünnhildes of *Die Walküre* and *Die Götterdämmerung*. I can frankly say I came close to killing myself with learning roles, on the one hand, actually singing other roles, on the other hand, and, on the third hand, singing in concerts. The following year, 1942–43, I learned the roles of Isolde and the Brünnhilde in the opera *Siegfried*. That season I finally qualified to sing the entire Ring cycle and one extra opera. That was the year when I made my first round trip on the Wagner merry-go-round.

My roles were few at first at the Met. I sang only four times the first year because when I joined in 1939–40 the season was half over. The season of 1940–41 I sang eight or ten performances. In 1941–42 I sang fifteen or twenty performances. In 1942–43 I sang twenty performances again. In 1943–44 I sang nearly twenty-five performances, which represented the tops of any year. It is as many, I believe, as have been sung by any other major Wagnerian soprano.

Such a schedule was a grinding performance—one that took more energy and stamina than most people think possible. It is my own opinion that a day at the docks with the longshoremen, working shoulder to shoulder heaving cast-iron pipe, is a picnic compared to an evening at the Met for a Wagner singer. As I once said to an ambitious student: "Singing opera is like baseball. It depends on your equipment—not only how well you can pitch but how long."

Wagner always made his roles at least twice as hard to sing as any others in grand opera. His librettos were calculated to strike the fear of God into any attempt at acting with their unnatural pauses and long declamations. I have a good solid dollop of

German myself—but his sentences! My God, his sentences! He has a trick of writing a line and then repeating it backward; he loved alliteration, using it whenever he could and a lot of the time when he could not. For a singer, it bends the vocal cords right around a post to pronounce the strings of German gutturals he sticks at the front of a melodic line.

In the celebrated sixteen-minute Immolation scene from *Die Götterdämmerung* the voice must be used to its utmost. The orchestra plays like crazy, all out, one hundred ten men blaring and blasting at the same time. The singer must do the same if she is not to be entirely inundated by the torrent of sound. I used to lose five pounds a performance, coming off soaked with sweat. I was actually exhausted from the emotional impact of the decibels of the orchestra, the fervor of the audience, and the wonderful music itself. If he could not write words, Wagner could certainly write music!

In the 1944–45 season I learned the role of Elsa in *Lohengrin*, the easy one that many sopranos start with—the one that Lulu would not let me touch before. Johnson at the Met had proposed this to me originally as my debut as far back as 1937 but had never mentioned it after our Sieglinde tussle. In 1946–47 I learned the role of Kundry in *Parsifal*. That completed my repertoire of Wagner, all that I was interested in. It meant that I could sing the three Brünnhildes in the Ring plus the Sieglinde role—and could take the leads in the other three Wagner operas. I had no liking at all for the role of Senta in *Der Fliegende Holländer*. She might have had a little sympathy from the audience but she had none from me. She came into the scene first in a dirndl. Do what you will with it, there is nothing heroic in a dirndl. I would have looked ridiculous with such a bib around my waist.

As for other operas, such roles as Aïda had not the faintest attraction. She had some beautiful music, it is true, but she sang forever under a cloud, her shoulders hunched forward. I have always found it impossible to inhibit my tones that way. I did learn three other roles: that of the gay Marschallin from *Der Rosenkavalier* of Richard Strauss; Santuzza in *La Cavalleria Rusticana*, though I never sang it; and I "learned at" the role of Leonora di Vargas in Verdi's *La Forza del Destino* and *Tosca*.

The reason I became a Wagnerian soprano, devoting virtually all my time in grand opera to such roles, is easily explained. I became such because there was no one else with the physical equipment to handle it. I kept asking Johnson: "Aren't you interested in putting me in something Italian?" *Tosca* is one of my all-time favorites.

"My dear," he would say, "we have Toscas by the dozen. We get little enough of your time as it is. We must use what we have to our best advantage."

I did manage to add to my repertoire about five hundred songs. I have never tried to do the so-called tone poems nor those operas such as the *Electra* of Richard Strauss where you are neurotic at the beginning, tear out your throat in singing in the middle, and go crazy in discords at the end. I think any soprano who tries this must be actually lunatic all the way through in order to make such horrible sounds with her throat. I myself have always known that, if I were useful for anything, it was to make beautiful sounds. I could not bring myself to perform such roles.

The parts I had first of all suited my equipment; that is, the quality of my voice, the meaning of my thinking, and the size of my person. It should be understood that I am not a small woman. I am very tall, with big broad shoulders, forty-six-inch bosom and a forty-three-inch waist. This reflects the structure of my rib cage: it has practically no slope going straight down. My hips are about forty-one and my weight then was one hundred and eighty-six pounds when in singing trim. I forget who it was who called me "an instrument expressly made by God for the purpose of singing."

I looked ridiculous in something like *The Man Without a*

Country where I played the soubrette and was a foot taller than the tenor. There was no dramatic reality at all. Too, I always looked for spiritual content in a role—whether it had sympathy and emotion, whether it had a message primarily for me and for the audience. Unless I could create the mail I could not deliver it.

That first season at the Metropolitan Opera paid me one hundred and fifty dollars a performance. There were only four performances. I sang ten concerts the same first season. Even before I joined the Met I got a thousand dollars a concert, so the total income of Bill and myself for that year was roughly ten thousand five hundred dollars. Bill was working on my not inconsiderable management problems, assisted by Columbia, and we acknowledged that our lean times were not over. For nearly two years we had to confine ourselves to the same program we had before.

One of the reasons was that we had to pay two commissions to two different outfits for three years. This, plus other fees, cut our income down to 75 per cent of its total take. I may add that 35 per cent and more of our income had to go for my wardrobe. In the first year and a half, for example, we jointly owed twenty-two thousand dollars for clothes to a single New York store. I was forced to dress up to my part, though I did not particularly care for it—fur coats, evening dresses, and all the rest of the armor which any opera star must have in her kit.

Meanwhile, Bill and I lived on as we had, with our friends and ourselves, and careered madly from seven in the morning until sometimes after midnight. I was practicing parts in opera, rehearsing songs, learning new parts, learning new songs. I was taking lessons in acting and drama. I was working continually on my vocalizing to improve the sound of my voice. I was shopping for food and clothes, cooking all our meals, and cleaning our apartment—and even doing our laundry. The days never had enough hours in them. They were used up like rockets, the hours only for all the work—and the good deal of fun which we insisted upon.

Bill and I have always felt that life must be spent rather than grabbed closely to your chest. We did what we could when we had it. We will never regret anything we did as spent in those days although sometimes, at the time, it seemed to my thrifty Teutonic soul that our outpourings were extravagant.

One of the most exciting experiences in my whole career came in that era of our lives. It was that first rehearsal, sitting on the Thirty-ninth Street roof stage of the Metropolitan, a story-and-a-half high, one woman with a hundred men playing away at Wagner. Me sitting in the midst of it, being wrapped in it again and again and again, enveloped in the tremendous blankets of delicious sound. I really had to fight very hard against a feeling that I was not human but a piece of wood or metal, an instrument contributing to this sound. For the first time I realized the mixing of tone and the magic it could work, the excitement that it must bring to any musician.

At this rehearsal I received my first rude awakening. We were singing right in our rehearsal of the opera. At one point, the singers had a break to enable the orchestra to practice alone. During our singing the tenor opposite me, a tenor who was new, one I had never seen before, kept clearing his throat and glaring at me. I never could hear his voice very much. I cannot remember to this day its quality. As for me, I was gone: I was having the loudest time of my life. It was one of the supreme moments of my existence to stand before the orchestra and be part of it, to really let loose what I had inside. During this intermission the tenor stepped over to me. He said, "Miss Traubel, why do you sing so loud? Why do you give too much of your voice?"

"I want to hear myself," I said.

"But so early in the morning?"

"I practiced before I came down. I am warmed up."

"Well, you mustn't give too much now."

"I have to. I have to give *now* in order to give *then*."

He glowered at me. "You must save yourself," he insisted.

"Not at all," I bristled. "I still want to hear myself to see what I am doing."

"But it's too early."

I gave him what I hoped was a look. "I sing just as well in the morning as I do in the evening," I said, and moved away.

I loved music so much that every time I had a chance to open my mouth I let go with all I had. Now I began to perceive dimly something which did not come to full flower until years later. It was that, tremendous as opera became in my life as a driving force and artistic experience, there were other people in the business who were mere pretenders. They, too, had been endowed by God. But they did not feel their responsibility to spend their talents as prodigally and as well as possible. This was to become one of the most bitter disillusionments of my whole life in music. It still is.

After the occasion of that first rehearsal, when Edward Ziegler had escorted me to the room and uttered those magic words, "Gentlemen, let me introduce your next Sieglinde," the whole orchestra had risen and applauded. It became an invariable custom for the musicians in the pit to stand and applaud when I finished my opera stint for the night. I was becoming known as a musician's singer. As one of them said, "There is nobody that can appreciate the qualities that you are bringing to opera, Miss Traubel, better than we can. We have spent our lives producing your kind of tone," one of the most beautiful compliments I have ever had.

After this first four-hour rehearsal the men in the orchestra stood up and applauded. Each one shook my hand. After this there were several stage rehearsals, with just the piano, down in the maw of the Metropolitan. I went on to my first performance a week later.

Singing in the Metropolitan I can only describe as singing in a wolf's throat. The red plush seats, the red carpets, and the boxes all remind you of a slavering animal ready to devour you.

It was here that my basic training by Lulu came to the fore. I found, in this immense cavern, as soon as I let loose a tone it vanished forever from my mouth. It never came back. But my training had been such that I never cupped my ear nor listened for an echo. I can actually say I "heard" the tone in my brain before I let it drive. I knew I was going to face the vastness of the greatest opera house in the world and the most sophisticated audience under the most difficult conditions—but it really held no fear for me. I paid no attention whatsoever to anything else as I worked. For me this feared auditorium then was a great bosomy protector, opening its arms. I suppose if I had allowed myself to think I should have been terrified. As it was, I told one of the singers: "All I need are a few deep breaths. If the orchestra holds out, I'll hold out. We'll both give out!"

In that first performance in late December 1939, for the first time I saw the real workmanship, real beauty, real artistic integrity that the Metropolitan Opera could put into its performances. As Sieglinde I never had to change a costume, so I used to hang around in the wings with my eyes, ears, and mouth open—watching and staring and looking. People had to push me out of the way to change scenery or to make their entrances. I was sopping up all I could learn, all I could see, all I could hear, feel, smell, and touch. Perhaps it was drinking me in, too, because I have never separated myself from it since.

December 28, 1939, I made my debut as Sieglinde in *Die Walküre*. This time the applause—without the aid of the customary hired claque—came from the connoisseurs of opera without stint. What had been confined to New York and St. Louis now became a country-wide affair. I was the home-grown Wagnerian big-time soprano, never out of the country, who had achieved her goal on her own terms—a goal set as long ago as when my pigtails were hanging down my back.

The Associated Press hailed it jovially BIG HIT and wrote: "Helen Traubel of St. Louis was cheered tonight when she made her Metropolitan Opera debut as Sieglinde in Wagner's immortal *Die Walküre* before an audience that strained the stout walls of the yellow-brick pile on Broadway." The account added: "In addition to being the center of numerous joint curtain calls at the end of her most important act, the first, she had two of her own, and the audience was reluctant to let her go even then."

Time, which a few years later put a somewhat strained painting of myself on its cover, declared: "Last week, singing Sieglinde opposite such champions as Flagstad, Thorborg, and Melchior, Helen Traubel made her official Metropolitan debut. Manhattan's debutasters trooped in droves to hear her, stayed to cheer, for they heard one of the finest Wagnerian soprano voices ever to turn up at the Metropolitan."

The austere *New Yorker* unlimbered its circumlocuted style and noted: "One of the big Metropolitan welcomes of the season went to Miss Helen Traubel when she sang her first Sieglinde hereabouts in *Die Walküre.* Earlier in the semester Miss Traubel had bowled over concert goers at her Town Hall recital and at her appearance as soloist with the Philharmonic-Symphony. She had exactly the same effect on the Metropolitan's audience."

The New York *Herald Tribune* warmly praised me with a bouquet of choice phrases: "One of the finest voices to be heard anywhere today" and "exceptional for sheer loveliness of its texture. Miss Traubel has achieved a technical perfection which few singers can match. Such tonal gorgeousness is in itself rare."

And the New York *Times* reinforced its previous opinions with still more blooming descriptions: "A voice of remarkable beauty and eloquence, dramatic and opulent," and "its range and power and essential quality are truly Wagnerian," and "intonation beyond cavil," and "can pour tone with thrilling prodigality," and "natural flair for the grand utterance."

Such reviews touched off my desire to go as high and as far as I could—as soon as I could. I felt as if I could take off with my voice and soar to heaven if need be. It was in this mood that I challenged the champion singer of opera, one whose recorded voice I still hear with humble wonder.

Ten days after Flagstad made a triumphal appearance in Philadelphia I also sang there—on March 14, 1940. I sang the identical program she had selected. I politely refused the tearful requests of the management to change my selections. I went out on the stage to make the concert a duel on exactly the same grounds with the same weapons, no holds or high C's barred. It was a little fey, perhaps. I was feeling in such fettle that I could not resist shoving out my young, tender freckled neck for the critical ax.

I received a collection of the finest compliments of my life from the critics. Some have lingered with me for many years. One wrote:

"Miss Traubel sang the *Götterdämmerung* music superbly. Recent rumors of Madame Flagstad's retirement next year have been coupled with hints that Miss Traubel may be groomed as her successor in the Metropolitan's German wing. On the strength of her performance last night, the suggestion is at least plausible. She has a voice of magnificent volume which last night asked and received little concession from the hundred musicians playing against her in the score. It was an impressive and affecting performance, the music laden with epic grandeur and monumental difficulty, and the audience gave Miss Traubel an ovation at its close."

A second critic wrote: "As for Miss Traubel, she projected the encompassing grief and exalted resignation of Brünnhilde with an intensity of utterance and eloquence of feeling not apparent in the singing of the vastly more celebrated Madame Flagstad. To say that in this day is, of course, a heresy, tantamount to taking one's life in a blitzkrieg with one's head in one's hands. But it represents an honest impression of Miss Traubel's pointedly impressive singing of the soul-searing scene."

A third: "Of Miss Traubel's singing of the Immolation [*Die*

Götterdämmerung] the reviewer can speak only in superlatives. No performance of this music within recent memory"—and Flagstad no more than ten days before!—"can compare to it in its qualities of vocalism and interpretive insight." He pointed out that I had been studying with Boghetti and that what I had wanted from his training I had apparently received. "Her singing bears certain unmistakable resemblances to Miss [Marian] Anderson's in the certainty and accuracy of the vocal focus and in the exceptional firmness of the legato. This Immolation scene was lyrical from beginning to end, even in the most forceful declamatory passages, but it was more than merely an example of *bel canto*. There was warmth and passion in it and a commanding authority."

The audience that night gave me a spontaneous ovation. The applause was shared by the members of the orchestra, the New York Philharmonic-Symphony men I had known so long and their leader, John Barbirolli. The illustrations that appeared with the critical reviews—they were called caricatures—gave me the enormous exaggerated shoulder breadth that was to become one of my trade-marks.

The whole affair, strangely enough, brought back to me my first review of any consequence in St. Louis. I dug it out that next night. I reread it. The anonymous booster said, among other things, that I had "definite gifts and great promise," and I had "two octaves of golden tones, all twenty-four karat, to be classified as pure soprano" refined by "pure musical feeling and fine insight." He added with amiable prophecy: "Would it seem exuberant under the circumstances to predict for the girl a distinguished career?" I had felt, at that time, with the brashness of a youngster, that it was not exuberant. It was merely a fact. Now, on the high plateau of my own mountain, I commenced to feel the dizziness and the doubt of high places that were always hidden in me. That same unknown critic had said, in St. Louis, that I was "tall, handsome, and very young." He was right: I was sixteen when he said it. Now I was thinking of the future—twenty years older, twenty years more experienced, twenty years more mature in voice and nature.

It may be conjectured that this barrage of pointed suggestions laid down at the door of the Met could not help but have its effect. I was not wrong in this belief: I was to succeed Flagstad. I was sure I was ready, but how well and for how long were thought stretchers indeed.

Within two years—though I could not foresee it at the time—I was to be cheered as the "greatest Wagnerian diva" of the Metropolitan. I was to be spoken of as great as Flagstad and greater than any other singer since the fabled performances of Johanna Gadski and Lillian Nordica at the turn of the century.

It was to be a stunning kind of praise to me. It was both dizzying and satisfying—and saddening. I felt that the voice of Flagstad was one of the most glorious voices I had ever heard in a human throat. One of the finest that any woman had ever produced. It was a tremendous compliment, I thought, to have such a comparison made between us.

10

Behind the Met Scenery

DIVIDE me into three parts—which is not too difficult for a person of my size—and they would be called, Artist, Critic, and Appreciator. It is a strange fact, but each is a separate personality, distinct and individual, united only in whatever is really me. As in the case of a good girdle (which, incidentally, I rarely wear), I get a three-way stretch out of my career.

I can say this because, for example, I like to listen to my own records. I can appreciate the sound as a detached audience of one. I can criticize the sound—knowing that purity and simplicity are the two wings that take one upward—and acknowledge my shortcomings in such items as classic songs and scat-talking modern music. As an artist, however, I feel uncomfortable with my records if anyone else is listening. I become self-conscious of what I am hearing. I regard my friends as a captive audience that must praise or else feel ungracious.

I cannot think anyone should be subjected to me—except Bill —without his permission. If I cannot be accepted on my own virtues—as they sound to others—I would rather not be accepted at all. I will sulk in a dark corner of my repertory. No one can hurt me by saying they dislike my singing; they can rile me by saying insincerely that they like it. If they say it from their hearts, why, God bless us all and *prosit!*

Accused of vanity about my voice, I can say humbly that I do not consider it altogether a part of me. I can hold it out at arm's length and study it—just as I would a recording of a Toscanini symphony concert. I have my own standards about my singing. When I fall short, I am much more violent than any professional critic. From childhood on I had to learn how to listen to myself detachedly. I have kept listening to myself all through years of scales, of simple songs. Even today my husband will say cryptically to some invisible sympathizer: "Helen is getting back to that bad habit of listening to herself."

If I do, I do not listen to praise. I must have my own opinion as a tool for improvement. I like my voice. I can see why people applaud—why they came to my concerts and to my opera performances—why they switch on their TV sets and play my records. There is nothing narcissistic about such a feeling. The hardest thing in life for a person to do is to estimate himself correctly: not to overestimate or underestimate. This I have tried to do. It took me a long while to get my voice where I wanted it, where I could make a simple set of scales sound like a solo just by coloring tone. I am not likely to forget what came out of that, nor the work that made it possible. Neither am I likely to underestimate it.

Next to this impersonal attitude toward my voice I value the people it has drawn to me. Because I could sing, I found that a whole new world fell open in front of me, like a wonderful hollow Easter egg. I could see the universe of art and living through the exquisite focus of people such as Fritz Kreisler, the great violinist; I could sense the extra radiations of that existence. Music—if one is part of it, either as artist or appreciator—is like living on another more glorious plane of sensation.

The friends I have made in this second existence have always given me a new kind of life. Here I must talk about a few of them, about what they meant to me. Lauritz Melchior was one of the first—and is still a good friend of mine. Possessor of one of the finest operatic tenor voices in volume and quality of all time, he was an experience in himself.

I met Lauritz for the first time in 1938. As a young, aspiring soprano, I sang a Wagner operatic concert with him in Minneapolis. He was a big, healthy, lusty, vital man. We talked less about music than we did about recipes and eating. We ate from morning until night—stuffing ourselves with all the good things you can find in the Midwest. The man was Danish; he shared that physique, endurance, and that vocal range which probably made the Vikings able to shout clear across the Baltic Sea when they wanted their wives to come in from pasturing the kine. It was a peculiar combination of temperament and tremendous physical vocal qualities, coupled with his beautiful voice and ability to sustain the most taxing role that made Melchior the world's greatest Wagnerian tenor of his time.

Much as I admired Lauritz, however, many things I learned from him were not musical. My real education from him came in handling myself on stage, not to be "Melchiorized." This grew to epic proportions as the years passed. It became famous among the backstage buffs. Bets were sometimes taken on where he or I would be at the end of a solo or duet.

With an inward glee known only to ourselves, Lauritz and I carried out grand maneuvers on stage for years. It was like a stately chess game, in full view of the Metropolitan Opera audience—but its moves were veiled in the heights of song. Those behind scenes knew it was going on; it caused amused whispers in more than one august corner. Strangely enough, Lauritz and I never mentioned one word about it to each other. It was one of the rules that any comment was *verboten.*

One of the most ancient contests in the world is that of jockeying for position. A horse in a race, a boxer in a ring, an actor in a movie, a politician on a platform—all of them know the techniques. Anyone in the public eye must learn it. The rule is: be noticed or die. In grand opera in my day it appeared in a somewhat different form. My great rival—and one I must bob a curtsey to—was not really Flagstad. Mine was Lauritz. Fifteen years my senior, he was my singing companion for a dozen years. He was a darling and a voice unexcelled this side of heaven—but he was a devil on the stage if he got loose.

This tug of war between Melchior and myself lasted for years. It became famous among backstage opera fans as the invisible battle between Traubel and Melchior. Gentle old Reidel, the prompter, with his lean, handsome face and spectacles, who sometimes led the orchestra on off nights, sat in his hooded cubicle just below the stage as prompter. He saw it all and used to laugh so hard that he would drop off his chair, wiping away the tears, and disappear under the stage to regain his calm.

Clad in our majestic, glittering Wagnerian costumes, we would come lovingly to each other in our duets. Lauritz would put his arm about my shoulders protectively, his huge cloak enfolding me. It all looked so warm and affectionate from the audience—but he was smothering me. Lauritz's arm weighed a couple of hundred pounds, it seemed, the cloak added as much to it. He would gently turn my shoulders as he sang—so that when I was delivering my aria I would be singing directly into the ear of some stagehand at the rear of the cavernous Met stage. I got around this by lovingly turning away and walking a few steps downstage, delivering my sorrow or ecstasy to the audience. I got back at Lauritz by maneuvering around him when he was supposed to be singing to me so that he had to fling phrases over his shoulder.

At another time Lauritz would move ponderously in front of me, between the spotlights and myself. His shadow would fall over me. It was a mighty shadow. It blacked me out until all I was to my hearers was a soprano blackface minstrel singing somewhere in the distance. Lauritz and I must have walked miles around each other each season, just singing our hearts out and casting shadows. Mine was hefty enough to make him worry. He would also walk away from me when I was singing my soul's love to him—so I would promptly transfer my affections to the front row center. Later, I would pay him back in kind.

One scene I did complain of to him. It was a moment when we rushed across the stage from opposite wings and clasped each other madly in our arms. It was exactly like a couple of two-ton trucks having a collision in the middle of Broadway. We rushed together, had our head-on crash with a rending of my brocade and a clash of his armor (I can still show scars), bounced apart from sheer observance of the laws of physics, then came together again. Lauritz crushed the breath out of me every time with his bear hug.

"Lauritz," I whispered pantingly to him one night, "we can't keep this up. The wear and tear is too much!"

"My love," he muttered, his eyes twinkling, "how can you speak so of our irresistible attraction for each other?" His arms enveloped me smotheringly again. I got out of that in subsequent performances by sidestepping, a couple of times letting Lauritz skid his way nearly into the opposite wing.

Lauritz also had a lot of fun trying to break me up when he was offstage and I was on. During my most serious arias, when I was solo on the stage, weeping my heart out for some hero or other who had gone away and left me or I had left him and gone away—whichever it happened to be in the libretto—Lauritz would be in the wings. He wore a little woman's hat on his head and was jigging around talking to the stagehands. Or he was wearing a derby and a bearskin strapped across his chest, winking at me, wiggling his fingers in his ears, and doing everything from a hornpipe to the Highland fling. On one notable occasion he secretly broke into the costume department. He got himself a grass skirt and some paper flowers. He did a hilarious hula in the wings in the midst of my most tragic moment onstage. It **very** nearly broke up my diaphragm control, but I am glad to say I retained a straight face.

The only person who ever put me out of countenance on the opera stage was a white horse. It was the heroic horse Grane in *Die Götterdämmerung*. Its name was really White Ghost, a stallion that was given to me by Robert Ringling. Most of the horses of the opera used at that time were the saddest, most swaybacked dray horses it has ever been my privilege to put an eye upon. But when this immense, spirited, trained stallion came on, the whole audience sucked in its breath in appreciation. The magnificent beast stood there dressed in his specially made white bridle and I sang to him. I sang to and from him, I sang all around him. Suddenly he pricked his ears forward. In time with the rhythm of the song he started to lift his hoofs. I saw he was dancing with the aria—tippy-toe, tippy-toe, in and out and around. The audience started to chuckle, a wave of glee that swept the house. I kept singing my brains out indignantly, but it made no difference whatsoever. The horse had stolen the show. Hoofs up, hoofs down, it was the first time that a diva had been outclassed by a stallion.

My first Met introduction to Kirsten Flagstad came at my first rehearsal, but it was not the first time we had met professionally. That had happened in 1938 in Chicago, when I had sung Sieglinde (with no rehearsals to speak of) in company with her and Melchior after the appearance with the Minneapolis Symphony. She had been very complimentary about the singing of such a "youngster"—and, I noted with pleasure, she was quite genuinely moved as she kissed me.

She was of medium height, plump figure, and rather quiet. She always sang, I thought, really to get enough money to go back and live peacefully at home rather than for the sheer pleasure of singing. She had one of those extraordinarily clear, clean-cut Scandinavian faces. Her strong, vibrant voice was one of the most beautiful I had ever been privileged to hear.

At the time I came to the Met, she was at the height of her career. She did not know that World War II was completely to destroy that career in 1941. She used to come down and talk to me as I knitted in my dressing room. She was terribly disturbed about the outbreak of war in Europe the previous fall of 1939. I had met her husband a few years before, during a tour of Flagstad's in St. Louis. He was a happy, tall, sandy-haired fellow with whom she was very much in love. He owned a lumber business, I remember, which the Nazis took over. He was later accused of collaboration by his own countrymen. In the temper of those times this destroyed the voice of his wife in the public ear three thousand miles away—a voice that women in my profession would have given anything to have, even with one fifth the quality, purity, and tone. She used to talk to me often *sprich durch die blume,* as the German phrase goes, "through the flower." She would seem to be talking to someone else but indirectly she was addressing me in all sincerity. I really think she was preparing me to take over her place in those days. She used to tell me again and again, "Traubel, I am so tired! I'm singing *so* much opera. We must change the parts around, Traubel. I will sing Sieglinde to your Brünnhilde, eh?" Or she would say "Traubel, I want to stop this foolish singing, I want to get back home!" It was pathetic to me and tragic to her.

I rarely saw her after her final triumph in 1941. She went back to Europe for the duration of the war and disappeared completely. She returned to the Metropolitan ten years later, in 1951. Her husband had died and I suspect that music had become her only love and solace. It was the first year Rudolf Bing was manager. He came to me and asked if I minded if Flagstad and I would each share singing the Wagnerian parts. "Of course," I said. "It will be all right, of course!"

I may say flatly that the absurd Flagstad-Traubel feud whipped up by the press critics never existed. Some people thought she was the greatest Wagnerian soprano that ever lived; some people thought the same of me. Still others thought we were equal. That was all.

Whatever the outside world thought, however the comparisons were, we never knew very much nor cared. The fact is we were doing the best job we could, at the tops of our voices. If one of us did badly, that was our own fault. We knew enough to correct it next time. Between us we were always the greatest of friends. On my side, at least, I was a "further-going" admirer. Envy and jealousy of a fellow performer often has the effect of curdling the good artistic instincts one has. This, in turn, affects the quality of one's singing. It is by far the wiser part if only for your own sake not to indulge in such childish histrionics.

The finest compliments I ever had in my life up to that time were those that compared me to Flagstad, favorably or unfavorably. It meant a great deal to me. For the first time the critics broke with the tradition at the Metropolitan that the great Wagnerian voices had to come out of the depths of Europe. I had never been to Europe; at that time I had no intention of going. I was a native, corn-fed product from the Midwest. I was and am proud of it. Here I could stand on the creaking Met stage and take my own. I could feel myself an equal with Flagstad, the greatest that the Old World had produced with all its tradition, talent, background, and training.

What I always wanted most was to be a *singer*—and a damned good one. I realized, of course, that to join the Metropolitan in any capacity was the top of the heap to most people in my profession. Even those who took third and fourth parts on stage had to be good. It was something to be in the chorus. But my goal was only to sing as well as I could.

"Where?" I might be asked. "It isn't enough to sing in the bathtub or on the rooftop."

"Anywhere," I would say, even today. "If I sing well—as well as I know I can—every door in the world will be open."

Yet, if the truth is known, I did have a specific goal. I wanted to be on Victor Red Seal records. As a little girl they had enchanted me with the miracle of their tone and fidelity—though it was not very good compared to the standards of today—and I knew they represented the cream of the singing world. I wanted my name to appear on one. Money never meant very much to me; nor did the fact that people might know me; I just wanted to show one single record with my name on it to my mother—something that never happened before her death.

I can admit that opera bored me as a performance. People used to talk about me knitting backstage, putting down my work on cue, stepping out and singing a difficult role, and coming back to take up my knitting without dropping a stitch. The fact is that although the music and the atmosphere of opera charmed me, the enactment never gave me a thrill. It was a job, and I did it well. I can say flatly that the total learning of my opera life has been nine roles. I never wanted to know any more: I wanted to sing these perfectly. They were mostly Wagner, the most difficult in the world, and I had one of the best opera coaches in the business.

He was a man named Ernest Knoch who was, like me, a perfectionist in opera. He was the spitting image of Wagner, very thin, with fluffy gray hair, a short, ramrod-straight fellow. He loved anything that was a challenge—as I suppose his taking me on as a student must have been. He was an ardent devotee of the cult of Yoga, standing for minutes on his head to meditate; he was also a dedicated mountain climber who had scaled most of the peaks in Europe. He taught all roles in opera, drawing upon his experience as a Continental conductor. Explosive in opinion, individual in his tastes—and perennially broke because he would not conduct or teach if he felt it beneath his peculiar dignity—Knoch gave me much of what I had hoped for.

I spent three hours a day with him. He taught me musicianship, tone, color, language. He was impressed with my physical qualifications. "Opera is not simple, but it should seem simple," he used to say. "If you have the size and stamina and equipment, it's easy; if not, it's the most difficult and terrible thing in the world." I soaked up everything he had to tell me, absorbing his gnarled wisdom like a blotter. His individualistic teaching and my own feeling that I must be myself no matter what tradition or the past dictated agreed. I never once listened to another singer to learn anything, though I listened to many to appreciate their art. I never did a role on the basis of other performances. My rule had to be: never copy.

For a dozen years after my first real season of 1940–41 I settled in at the Metropolitan. In the first couple of years the opera fans divided into three groups: the pro-Flagstads, the pro-Traubels, and the pro-Flagstad-Traubels who thought we were a dead heat in ability. As the years went on, my own position became assured. No genuine rival appeared up until the time I left the Met in 1953.

I have heard many things about myself. Various surveys of that era—and some over the whole period of such music—describe me as "the greatest dramatic soprano of all time." If that is true, I must confess that it deals almost wholly with Wagnerian roles. My own claim to fame is simpler: no matter what my talents, I changed the whole picture of grand opera simply by being myself.

By that I mean I was American-born, -bred, -raised, and -trained. I never saw Europe nor even thought much about it until long after my triumphs in the operas of Wagner. Put it this way: I proved that a spoiled brat out of the Midwest, endowed with lungs and persistence and great teachers, plus whatever talent God gave, could make a fool out of those who insisted that opera was the greatest thing in music; that only Europeans or European-trained artists could do it; and that it was the only open sesame for a career in that world.

Let me make a confession: I never aimed for opera from the beginning. It was never my soul's desire and it never inspired me to sing—a dream of myself ascending the golden stairs at the Met.

Some people have wondered (from time to time, aloud) why I insisted so rigidly on singing the part of Sieglinde for my debut. It is true I preferred it; that I had learned it because it appealed to me so strongly, but it is also true that the role, at the time, was the sole Wagnerian part I knew.

My theory had always been that I should make beautiful sounds in the best way I could—and that everything else would follow. This, though I did not know it at the time, was contrary to the then-current ideas of opera. Opera was dominated by a clique of managers, agents, and impresarios who were in turn supported by the wealthy specialists in music who liked to exhibit their protégés as if they were trained seals. This group, small and powerful, had never relinquished their tight rein over the opera. It decreed that each singer should know at least a dozen roles, sometimes in four or five languages.

Possibly because I did not know any better, possibly because I would have done just the same if I had—someone told me later, "you either had a lot of guts or were just plain stupid"—I went against this tide. I jumped into it without fanfare, and instantly became one compared with Flagstad, the leading voice of that generation. I once asked a writer why such comparisons were necessary. He told me: "If I wrote five columns about you alone, no one would read it; it is only when I compare your performance to standards already known that people become interested."

In singing the role of Isolde, for example, it is not generally known that the vocal demands are so tremendous that Wagner himself had more than fifty rehearsals before he could launch it and at one time actually thought of two sopranos—dramatic and lyric—to conquer the portrayal. A dramatic voice in that sense is one that is powerful and stunning, capable of long bravura passages, full of drive and sustained tone; a lyric soprano is lighter, capable of more vocal gymnastics. Isolde had to be both: so did Flagstad and myself. I was thought by many from the beginning to be her superior in the demanding dramatic character of the first act and the beginning of the second act, and her equal in the lyric necessities of the last of the second act and the third.

This is not to say that I can compare with lyric sopranos. It is like trying to compare an eagle with a dove. Sixty years ago a young Maine singer who took the name of Nordica was supposed to do both Wagner and such light roles as Violetta in *La Traviata* with the same ease. That is hard to judge at this distance, but the recordings I have heard of her voice—even allowing for recording deficiencies—do not bear this out.

In the future, when other voices are heard by other audiences, there will be critics of that faraway time to judge me as rigidly as I judge others. At that time I can only say, as I once said to my dressmaker as she was measuring me: "I do not ask for justice; I only ask for mercy."

Nothing is more melancholy to the singer than to know that her voice is doomed to be no more than an echo on plastic or a fading cry within a machine. But it is comforting as well to know that there will be others with my own dream and with their own passion for tone and for music that will carry on the massive tradition of art.

11

Costumes and Critics

IF any one performance of mine was commended by the critics, I could usually count on being knocked for six, as the British say, by the comments on my costumes. Here, as in music, I went my own merry way. For example, I felt that as long as Isolde was an Irish princess in the opera, it was perfectly logical for me to wear a brilliant green dress in the first act. This did not come off very well and I discarded it. But I did rebel against the traditional pigtails of the woman and put my own hair up atop my head, a crown hairdo which set a style from then on.

The greatest costume furore came when I monkeyed with the Brünnhilde costumes. These were the frumpiest possible kind of dresses, made by the harried, penny-pinched costumers of the Metropolitan. I decided to have mine all redone by Adrian of Hollywood. His chosen fashion trade-marks were broad shoulders, straight lines, and simple taste. They suited me down to the ground.

The traditional dress of Brünnhilde in the first act of *Die Walküre* was a tunic of tin armor. I put it on. I looked exactly like a canned lion. Not only did I have to wear this coat of fake armor plate, I also had to don a flyaway helmet of metal with huge wings. In general, including a huge cloak, I looked like a relic of the Hundred Years' War. Adrian changed all this by taking me out of my prison of what-was into what-should-be. He reprieved me by designing armor of silvery suède leather rather than tin plate, and attaching it only halfway round instead of *all* the way around. He designed a light and stylish helmet for me of the same stuff. He changed the lines so they were simpler and more impressive. Most of his costumes, I may add, are now in the various New York museums as supreme examples of tasteful costuming.

I suggested three new costumes for the role of Isolde—every one of them against tradition. One was a pink dressing gown of light silk jersey for the second act that looked as if I had just come out of the boudoir—which was exactly what the role called for. For the role of Elsa in *Lohengrin* I had a simple white gown with a bolero jacket. For the role of Elisabeth in *Tannhäuser* Adrian designed my most spectacular costume: a lavender dress in full, sweeping curves with a cape of orange-gold and a jeweled crown of gold leather. There were others—such as the gleaming dress of gold lamé that made me look like a torch even in the dimmest light—but these were the highlights. The total cost for me, in 1941, was more than thirty thousand dollars—at no expense to the Met.

As a matter of fact the Metropolitan costume department at that time was a poverty-stricken, staggering affair. It had a great deal of talent but it was so immersed in tradition that it never dared raise its head—and it had only "scraps and rags" to work with. In those days most of the Met singers came with their own costumes; even a lot of the chorus had to appear with what they had and the whole had the appearance of something like a confused Chinese fire drill. I must add that in recent years the whole affair has been reorganized and put on a sensible basis—of which I highly approve. Why, even the operas themselves, in these saner days, are organized as productions instead of being thrown together at the last minute like a Tammany picnic!

Together with the costuming difficulties there were those that always come with a fresh singing role—those of proper interpretation. I had never believed much in a fusty traditionalism of the Met. I had thought out my own ideas of how a role should be sung. It became far more realistic than the usual treatment but it was rarely accepted when I introduced it. As an example, in *Die Walküre*, as Sieglinde, I was supposed to come onto the stage and discover some man—I don't know who, except he was supposed to be half-wolf and half-man (no neophyte could ever follow the plot of a Wagner opera and I had a tough enough time with the reversible, back-to-back words) sleeping on the hearth. The traditional way of entering had always been to come on stage in a loud, very dramatic entrance, singing: "What! A strange man lying on the hearth"—and he was supposed to sleep through it. I thought this was silly. I determined to come in singing softly, obviously not to awaken him. It was very soft, well controlled, and, I thought, very effective dramatically. I am damned if the critics to a man did not think I had stage fright—something I have been fortunate enough to escape all my life—and accused me of "tentative" or frightened singing.

This kind of critical nonsense has always irritated me. It is unfair to the singer; the mass of the audience generally follows slavishly the critics' opinions. It is true that later they became accustomed to my renditions—and even complain when they are violated today—but in those times such an innovation generally was misunderstood.

This business of what might be called "comparative singing" is difficult to work out. I have always tried to adapt the quality and volume of my voice to fit the dramatic moment—not without a struggle with conductors and stars. I recall in 1942 I was working out a role with Leinsdorf in Hollywood—I was recovering from an operation, a cartilage splice in my kneecap—when this difficulty came up. I was singing at rehearsal and keeping my voice soft and low. Leinsdorf stopped.

"What's the matter?" I asked.

"You'll have to sing with more volume," he said.

"The part doesn't call for it," I protested. "It calls for just this kind of singing. The score is marked that way."

"Your partner can't sing pianissimo that way and still maintain his tone," Leinsdorf explained.

"I can't worsen my own performance to make his seem better," I said. "Let's sing it the way it's written by the composer." And so we did.

Tempo and sound. How many arguments these have touched off in opera! In *Die Götterdämmerung* the tempo doubles and doubles again in one place. I have seen tenors start off so fast in this scene that by the time they got really coasting down the torrent of notes, the horns in the orchestra could not blow the separate notes to keep up with them. It is quite easy to sing loud and fast, but the singer must remember that there are spots in any opera that put him at the mercy of the orchestra, and that the orchestra is not above taking revenge on the singer at such spots. Contests of this kind between voice and instruments do not improve the quality of a presentation. I was always extremely conscious of the necessity of collaboration with the orchestra—and I was happiest when the musicians themselves were pleased with my singing.

I used to practice the whole role of an opera in my apartment, going over it phrase by phrase as many as four or five times before I even entered rehearsal in order to develop the controlled interpretation I wanted. I never paid much attention to the traditional superstitions about eating and drinking certain things just before a performance. At one time, before a Hollywood Bowl concert, I had myself a fine time strolling down the boulevard with a sack of peanuts under one arm and devouring a chocolate ice-cream cone on the side. It was only a few hours before I was scheduled to sing.

My companion, Mario Chamlee, an excellent tenor, was on the verge of apoplexy. He knew that salted nuts and cold ice cream were supposed to produce acid and mucus that would foul up a voice. He kept muttering to me about how reckless I was, what a terrible thing it was to eat such comestibles just before a critical rehearsal. I crunched away and lapped up the cream—and went out to sing that night. When I came off the stage to my dressing room, I found my companion of that afternoon's stroll waiting for me, glowering at Bill. Mario drew himself up. "Exquisite!" he shouted. "Give her nuts, give her ice cream, give her all she can eat! I may take up eating them myself!"

I used to drink milk in my dressing room at the Met just before a performance. The people who saw me would run shrieking from the room, but I felt that I knew my own capabilities better than anyone else. I knew that there was one famous singer who had to have a lozenge in his mouth during a performance or he felt he could not perform successfully. On one occasion he accidentally spat it out and was lost. He edged toward the wings and hissed at his valet: "Toss me a lozenge!" His valet had none—but he did have presence of mind. He ripped a button from his coat and tossed it. The tenor went back, delivered a superlative performance, and then found he was singing with a mother-of-pearl lozenge in his cheek. He was completely cured by the shock. Other singers insist on hot tea in their dressing rooms; or they have a table lined with sprays to clear their passages.

The only thing I tried to do in my career to prepare for a night of singing was never to see anyone or do anything besides rest and listen to the radio or chat; and to keep singing. I realized that the talent I had was like a big motor. It needed to be worked and warmed up. It was not delicate (I rarely had laryngitis—outside one notable time—or enlarged lymph glands). Where other singers would not even talk, writing notes to their friends, relatives, and servants for a day before a concert, I was constantly doing scales, vocalizing, testing my tones—even while putting on make-up or costumes. I would go over the whole opera the day before I was to sing, at full volume. I went to bed at ten at night, usually with the scores in my lap, and studied them until I fell asleep. I never worried about resting nor took drugs of any kind to induce it—I calculated that if I needed sleep it would come to me; if it did not, I would get up and read or turn on the late radio musical programs. All this, of course, was not too radical a departure from my usual training schedule which consisted of getting up at seven thirty in the morning, getting breakfast and doing the dishes, then working with three teachers, each for two or three hours a day—and ending up with my own experimenting at eight or nine at night. I never appeared to need relaxation: immersing myself in the imagery and sound of the music was apparently enough to give me endless pleasure.

Acting was always a problem with me. Some people, whose reputation has led me to believe them, tell me I am quite competent as opera singers go. But I was always confounded by those long-drawn waits and postures in Wagner's works. He fancied himself not as an opera writer, as most people know, but as a writer of "musical dramas." In the scene where Wotan and Brünnhilde say farewell in the last act of *Die Walküre,* a scene replete with suggestions of incest, we used to stand perhaps fifty feet apart and signal and shout our love for each other like a troop of Boy Scouts practicing semaphore. It took an interminable period just for us to get together to clutch each other. The same thing used to happen in *Tristan und Isolde* where I, as the tragic heroine, had to say something like: "Give me a coke with a love potion in it"—and then kind of fade out, waving, as the hero departs. Adrian designed me a special scarf to wave with. I cut down the number of traditional heaves despite the usual argument with the conductor. As a matter of fact, I tried to minimize all of my action and to concentrate the attention of the audience on the music rather than on the lines or the stage movements. Lauritz felt the opposite—and it occasionally annoyed the stagehands who on at least one occasion sprinkled carpet tacks on the floor where he was supposed to kneel.

The whole idea of musical, emotional communication has a sobering effect on me. I feel even more strongly now the vast distance that lies between any artist and his gift—how much is owed to a source that is never consciously tapped by a singer. When I sang at the Metropolitan, it was commonplace for the box office to hang out the SRO sign: for five years there was never a vacant seat at one of my performances, I was told. Yet I cannot say that I ever "suffered" for my art; the reserve was merely there for me to tap when I needed it. Lulu, my old teacher, used to work on me until I would be driven to complain: "I'll never be able to satisfy you!" to which she would snap: "When you do, I won't be around!" I got the habit of driving and working from her, changing me from what most people might call a spoiled brat into a person who sometimes can be a slave driver in musical things. I drive myself as hard as anyone, but I do not "suffer." This business of putting the artist into the attic or vice versa— bringing a good soprano out of the shower—is nonsense. I got the love and care I needed when I was young—and I got the discipline, too. Work and play were right there when I had to have them. This so-called "suffering" doesn't make you a better singer or anything else; it just makes you suffer. I used to tell Lulu defiantly: "You'll never make me cry!" No one has ever done it to me yet.

Such thoughts were constantly with me during my first years at the Met. I was even more conscious of their importance when I was free to go out on tour and meet people much more closely— something I enjoyed so much that I have never abandoned it since. I could sing at full volume with assurance that the economics of the situation were under control instead of leading the parade. Whatever the Met was not, it was certainly a magic ticket seller and open sesame to engagements if you could put . . . "of the Metropolitan" after your name.

In the spring of 1940 I did a few concerts. Not many: it was difficult to schedule me. Concerts were arranged as far ahead as eighteen months. "Too big, too quick," was the opinion that one agent gave me. Bill and I changed our agent to another, larger organization to facilitate this handling—the Columbia Concerts Bureau with whom we stayed fifteen years under the direction of Jack Salter, Lawrence Evans, and Kurt Weinhold. At that time I was getting between twelve hundred and fifty and fifteen hundred dollars per concert. I got the same for radio appearances.

Bill and I then went on our first tour. It was the most incredible arrangement we have experienced from that day to this. From New York we went to Toledo, Ohio; from Ohio, we flew to Seattle, Washington; from Washington, we went down to Tucson, Arizona; from Arizona, if I recall correctly, we wound up in Cincinnati and then went down to Miami, Florida—and somewhere in between all these we appeared on the Bing Crosby Show with Bob Burns, the bazooka king, in Hollywood on a radio program. It was a really exhausting trip in which we crosshatched the whole of the United States. I enjoyed it; I think Bill did—but poor Cooney Bos! We did not know that he suffered from altitude. I can still see my dignified accompanist sitting up all night miserably staunching his nose bleeds in the rear of the plane. (It did not affect him too seriously; he died in 1957 at the ripe old age of eighty.)

Not even those closest to me always agreed with my ideas about music. I thought of singing largely as a method of communicating emotion by sound. They thought of it as a sacred traditional form, like a rite performed by high priests before an altar shaped like a high C. Cooney Bos, my accompanist, was a traditionalist when he first worked with me. We were experimenting with lieder. I suggested singing some of the songs of Beethoven—and cutting them down drastically. He became very excited.

"You can't do that to Beethoven! No, no!" he cried. "I can't allow cutting Beethoven to death!"

I talked to him awhile and finally persuaded him to edit them if I would sing them to him as an experiment. We took out many of the repetitions and meaningless phrases. Cooney, with enormous doubts, sat down at the piano and we rehearsed our new version. After it was over and the last lingering note had died away, Cooney turned slowly on his stool. He said wonderingly: "You know, I like it this way much better. But the critics, they will murder you in cold blood, they will knock you down."

"Let's see if we can give them a blunt instrument," I told him cheerfully. We went out on the platform a few days later and sang the songs just as we had rehearsed them. The critics were in raptures. They said they had never heard and understood these songs so well before. Not one mentioned that they had been cut—I do not think any one of them knew it. From that day to this our editing of the "sacred" Beethoven works has gone unnoticed but is thoroughly appreciated.

Such a tampering with the works of the masters is not to be construed as sacrilegious criticism. Only recently Erich Leinsdorf, the first conductor with whom I sang at the Met, has declared himself —nearly twenty years after Cooney and I first did it—in favor of abridging certain pieces of classical music which he feels dull and tedious. This is not the only reason for such editing—but certainly it is a good place to start.

Encouraged by our early success at presenting Beethoven's songs intelligibly by using musicianship and common sense, Bos and I cut many more without the knowledge of the critics. Indeed, everyone went along with our versions except those who forehandedly brought the music and read score against us. Cooney was always a little cautious about doing it but he soon became converted.

"Ah, you can do that in America," he would say, shaking his head, "but in Germany they would never allow it."

"I'm not singing in Germany," I would say. He would shake his head again. After we had done the songs, he would shake it differently. "I like this," he would say, "but you could never do this in Berlin."

"I'm not worried about Berlin," I would assure him. Finally, after a particularly successful recital, he would nod in approbation. "This," he would declare, "you could do just as it is in Berlin even!"

In this concert work I learned that I disliked overworded songs. Words are good to sing, but they are far from necessary. I could make lyrics out of simple scales, songs that existed simply because of coloration without a word to their name. I found that although Ethel Merman can belt these out—and no one admires this talent more than I—it is impossible to make a really true *sound* while jabbering at the top of your voice. I have always felt that a singer must make her choice between talking and singing. The two are not synonymous. Since the modern rash of "talk singers," I am more sure than ever of my conclusion.

At the same time I discovered that it was possible to create an unsurpassed dramatic effect simply by the prolongation of a single tone. In the Richard Strauss composition, "Rest, My Soul," I created a ten-second pause after a high sustained note—then delivered a long, low, soft note while standing absolutely still. It made people hold their breath. Somehow a feeling of pure drama crept into the rendition. It became famous as one of the most outstanding renditions in my repertoire. After one performance a critic came up to me and said: "I've heard this Strauss before but never this way. I can't understand what makes it so compelling, so affecting."

"I've learned that the pause counts as much as the note," I said. He nodded, but I am sure he did not understand.

Wagner and Strauss are among the great proving grounds of a voice. It is not enough to be heroic on the stage. The voice must endure the extremes of extraordinary range and must be capable of the most delicate coloring of tone. In addition, in order to offset the typically Teutonic sentimentality of expression, the singer must be able to inject her own crispness of interpretation. This, coupled with the endurance to appear in works that average four hours in length, enables anyone to appreciate the value of a pause. Sometimes it is not so much for dramatic effect as it is merely to get a rest.

When Bill and I went to watch other singers, I was driven to distraction by their presentations. There was—and is—one famous songstress who has three different registers—and holes in all of them. I could not understand the critical applause for her voice, though I was highly appreciative of the intensity and the interpretation she gave a song. I modeled my own phrasing and dramatic pauses after hers (I could afford a little longer wait, as I was more imposing) but I ignored what she had in voice quality. "The trouble with you," said a friend to me at one point as I analyzed my own work, "is that you know all there is to know about your music—and yet you keep sweating over it." The business of keeping the illusion of loveliness on tiptoe is a constant backstage wrestle. I have always needed all the help I could get from people such as Bos and Knoch.

Like Knoch, Bos was a man who meant much to me in supporting my musical career. His impeccable taste and guidance were my criteria for nearly all presentations, especially in the broad selection of lieder, those small delightful songs that are so important a part of any singer's repertoire. He and I used to loathe the usual approach of a concert singer to a program. Anyone acquainted with the musical world will know what I mean: the cat-and-mouse attitude of diva and accompanist. All the items of curtseying, grinning, milking the audience for applause, pointing to the accompanist and having him take a bow—these and the other impedimenta to hearing music were in the way of what we wanted to do. It seemed to us like a deliberate vaudeville act, insulting the intelligence of audience and artists alike.

We were very casual about our approach to a concert occasion. I would stride out on the stage and take my position. Bos would come out, spread his tails, and sit down. Without further ado we would sail into the first song. Once I began with the wrong lied; Bos pounced like a bird dog into the right chords and we moved along divinely to the end. Once in a while he would get off and I would keep right on and he would chime in. We really never knew who started what or picked up the other, but from long practice together our reflexes were so fast that we could cover our mistakes before a critic could pick his teeth. I do not think anyone ever caught us out on this particular phase of concertizing.

All this impromptu was pleasing to Cooney. He loved it. For years he had wanted to be a vaudevillian on a stage bill. He could do tricks such as balancing a glass of water on the back of his hand and slowly turning over his hand underneath it until it was in his palm. He could balance a long-stemmed flower on his nose for minutes while playing the piano—and once horrified the assembled press of Worcester, Massachusetts, by doing just that.

I am known in the singing profession as a careful prop checker. That means I like to go around the stage—as I always did at the Met before a performance of any kind—and check each object with which I have to act during the scene. On my concert tours, I also liked to visit the halls beforehand to find out where to enter and exit, to test the acoustics, and to strum the piano. I had no embarrassment about performing functions that were not the duty of a prima donna. Occasionally I got into trouble about them. I recall once in Troy, New York, I went to the hall and found the piano in the wings. I wanted it on the stage and so I pushed it out to the middle all by myself. This fact was seen by the janitor and reported to whatever union oversees the destiny of the piano movers. They came in a high, eight-cylinder dudgeon and took it away. We had to get a new piano propelled by union pushers—inasmuch as I had no time to join the organization.

In Topeka, Kansas, there was a mixup in dates and the piano was taken away before we arrived. Since it was Sunday, it was impossible to rent another. The audience and I waited half an hour, chatting informally, until one was taken out of a private home and brought into the auditorium. Which reminds me of the time Cooney and I were singing a short ditty as an encore written around Shakespearean words—musically an abortion, but it seemed to please the listeners. It had two endings, one for encore and one for finale. Cooney went one way and I went the other but we ended up harmoniously. I imagine it may have sounded a little like Schönberg's stuff anyway.

"Why did you do that?" Cooney asked me afterward. "What were you thinking of?"

"It was the last concert of the year and I was thinking about getting this tour over and going home," I said defensively. To be sincere about it, that was often in my thoughts: a home of my own and a place to settle down after all the roving.

12

The Diva Settles Down

IN the 1939–40 season—opera usually lasted from November of one year to April of the next—I performed two or three Sieglindes. I also did one Elisabeth in *Tannhäuser*. I learned the latter part in the late winter. The impact of the Philharmonic concerts had taken the bigwigs of the musical world by surprise. The Met officials privately admitted that they were "forced" to take me because of the newspaper reviews and the clamor of the opera buffs.

What they did not know was that those in the inmost circles of music—the true artists without whom nothing good could have been produced—had already given me their cachet of approval. It came to me really as a surprise. It was the finale of a series of rather amusing incidents. The first arrived at the time that the great friend of Bill's and mine, Mario Chamlee, was visiting us in our cheerful little apartment catty-corner across from Carnegie Hall. In those days we were young and opinionated. We were in love with what we were doing and nothing seemed to matter too much except good music. Those were semi-depression days. Not many in our crowd had anything to spend except their own fun and ideas. We used to talk, Bill and I, about what we would do in the future if my voice—on which we had bet our dimes and our hopes—failed to prove out. We kidded on the level about running a gasoline station with a hot-dog stand or being a butler and cook. *Monsieur and Madame William Bass*, cooking and buttling—the very best in international cuisine and Old-World manners! Or perhaps: GET YOUR GAS HERE AT THE BASS'S STATION! SERVICE AND SAUERKRAUT WITH A SONG!

One of our recreations was to cross the street to Carnegie and pay seventy-five cents to sit in the top-gallery seats to listen and criticize. I recall coming home night after night in as near a depression as I could get. "If they're good," I would say to Bill, "then I'm on the wrong track." The next morning the critics would call them "great" and my hopes would go down another notch. One evening early in 1939, when Mario came to supper, I asked him point-blank if he thought I should do a recital in New York. Mario clapped his hand to his head and said: "Just get up there, open that mouth, and let the tones come out!"

"I've never given a full-length recital," I said.

"Can you do 75 per cent as well as you do in your singing right here?" he asked dramatically. I nodded. He leaned toward me. "I tell you," he said impressively, "if you do 10 per cent of what you do here, you will do better than anyone in the world." Whether I believed him or not, his enthusiasm was heartening.

I got another boost from another admirer not long after. Bill was angling to get me a radio broadcast spot on the famous Telephone Hour. At that time it was one of the top prestige programs —and Bill had a friend in a New York advertising company. He pulled all the strings he could and got the same answer: "Let her get famous and we'll think about it; we use only the biggest names." This left Bill frustrated to the point of frenzy, but there was nothing he could do about it until one evening we had dinner with Giorgio Polacco. This dapper little man—who resembled the epitome of all maestros with his lapel flowers, white hair and mustache, upright carriage, and impish traits—had been a great conductor of opera and symphony in his day. He had been general manager of the Chicago Opera Company in the long-gone years when that organization was really great under the millions of Samuel Insull. He was a close friend. One night he declared he would cook the chicken *cacciatore* at our apartment. I told him to bring his daughter, a charming girl named Graziella. We were going to have Robert, another old friend—so I asked Giorgio to get a friend for his daughter. He looked at me queerly and then, with a twinkle I had never seen before, nodded. "I get one," he said, and went off.

That evening he turned up with his friend. It was a young, handsome man in his thirties—John Barbirolli, who had just succeeded Arturo Toscanini as conductor of the famous Philharmonic. I suspected at that second that our beaming Giorgio had some scheme in his head. I never expected he would ask me to sing. He knew I loathed it at private parties and always tried to avoid it—but he also knew that I had been denied any auditions of consequence in New York. Here was my chance in private. He was determined I should take it. It was a wicked thing to do— especially as Barbirolli (who later became a genuinely close friend of ours) looked exactly like a Christian thrown to the beasts of the arena. I could not blame him. I objected as long as I could without being obnoxious. "This is a case of bringing my harp to the party and being told to play," I muttered despairingly to Bill.

Our friend Robert was feeling no pain after the post-prandial drinks. He sat down carefully, with great expectation. Barbirolli picked up the score of a song lying on the table. He started to turn it over. Instantly Robert pounded the table.

"Put away that book, you fourth-rate conductor!" he bellowed to my acute embarrassment. "Don't you know you're going to hear the greatest voice in the world?"

We calmed him down, and the room took on the aspect of a torture chamber for me. Barbirolli, in my opinion, was then a young conductor of great promise since fulfilled. He never played the newspaper-society-arty game; he was a pure musician to the core and wanted none of it. It seemed he had been trapped by just such a deadfall.

I started to sing, and he paid instant attention. By the time I finished, he was glowing. On the spot he confessed that he was entranced. He added that he wanted to sign me up to sing on his Philharmonic program that coming fall. After he left, I turned to the radiant Giorgio in terror: "He wants me to sing the Immolation scene!" I exclaimed.

"So?"

"So I don't know it!"

"So neither does he," said Giorgio placidly. "Don't you tell him and he won't tell you. You both have plenty of time to learn it."

"Oh," I said feebly.

"And from this time on," added Giorgio severely, "if anyone asks you if you know any piece of music, including cadenzas from the Eskimo, always say yes"—advice I have followed to this very minute. I learned the part in a week in April 1939—and spent the following months until October polishing it.

The news—which Bill was careful to spread around in the right places—began to work like yeast in the ferment of the musical world. It proved to be exactly the right enzyme for my career. Soon after that I was notified that I would be allowed to perform an unheard-of audition for the Ford Hour.

The day before the scheduled "tryout," Bill and I went to Connecticut to visit friends. They had one of the cutest black kittens I have ever seen. I picked it up to cuddle it under my chin. Within a couple of hours I broke out in every direction in blazing red spots the size of fifty-cent pieces. The kitten had been rolling in poison ivy!

There was no particular rejoicing in our New York apartment that night. The next day my arms were so swollen we had to cut the sleeves off my best dress. I was loaded with gobs of white lotion—arms, chest, throat, face. But I was determined to sing, even if I did look like some strange spotted being from Mars. We arrived at the studio and I was taken tenderly to the audition room—only myself, a piano, and an accompanist. The bigwigs were supposed to listen to me somewhere upstairs via their desk sets.

I started to sing. In the middle of my selection I suddenly noticed that the engineers in the control booth were laughing. I suppose I was oversensitive about my appearance. I halted in the middle of a high note and said into the microphone, in a voice cold with anger: "I'm sorry this amuses you." I started to walk out.

Instantly one of the engineers flipped a switch. His contrite voice boomed out: "Please don't go, Miss Traubel. We'll tell you *why* we were laughing when you finish." Only half-appeased, I went on to the itchy end of my song. I waited for their apology—but it never came. Instead, they told me the reason they were laughing. It seems that the brass upstairs had phoned down to them. "Stop your kidding," they had ordered. "Turn off that Flagstad record and let that kid you're going to audition start singing." I can imagine that statement today as a compliment, but at the moment I was still mad. What soothed me considerably was the fact that I was signed up for two appearances on the Ford Hour for that fall.

I sang one broadcast in 1939 and I sang three or four the next year. The results of my salesmanship-by-song must have been good. Altogether, before I finished I sang perhaps fifteen such appearances for this commercial sponsor.

I must add at this point that after my Metropolitan appearance in the 1939–40 season I had a special treat in store. I visited the West Coast and sang in Los Angeles. The audience was kind enough to give me a rousing, movie-star standing ovation that lasted for minutes. It was tremendously affecting. It caused the Hollywood Bowl group, through the person of Mrs. Leila Atherton Irish, to offer me a concert in the vast, beautiful reaches of the twenty-one-thousand-person arena in the Hollywood hills. That was my first concert booked for the 1940–41 season.

That season in opera was marked only by the fact that I had a very bad case of flu. Much of it settled in my throat. This was a peculiarly ominous happening because I was scheduled to sing the first Brünnhilde of my career in *Die Walküre* late that season. It was grim, raw weather; I had just learned the role. I was determined to go on, but Bill was just as determined that I would not. He pointed out to me that it was either physical or critical suicide for me to appear under such circumstances. "If you sing well, you'll kill yourself," he said. "If you don't, the critics will kill you."

I went to bed with a fever of 103°—and the telephone commenced ringing for Bill. He endured (I was listening from the bedroom) the most god-awful barrage of demands that I ever heard. Mind you, this was three days before the Met presentation and I was scheduled to go through two days of full rehearsals. Their stage director was with us in the Essex House—where we had moved in 1940 and remained until 1948—on Central Park South. He had come to rehearse me in my role. Bill told him: "No rehearsals," he said, "and no performance. It's impossible for Helen to go on." The wretched man looked at my husband and sighed. "All right," he said reluctantly, "I agree with you. But I can't go back and tell them so. You-know-who is going to raise hell."

He was quite right. The telephone rang like crazy night and day. Without me, unhappily, there was no one to sing the role. Flagstad was on a concert tour as was Marjorie Lawrence, that stout-hearted and ill-fated girl, who got polio the next summer of 1941. I felt as bad as they did on the artistic side—but much worse on the physical. But we were adamant all round.

"How dare you!" crackled Johnson into the phone. "Never in

the history of this opera house has a performance been canceled!
The people are expecting Traubel to appear and she *will* appear!"

"Not unless you have someone else of the same name," Bill
responded cheerfully.

There was much dialogue of the same nature. But it all came to
nothing against our determination that I would not be allowed to
endanger my health. The whole tempest in a larynx wound up
with the Met changing the performance and shoving my debut as
Brünnhilde into the 1941–42 season.

By the fact of the sheer concentration that develops the ability
to shut out everything extraneous to one's work, an opera singer
finally achieves an invulnerability to the world. In most cases a
flat note on the scale will pain her much more than an earthquake
in Peru; and the fit of a dress around the diaphragm is likely to
cause her more tears than the tribulations of the American Indians. I say this only to illustrate the fact that I sang my first
Brünnhilde in *Die Walküre* at a Saturday matinee December 6,
1941.

That night we left for the country and had a peaceful open-
air day in Connecticut, away from any distractions of news or
world events. We motored back to New York to the Hotel Plaza on
Sunday evening and our lawyer friend, Sullivan, came in to join
us for dinner. He was agitated, as pale as his ruddy face could get.

"Isn't it terrible!" were his first words. "Isn't it dreadful!"

"What?" we asked in astonishment.

That was the way we first learned about Pearl Harbor, so far
outside our lives were the catastrophic events of history. As an
anticlimax, the review of that first Brünnhilde said:

"Miss Traubel's opulent voice had the heroic ring and ampli-
tude Brünnhilde's music requires. The 'Ho-yo-to-ho' at her first
entrance was splendidly delivered, with completely free, resonant
top tones and an exemplary sustained trill. There was tender expressiveness when needed in the following scene with Wotan and
the 'Todesverkuendigung' was nobly conceived. As the opera pro-

gressed, however, Miss Traubel became somewhat less secure in her vocalism, some of her later endeavors finding the lower part of the compass a bit unsteady at times and the upper register somewhat metallic when stressed.

"In dealing with Miss Traubel's impersonation it must be remembered that she was new to the role of Brünnhilde, and no one can be expected fully to grasp its histrionic possibilities without prolonged experience in the difficult part. Taken in its entirety, Miss Traubel's work was a serious and distinctly commendable first try at this most exacting role."

The conflict that changed so many lives, strangely enough, did not change ours at all in essentials. I found myself doing more singing, possibly, and there were more uniforms in the audiences— but that was actually the extent of the artist's direct involvement in the chaos of the day as far as the Met was concerned.

But my close involvement with World War II on other fronts was extreme. In those times the problem of morale was intense. I made dozens of records for overseas use. I sang on the armed forces radio, I made appearances and took trips, it seemed, to the ragged edge of nowhere. Some of the details might be interesting.

In those days, of course, it was common knowledge that the favorite music of Adolf Hitler was Wagner. I, though of German descent, was solidly in my own mother's tradition: American first and *raus* with any other ideas. I was commandeered to sing Wagner in German and get it short-waved to Nazi Germany. This was in order to demonstrate to the people, at the very time Paul Joseph Goebbels was shrieking there was "no culture" in our "barbarian" country, that Wagner was doing all right in America. I also sang lieder and popular songs at troop encampments whenever I could. At each concert performance of those years I made it a practice to locate the camps within forty or fifty miles' radius of the concert city and drive out there for an impromptu song fest.

In fairness, I must say I got as much out of the concerts as the soldiers. I guessed it must be boring for them to listen to operatic excerpts and started singing popular tunes—spirituals, pop songs, and old favorites. The response to these was so great that it set me thinking seriously about reaching another, greater audience than the opera group. I made several experiments. Once, in Philadelphia, I arrived at my hotel and found three women's society groups were competing to sponsor my appearance at a certain base. I decided to duck all of them. I went down to the USO canteen in the basement of the Academy of Music. No one knew me there. I offered to sing—but not as Helen Traubel. I went on the platform as Helen Bass.

It was wonderful to be received for myself, not as an impersonal reputation. The applause was warm and real; they stopped dancing to listen; they came over to me afterward and more than one of them said: "Where have you ever been, ma'am? With a voice like that you should try to get yourself a job in opera!" Bill—who was on draft call but never got tabbed because of his age and weight—decided with me to make something of a career of this. We visited many spots in the United States. Lauritz and I did a concert for the benefit of the Danish resistance—and he and I received a decoration from the King of Denmark for our aid.

As the war went on, there were more and more trips—but the Met went on its way, the sphinx of music, always there and always impassive with its repertoire and its reputation. Bill and I never took such a position very seriously, least of all in the war years. Some of the members of the ruling circles took this to heart. There was a mild form of revenge taken on Bill and me for what the Met officials evidently considered an outrage to custom.

It was the custom in those years—though it is true no longer —that the four great operas of Wagner, the Ring series, were given each year. I had been doing the role of Brünnhilde for a couple of years and I wanted to vary my repertoire. So, in the months preceding the season of 1941–42, when the opera front office came to me and asked the usual and meaningless question: "What would you like to do next year, Helen?" I overturned their calculations by saying: "Isolde."

This caused a scurrying around unequaled since the Civil War riots in New York—at least in the privy music circles. The Met brass gave me lip service. "Of course, if you want, Helen," they soothed me, "but if you do, we can't do the Ring series at all. You are the only one who can do either Isolde or Brünnhilde or both. If you insist on Isolde, we will lose all four operas of the Ring." It seemed a reasonable argument and I was not stubborn. I agreed to put off Isolde until the next season. What was my total surprise and outrage, then, when they did announce the coming Ring series, bypassing the idea of presenting Wagner's *Tristan und Isolde.* The announcement said that the real reason was that no one could do that role of Isolde in the shadow of the incomparable Flagstad—therefore I would appear in the Ring. This had the effect of chastening me, I suppose. The management had no idea that such an announcement would really be bad for business and a confession of the inadequacy of the Met to meet the demands of its classical audiences. It also made me so furious that I sang the Ring that year with such grim vigor and determination that the response of the audience and the reviews were better than ever. One critic announced that I had the "true revengeful aura of Brünnhilde." He was right, but he did not know the real reason.

It was on December 4, 1942, that I sang my first Isolde—the favorite role of my predecessor, Flagstad, who must have gone through it hundreds of times—on any stage. It was almost exactly a year after my Brünnhilde debut. The reviews were good; the most restrained in many respects was that of the *Times:*

"She sang it very carefully, very intelligently, always with a lofty purpose and with a sincerity that was manifest in every measure. Naturally, she is not wholly at ease or completely her artistic self in a part just emerging from the study and rehearsal stage. But the first act was admirably proportioned, more than competently sung, and well worked out in detail.

"In the second act Miss Traubel sang most of the love duet so discreetly that at times she was hardly audible. She and Mr. Melchior held the passage down dynamically so that there was a real impression of intimacy and it was refreshing not to hear this superb music bawled. But the phrases needed the freedom, spontaneity, and warmth of color they readily can have when Miss Traubel sings, for there is plenty of that in her voice."

This is the kind of critical self-contradiction that used to drive me nuts. The critic here liked the idea of the music being intimate and he could not stand it, either. I was damned if I was low and damned if I was high.

"For the voice [mine] is more than a soprano with exceptionally brilliant high notes. In fact, the high notes were made less of than is customarily the case and Miss Traubel can confidently make of them. She avoided the high C's and she kept well within her powers as far as sonority is concerned. It was a restrained interpretation, one that went very carefully over difficult ground and left nothing to impulse or chance."

The intimation here was, of course, that I was scared to tackle the high C—but then the critic admits that I was not! The fact again is that I agreed with the writer that the music is "superb" and as in the *piano* effect of the duet, I wanted to sing it for its own sake, not for an acrobatic stunt like hitting a high C. I had always noticed that after a performance the discussion nearly always revolved around whether a high C was hit and held badly or long or whatever. I felt that to single one note out of thousands —with the extreme importance of each one and the pauses between —was silly. I determined to make the high C's less conspicuous by not taking them.

"At present, Miss Traubel's Brünnhilde of *Götterdämmerung* has a dramatic line that her Isolde has yet to gain. In acting Isolde, as indeed in most of her acting, she is now limited. Fortunate that she did too little rather than too much!" Dear sir: did you think I did this without recognizing my own limitations, simply by happenstance?

"To what degree we can expect romantic illusion of her is debatable. She can and we believe she will do much more in this direction than she does now. Her gestures are exterior.

"Let us wait a little. Here is an American soprano, very gifted, who in three seasons has learned the Sieglinde and all the Brünnhilde parts of the Ring, and last night essayed a first, thoughtfully studied and competently realized Isolde. This takes account of Miss Traubel's performance up to the end of the second act. It does not chronicle her singing of the 'Liebestod.' "

The opinion of the other critics was somewhat better than that of the one who had not stayed to hear the "Liebestod." His deadline had kept him from hearing the high point of the whole opera. It was impossible to judge it as he did. After all, the "Liebestod" is the greatest single aria in the whole production and I had paced myself carefully to make sure I did it full justice. I was satisfied with what I had done—and only Bill and I knew that I was on my way to a singing record. The Isolde was the start of it: I was to become unique at least for my endurance.

As one review put it, "Rated by some critics the vocal equal of famed Kirsten Flagstad (whose roles she inherited), Helen Traubel is far and away the finest United States Wagnerian soprano of her generation and one of the three or four finest in the world. Last week, as the Metropolitan's annual Wagner cycle came to an end, Traubel could claim an added distinction. No other United States soprano since Nordica had sung the three-volume role of Brünnhilde (*Walküre, Siegfried, Götterdämmerung*) right through in successive performances."

That meant since somewhere in the twenty years of Nordica's 1890–1910 career—not for a minimum of thirty-three years or more—no one had achieved such a singing feat as on that occasion. I was both happy and exhilarated, because I knew that my quality had been as good as my quantity. I was reassured by another critic: "She sings her Brünnhildes and Isoldes like a veteran of Bayreuth." That was something that counted—since I had never been to the famous Wagner shrine in Germany and barely knew how to spell it.

13

Olé, South America!

MY traveling days commenced in 1940. That was the year I went to Canada, and became an honorary member of the Queen's Fusiliers. I have become an honorary this and an outstanding that many times since but I can honestly say rarely have I been as thrilled as I was at that moment. The band played, the big, braw soldiers marched past, I got tears in my eyes and sniffles in my nose—and the general stuck me in the chest with the pin of my honorary decoration.

Such an award would generally be a publicity stunt in this country but it really meant something to the Canadians—and to me—in those pre-World War II days. I had sung a number of concerts for the soldiers that winter and such a non-drilling membership was their solemn way of showing their appreciation.

I have always liked Canada very much. The only large city I have not sung in, as far as that whole country from stem to stern is concerned, is Montreal. Otherwise, I have blanketed it: from British Columbia to Nova Scotia. I find the people invigorating. They have all the stout English virtues—directness, honesty, and openheartedness. They also seem to have a freedom and lack of side that stem from their own country spaces and independence.

Whatever it was about that first Canadian trip (Bill hates the snow, I am fond of it) it hipped me on travel. I commenced to long for places and dishes and sights and ideas that had never yet hit my palate or my consciousness. The outside world had been in dim focus up to that moment. Now it popped into full view. I was eager to experience it.

Besides, I wanted to continue my experiments in music. I wanted to find out what I could sing that would make people happy to hear. I wanted to see how many would listen to me—and on what basis. Instead of the often-quoted idea of "lifting people up to my level," I really wanted to take them on their own terms and see what made us alike—a highly reprehensible idea for one considered a Met artist.

It may be more understandable if I explain my feelings in a roundabout way. One of my favorite rites in returning to St. Louis, as far as I was concerned, used to be to visit the famous St. Louis Zoo. There I knew George Vierheller very well. As the head man of the animals, he introduced me to most of the trainers and beasts besides. I was fascinated with everything he did—from picking scales off snakes to feeding lions. My favorite relaxation there was talking confidentially and humming opera arias to the chimpanzees. They used to howl right back at me or whirl around, exposing their red-and-blue bottoms. I let them hug me whenever they wanted—they were supposed to be little devils but they were more like little babies to me. One of them snatched Bill's dark glasses when he got too close, popped a cigar into his mouth, and crossed his legs. I screamed with laughter—he looked exactly like a caricature of a Hollywood producer.

My point is that my conduct in the zoo was considered highly irregular and on the verge of being illegal. It was something no one was supposed to do. "Just imagine if one of those chimpanzees hugged you too tight," George nervously told me one day. "My God, we haven't got enough insurance in the whole city to cover what they could do to your diaphragm!" I went on doing it because, to me, it seemed eminently proper and natural.

My attitude toward the Met was much the same as my attitude toward the monkey house. I felt that certain things were right, and when I had the power I put them into effect. One of my constant complaints, over which I had no control, was that I was an American first and an opera singer second. I thought that the operas of tradition should be rewritten in good Americanese and sung that way—something which I am glad to see that Rudolf Bing, the present head of the Met, has acceded to long after I departed from those precincts. My argument was simplicity itself: each European nation has its own operas done in its own language. The French hear them in French, the Italians in Italian, the Germans hear Puccini in German, the Russians hear *Otello* in Russian. Why not the Americans in American, since we are numerically the greatest patrons of such music in the world? It would seem to me wonderful if such a musical as *Annie, Get Your Gun,* would be done over in German gutturals or French sibilants. Wouldn't it be something if the Russians insisted on hearing *South Pacific* in Russian? How well the *tovarich* boys would understand "I'm gonna wash that man right out of my hair"!

Actually this country has far more musical consciousness than is generally appreciated. Most people are afraid to talk about what they like, intimidated by the amateur critics over the back fence or at dinner parties. Yet our whole daily experience is drenched in the great motifs of classical ideas. Simply because our popular composers have borrowed so prodigally from the masters, they have done a service to democracy. Advertising jingles, church hymns, motion-picture music, rock-and-roll tunes, the so-called modern jazz, the music to listen to and go mad by, the drone of the constant piped music in factories or restaurants—this country hears more and absorbs more of this kind of melody than any other. Very nearly all of it is classical, however distorted it may be. I have found that the musical instinct of the average person is capable of selecting and purifying the great themes. I know: I have heard the school children whistling their own versions as they pass my house.

Knowing this, my expectancy of what I would find outside this fortress of music where I was born was enhanced tremendously.

In line with my new-found hobby of exploring for myself Bill and I went to Cuba in the winter of 1941. We admired the new and the old in that island country—that has so many strange and wonderful customs—more than I can say. Especially, we liked the beat of the music, the food, and the sport of jai-alai. It was not so much those balls bounding back from the concrete walls with cannonball speed or the dexterity and strength of the players—it was the betting. We used to go to an ancient court in Havana and scream our bets to the bookies with the little red hats. We would use sign language—my voice was the only one that could be heard much of the time and Bill used me as his personal amplifier—or else hurl the bets around in split tennis balls. At times we had an interpreter to tell us the constantly changing odds. Every second counted in *that* game. We could afford it because the concerts in Cuba were paying us three and four times what I received at the Met.

Our most interesting travel experience in those years, however, was our trip below the equator to South America. I was supposed to open the winter opera season (in July) with Lauritz. In those times we were under war restrictions, of course, but we were a commodity like munitions. We were supposed to show that things were going along as usual in the United States—and to bring whatever prestige we could from our native country to our neighbors. The trip was customarily made in five days, flying by day in the ancient DC-3's. We set down at night in some prearranged spot. Flying in those dark hours over the jungle and the Andes was considered too dangerous.

Bill and I never applied for priority on these flights. We were classed as "propaganda ambassadors," but I assure you we never felt the weight of our so-called classification. The South American route by air at that time was being used for munitions and supplies to Africa. I cannot recall the scores of times that we were bumped for loads of guns and food and similar supplies. We made it a rule never to complain or demand no matter what happened. As a result, the trip to Buenos Aires took twenty-five days instead of five—and the opera season opening there had to be postponed three times!

Red tape was almost entirely responsible for the delays. We arrived at Panama, and spent nearly two weeks in the sweltering heat there with only winter clothes since we had expected to land in Argentina within less than a week. We sat in our suite, wearing as few clothes as possible, sweating all the time, staring at each other or the heat-shimmering views, drinking pineapple juice. We finally got out via the good offices of friends and landed in Lima, Peru. At that point we were "off-loaded" for five days— a necessary delay, we thought, but it was merely the usual official mixup. A call came through from Buenos Aires, the formalities were gone through, and we got out. We flew to Santiago, Chile, and took off again but flew only to the top of the gigantic Andes ranges— that look so much bigger when you are creeping up on them by plane—and had to fly back to Santiago again because of the fog and clouds.

When at last we managed to land at the airport at Buenos Aires, a literal cavalcade of people met me at the airplane. They cheered, they threw flowers, they escorted us to the car, and met us again at the hotel. In the hotel suite—exhausted as I was from the delays and the trip—I learned that the first performance of the opera was due on Tuesday. That day, the day I had arrived, was Friday. This meant rehearsals, stage business, practice of all kinds had to be done—and not only that but the preparation of costumes and all the other paraphernalia necessary to opera had to go forward.

My hotel became phantasmagoria in the midst of bedlam. It was the first time I have ever seen a real-life occurrence acting as if it were a movie-drama script. There I was, lolling in the bath surrounded by clouds of steam and perfume, trying to perk up my mental tonus, and outside the door, in the living room, there was a mad confusion. There were people swathed in various gorgeous fabrics; a shoemaker with samples and lasts, a wig-maker, a hairdresser with her instruments of torture, a dressmaker with tape measure and an agonized expression, a couple of interpreters, gobs of the Spanish-American press, and even an orthopedic expert. They shrieked at each other in a blend of languages that had to be heard to be believed. My maid kept slamming in and out of the bathroom seeking my approval on their moves. Meanwhile, someone kept playing my records outside.

It might have been a highly nerve-racking session for some— for me it was almost pleasant. It was nice to be soothed and looked after following those sweaty, do-nothing days in Panama City and Lima. I knew I was in my element again when, through the billowing vapor, one of the jostling crowd slipped through and tried to enter the bathroom. As my maid slammed the door in his face and as I vainly tried to shrink down in the hot water, he cried from the other side: "Madame will sing like an angel in this material!"

That was a wonderful time and a wonderful town. Lauritz and I gave fifteen performances there that summer (or winter) in six weeks. Our fees were paid. So were our round trips there and back. Besides this, the Argentinian opera fans showered gifts on us. Nothing expensive, but items so charming that they indicated that their hearts went with the present. Handwoven blankets and shawls, fans, and flowers—almost everything indicating loving care and a response to the feelings that were projected across the footlights.

More than that, our trip had shown us some grand new foods. I kept many of them in my memory for my own concoction, though I have had little time since to work on them. I think—and Bill agrees—that there is some of the finest food in the world in South

America and the most inexpensive. We ate until we were glutted, experimenting with each new dish. One was *cerviche,* a very hot raw fish dish with onion, literally cooked in the acids of lime juice. Another was *puchero,* a family dish that was not anything like a stew. Instead, it was rather a South American boiled dinner. This was not the only kind of nourishment we indulged in: for those that have not been there, Buenos Aires has German, French, Italian, East Indian, Scandinavian—all the restaurants of all the countries in the world to cater to its citizens. The Hotel Plaza, in which we stayed, has a kitchen on every floor. The room service functions for twenty-four hours a day—for any kind of food, even the most exquisite and carefully prepared. The town itself, even at three in the morning, keeps wide open in every sense.

The reviews of the South American performances—the Ring and some others of Wagner—were ecstatic. One critic said there had never been such a musical experience in the last forty years. Our trip became such a *cause célèbre* that it was reported as news.

The story in *Time* pointed out that, after the Metropolitan, the Teatro Colón was the most important opera house in the western hemisphere. It catered to the high society of Buenos Aires in a season that lasted from May to October, in a perfumed, highly formal atmosphere which was usually rose-plush upholstery matched with gilt opera boxes.

At first, they said, the invasion of Americans—taking the place of the usual imports from the European stands—was not cottoned to by the inhabitants. But they gradually niggled us to their bosoms. By the time the opera season was in full swing in that city, the box office—always as good an indication in South America as in North America of comparative popularity—had soared more than 30 per cent. The pungent comment on my own singing was wryly reported:

"Number 1 artistic hit of the Colón season has been St. Louis-born Helen Traubel's massive Isolde. 'She looks like a cow,' commented one *aficionado,* 'but her "Liebestod" leaves us paralyzed.' "

Considering everything, my fee was ample for a moo from Wagner.

It was during these early war years that I became conscious of what was, to me, an amazing fact: no one, not even Americans, really believed there was any culture in the United States. In the applause of the armed forces camps, as well as in the hand clapping and *bravas* of the audiences below the equator, I detected the same note. It was one of astonishment; a note of blank surprise. I had no idea I was such a *rara avis,* a home-grown American soprano. Lauritz and the others in our entourage they could accept as great singers without feeling taken aback simply because they hailed from Europe. In my case, it seemed to them nearly unbelievable.

No one had sold this country to the world on the cultural level. Instead, they had abandoned the minds and imaginations of foreign peoples all over the world to the gangster film and gossip column. To us the word "culture" has almost an effete connotation. Not so to the citizens of other countries. I recall one man in my audience, a highly educated and musically sensitive person, coming up to me after a concert and saying: "I cannot believe that all Americans are as cultured as you are." Me, a druggist's daughter from St. Louis, who never got through high school!

To most of the world outside our borders the United States is a gigantic focal point of curiosity. The interest in what we do, what we say, and what we perform, is immense. Even what we sing is of surpassing interest to the other nations. But to most of them, having only the distorted mirrors of the commonplace to look into, we may as well be still a land of cowboys and Indians. More than one immigrant, I know, still arrives at our shores with fear and trembling—and armed with guns to repel the hollering hordes.

It appeared to me that the best ambassadors we could have were not the officials in the cutaways at the receptions, but the ordinary touring people of America themselves. I have no idea if I impressed anyone with what I myself was, apart from my singing, but that was what I wanted to do in South America. It was what I wanted to do to the troop audiences in my own country; we have become so deeply compartmentalized in our lives that we ourselves do not know how or why the next-door neighbor lives. In many cases we do not even really know our own husband or wife or children. Ten years later I was to go on two world tours. I was to find the same conditions prevailing in some of the brightest capitals of Europe and Asia as well as those of the relatively unknown countries.

The second thought I could not escape was that, at least in the art of music, some malign influence was driving the talent of America to seek refuge elsewhere to display their art. In South America—and later, I was to find, in Europe—there were scores of American singers on the stage, accepted as local artists. There were hundreds more working and waiting for a chance in the same country. Government subsidies, popular enthusiasm matched with publicity and prestige, plus cheap admissions to open the doors to a majority of the people, kept opera modern and on its toes—rather than making it a display of snobbery for the self-chosen elite. The great theaters of the past had long ago vanished from the United States—such as the New York Hippodrome, the Century Theatre, and the Manhattan Opera House, names that are not now known to the younger generation. The old New Orleans opera house burned down years ago and no one bothered to replace it. The Boston opera center, supposedly in the midst of one of the greatest concentrations of pure culture in the world, was neglected so long that it was eventually broken up for firewood.

If my feelings about this still-uncorrected situation seem intense, it is for a reason. My thinking finally became so involved in it that it was a direct cause of my leaving the Metropolitan in 1953. I imagine that my approach to music is purely utilitarian: the best and most music to the most people. But I cannot worry too much about the *how* of it. My job is to produce it.

Bill likes to tell a story about me—an incident that happened at the Teatro Colón in Buenos Aires on our South American trip —to indicate just how many kilometers I seem to be removed from the ordinary mechanism of what makes a singing tour tick. I am impressed only with the problems presented by the music and the most perfect performance I can give. Nothing else matters. In this case, Bill visited me at my dressing room. I complained to him about a shadow.

"There's a little man that keeps following me around," I said. "He's a nice enough fellow, very good-looking and polite, but I wish you'd get rid of him."

"What does he say?" Bill inquired.

"I don't know," I said. "I've never stopped to let him say a word. But he always wants to."

"What does he do?"

"He just stands outside the stage door and stares at me." I pointed. "There he is again!" I cried, and ran inside.

When I came out after the performance, I saw that Bill was talking animatedly to the same man. I was amazed; instead of brushing him off, he had taken him to his bosom. So I ignored both of them, sailing past on my way to the car.

When Bill got back to our hotel, he was choking with laughter. "What's so funny to you?" I demanded.

"You don't know it, dear," he informed me, "but you not only snubbed your husband but also the top man in the South American opera world—the impresario of the Teatro Colón who planned this trip, got you here, and financed the season!"

14

The Golden Chords

THE episode of somebody else's ground glass in my cold cream never hit the newspaper. It caused as much furore around the Metropolitan Opera in those days as anything that happened in the annals of the opera. It was a premonition of some stormy days to come.

I had come into the Met under the bright cloud of Flagstad. I had immediately been compared to her in the heaviest roles—reversing the usual European development that is like a ballplayer warming up, doing the lighter vocal calisthenics in other operas first and finally graduating to the heaviest of the heavy in Wagner. I had almost literally come out of the sticks in Missouri and been shoved to the top of the flagpole. All this had not contributed to my popularity with others who had been working for years to do the roles of Flagstad. At the very moment of what seemed to be success, they were seeing a newcomer snatch away from them what they treasured.

I was unconscious of the offstage feuds at the time. The cross-currents of politics and jealousy that run like unseen rip tides through any such profession were unknown to me. I had had some samples of the intensity of operatic rivalries: in Minneapolis, in

1938, when I had sung with Lauritz, he had cautioned me against holding a note too long. "Give each note its proper value," he said slyly—and then proceeded to hold his own notes so long that you could have pinned a week's wash on them. "If that's the way it's to be, it's every man for himself," I said at the time, and matched him note for note.

It must be remembered that the Metropolitan dressing rooms were something inherited direct from the Middle Ages. I was put in what was called the "plush" dressing room. It was one used alternately or together by about five of the leading stars. It was a battered, thin-walled place with a mirror on the hall opposite so everyone could look in; it had a small anteroom with a toilet in it that thundered like Boanerges when you pulled the chain; it had an intricate curtain and inner door arrangement that reminded me of trying to get out of a safety-deposit vault every time I left it. To make it worse, its windows were little squares with thick bars opening onto the street.

The joint gave me claustrophobia in one respect and, in the other, no privacy at all. If I had friends, it was hard to get more than a very few inside; if I wanted air (and I love all the ventilation possible) I had to chin myself up and peek out at Seventh Avenue. My maid, Marie, a very solid, able type of woman who was with me for fourteen years, was my shield and defense in such matters. She was always with me, even on my eight or ten weeks on the road. It was she who watched over me and assisted with such things as make-up—who was blameless as far as the incident was concerned—but who took it to heart even more than I did.

I used very little make-up on stage—in contrast to most of the make-up customarily used by opera people of those days who loved to daub on the rouge, eye shadow, mascara, and powder. It simply did not suit me. I felt overloaded with so much gook on my face. One of my stand-bys was a tin of commercial cold cream that I could pry open with a coin and dive into with both hands. As most people know, the first motion after you dig into cold cream is to dab it on your eyelids, working it into the skin. It was this motion that would have ruined my sight—if I had not been stopped by some sort of providential instinct.

On that fateful occasion—one night in early 1941—I pried off the can top, got my fingers loaded with cold cream, and went for my eyelids. I stopped a half-inch away; I worked my thumb and finger together a little and suddenly emitted a little gasp. Marie rushed to me. We examined my hands. We found that the cold cream was literally crammed with minute bits of carefully crushed glass!

Boghetti, who was with me at the time, gave a yelp. The news raced upstairs to the head office. Johnson and the rest tumbled down.

"My God, my God!" Johnson kept repeating. "Who would do a thing like this?"

No one knew. No one knows to this day, though some have a fairly shrewd idea. It was instantly agreed that the news should be smothered and never appear in the papers. A private detective was sent for to prowl the premises and try to solve the case—which he never did. I was told either to make sure someone was in the dressing room or lock it at all times. For two years after that I not only carried my own dressing and make-up kit, I also toted my own sealed water jug for drinking purposes.

"If they'll go so far as to try to disfigure you, Helen," said Johnson earnestly, "they might try to poison you, too."

I will not say that this kind of tactic frightened me; after the first shock, it made me furious. Following that episode, nothing could have kept me off the Met stage. If there was someone in the company—and only someone in that sacrosanct group could have had the opportunity—who hated me so much, I was going to accept the challenge. Nothing of the sort has ever recurred in the whole of my career, but to me it was a revelation like a flash of lightning on a pitch-black night. It seemed there were people to whom singing at the Met meant so much that they would stop at nothing to achieve their goal. My preparation and aim had not been for the Met. It had merely been to sing. Yet I was much more secure than they. Envy and jealousy could not shake the foundation of training I had laid so long and well with Lulu and my other teachers, the countless hours of rehearsal and planning.

One of the remarkable things about the singing business is that it is not very tolerant of child prodigies. Child musicians, tap dancers, actors, even child maestros, have come along in the world, but never to my knowledge has there ever been a child singer who has enjoyed a career. I am not unmindful of the children's choirs and soloists, but I think these groups can be relegated to another category. The reason for this is quite clear. There is an outstanding amount of purely physical equipment needed for any person to be a singer. In order to sing, you must remember that condition and pace, as in an athletic contest, are all-important. Intelligence for interpretation is necessary but so is a technical foundation that is more habit than instinct. Sound must be produced on a standard level of quality, even when you are feeling sick to death.

Marion Talley, the singer who had the fastest rise to the top— and unhappily the fastest coast to oblivion—was invited to the Met at nineteen; I never even thought of it until I was twenty-three— and at that time I turned it down. The Met manager, Giulio Gatti-Casazza, the greatest judge of singers in the world at that time, telegraphed me an offer after my New York concerts in 1926, and I turned it down. I was not ready to do justice to myself or to the music I would have had to sing. Miss Talley, appearing in the same year I turned it down, retired permanently from the Met in 1930, because she did not have the basic utensils to keep cooking with. I have been singing at the top of my bent for the last three decades, simply because I did—and I was trained the hard way. Yet I could not allow myself to do Wagner at the Met until I was nearly twice as old as Miss Talley.

My own debut had been welcomed with even kinder words than

those extended to Nordica. Nordica's first appearance, in a performance of *Les Huguenots* (very rarely seen today) on December 18, 1891, had been countered by the critic in this manner: "The quality of Madame Nordica's art as a vocalist, as well as her interpretation of the part of Valentina, is familiar; her performance last evening was an extremely creditable one under the circumstances. She was in excellent voice and acted with great spirit; the audience was prone to forgive one or two disasters of a lesser sort."

The strength of my personal feelings about music is perhaps involved with the love I had for my father and his early death. After he was gone, something had to fill the void: a renewed emphasis on singing was the natural replacement. Lulu, the celebrated teacher of St. Louis who taught all the society girls, was the natural selection. It was natural for me to quit, my third year at McKinley High School, and never to go to college. It was natural, though I got only about forty-five minutes a day with Lulu, for me to haunt her from nine to five, sneaking in between other pupils (who always snooted me and I snooted back), taking up the cancellation slack and kibitzing.

So it was equally natural that I would absorb the idea that I could get all I needed in the United States in the way of musical training without going overseas. It was in 1938 that I won my point. Geraldine Farrar, who had been one of the most famous singers in the world, heard me. She came to me one night at Sullivan's house in Connecticut and in her rich, kindly voice said: "My dear, you must go to Europe!"

"I really don't want to," I said.

"I will sponsor you," she said. "You *must* sing in opera. No one can have such a career unless they do study abroad," she told me.

"Thank you so much," I told her, "but I really don't want to go."

After my first year at the Met, I got a letter from her. It said: "You were right and I was wrong. You didn't need Europe."

Ill feelings in an artistic medium are inevitable. They are generated by conscious or unconscious acts. Those people who are independent of authority and in favor of art rather than social gimmicks are quietly cut down. Anyone can find a sample of some of these opinions, tacitly expressed, in the *Metropolitan Opera Annals,* the official book and permanent record of the Met history.

It is odd that though I was the leading soprano at the Met for a dozen years the summaries given to my work are comparatively so inadequate. As one friend remarked to me, "Your friends, Helen, are all in the audience; the others have their friends in the executive branch." These are errors for the record: but in view of the fact that I was also one of the leading rebels against the stuffy Met traditions and the ludicrous musical attitudes, it is understandable.

Here, in justice to whatever part I have played in musical achievement, I think I must quote a review of the February 12, 1942, presentation of *Die Götterdämmerung*. It was the first time I had done this particular Brünnhilde part, though I had been singing the Immolation scene alone for three years. According to the critic of the *Herald Tribune:*

"A superb performance of *Götterdämmerung* brought the annual presentation of Wagner's Ring cycle in unshortened form to a close at the Metropolitan Opera House yesterday afternoon. This was one of those rare occasions when the principal singers, conductor, and orchestra were in their best form, so that aside from minor blemishes, the unfolding of the Bayreuth master's colossal music drama, which for me is his greatest work and both as music and tragedy unequaled in the annals of musical art, was one to give the highest satisfaction.

"The focal point of interest was in Helen Traubel, who assumed the role of this Brünnhilde for the first time on any stage. Her delineation proved a far more convincing one than that of the *Walküre* Brünnhilde vouchsafed here earlier this season and was in many aspects quite remarkable. The soprano's work grew cumulatively in assuredness and tonal beauty. There was much that was fine even in the prologue, but here the singer had not yet attained a complete control of her unusual resources and the final high 'C' was only tentatively projected.

"Much of the scene with Waltraute was admirably sung, but it was with the second act that Madame Traubel became complete mistress of her voice, and from then on she accomplished some truly stirring things. Her delivery of the music of the Oath on the Spear was both intense and gleaming, and her portion of the Conspiracy Trio was impressively conveyed. One has heard some of the high-lying phrases invested with greater tonal expansiveness and a more glowing texture, but there is no other soprano this side of the ocean today who could equal Madame Traubel's achievements. The final Immolation scene was a magnificent piece of work. I have heard Madame Traubel sing it several times in concert and always found it her finest contribution; but she has never reached the interpretative heights therein attained on this occasion. It was not only astounding from the tonal facet, but profoundly moving as well.

"Until yesterday Madame Traubel had given little indication of talent as an actress. But with this Brünnhilde there were definite signs of awakening along histrionic lines. Her portrayal already had many genuinely perceptive touches. Her gestures and facial play revealed a distinct advance over her previous attempts in this direction, and with further experience and with a costume which resembles less a gray nightgown covered with a Prussian-blue kimono her characterization should develop into one which will bear comparison with the most distinguished from every point of view.

"There were several new departures in the stage direction for which, although his name was not mentioned in the program, Lothar Wallerstein was said to be responsible. Instead of shrinking back from Siegfried disguised by the tarnhelm in the second scene of the first act, and fleeing to the corner of the stage,

Madame Traubel climbed up the Valkyries' Rock to meet him. Instead of going off the right side of the stage to make her rush for the spear in the second act, Madame Traubel retired to the dwelling of the Gibichungs, on the opposite side of the stage, and in the final scene the body of Siegfried, formerly placed right stage, was placed in the center so that Brünnhilde delivered the Immolation scene quite appositely over the corpse of the slain hero instead of advancing to the prompter's box as heretofore and singing it like an old-fashioned Italian opera aria. There were other changes, too, but they were of less importance."

In the above I got my usual whacks in the costume department. It must be added that I did not quite get full credit for the stage maneuvering. I worked out most of the actions with Wallerstein. These came about as a result of my continual moans that the staging of the whole scene previously had seemed to me totally naïve and idiotic. The only changes made were those in the performance of my own role. They could not have been made without my agreement—and, actually, my suggestions in the first place. I refused to play Brünnhilde as an Italian diva any longer —nor did I think I should be frightened of Siegfried. Instead, I determined to be glad to meet Lauritz. On this occasion he almost made me blow my helmet when I bent over his recumbent form in the middle of the stage. As I started my agonized solo, he muttered: "For God's sake, Helena, hurry it up! I'm hungry and I need a beer!"

In the opera season of 1942-43 I became the singing workhorse of the Met. That season I sang my lungs out in nine top performances of Wagner, three of them the superlatively demanding *Die Götterdämmerung*. This was only the beginning. In the 1943-44 season I was called on to sing in fourteen performances—all of them Wagnerian and all needing every ounce of musicianship. But it was only in the season of 1944-45 that the peak demand came: that year I sang in fourteen performances, too, but three included the Immolation scene, the most racking of any aria to the soprano voice.

As a matter for the record, the early years of my career are in something of a dispute. The official Met rolls carry my debut as of May 12, 1937, when I sang the role of Mary Rutledge as a favor to Walter Damrosch in his *Man Without a Country*. The press contended it was with my singing of Sieglinde in the 1939–40 season on December 28, 1939—but such arguments settle nothing but personal convictions.

I had sung Damrosch's work three times in May 1937—on the twelfth, seventeenth, and twenty-second. Someone else had done it on the twenty-eighth. The New York *Times* review had said of me: "Miss Helen Traubel, a newcomer from St. Louis, a woman of noble and gracious beauty, brings to the role of Mary Rutledge a voice of power and fine quality, and her embodiment of the heroine was moving through its restraint and sincerity." I sang the role for the last time in my life the next winter, February 17, 1938.

Naturally, I did not appear anywhere on the official rosters during the Met season of 1938–39. But in the 1939–40 season, after the December debut, I sang Sieglinde on January 29, then Elisabeth in *Tannhäuser* on February 15, and Sieglinde again on March 2. The next season (1940–41) I opened the season on December 4 singing Sieglinde with Flagstad's Brünnhilde. I repeated it on the sixteenth—and on January second Flagstad sang Sieglinde while Marjorie Lawrence sang Brünnhilde. At that time Flagstad—perhaps exhausted by the enormous season she had sung during 1938–39, including a special Wagner series at the New York World's Fair—was alternating roles with such artists as Rose Bampton, Lotte Lehmann, Astrid Varnay, and Miss Lawrence. These took on many of the lighter assignments in Wagner, such as the feminine leads in *Parsifal, Tannhäuser,* and *Lohengrin*.

In the 1941–42 season I appeared only five times—four of them as Brünnhilde, twice essaying the strenuous *Götterdämmerung* role. In 1942–43 my performances started piling up. I was nearing my top in repertoire and I sang ten times—six of them Brünnhildes, three Isoldes, and one Elisabeth. It should be remarked here that I have never appeared in the prelude opera, *Das Rheingold*. It has really no major role for a woman.

After my chores in the succeeding couple of seasons I had a 1945–46 breather—I did only eleven roles. But the Met front office stepped up my schedule for 1946–47—in that year I did fourteen once more. I appeared in seven Brünnhildes, four Isoldes, and three Elsas. I was deep in my Wagnerian rut and was beginning to feel the strain. Much as I enjoyed singing opera —particularly the Ring—I could not help the uneasy sensation of becoming a one-composer singer. I commenced to feel the urge to get out and seek new musical horizons that was to culminate in my leaving the Met six years later.

15

Wagner, I Love You!

I CONSIDER myself a Wagnerian soprano. Most of my musical
life has been concerned with the works of this German genius.
Whatever claim to being known I have is largely bound up with
his greatest achievement, the immortal Ring series of four
operas. Of these, I have always believed—and generations of
opera lovers confirm this—that the finest single piece of composition in the entire Wagner repertoire is the climactic Immolation of Brünnhilde in *Die Götterdämmerung*.

It is one of the most difficult scenes in world music for a soprano, if not indeed the most rigorous for any voice. It lasts sixteen minutes by the clock. It is done from pianissimo to fortissimo and it covers more than two octaves in range. Its notes
must be the finest shadings within the longest, most swelling
chords of sonority. With all this, it must be sung with supreme
dramatic intensity.

Yet the Immolation scene is one of my favorite solos. It is one
that I have worked over and over since 1939. I have sung it, in
practice and in public, hundreds of times in its entirety. I have
never sung it quite to my tonal satisfaction but I have done it
well. One of my best-known renditions of it came when I made

an original recording with one of the genii of the baton, Arturo Toscanini. Toscanini had ended his long reign—from 1908 on—as conductor of the Metropolitan and New York Philharmonic-Symphony three years before I arrived under contract. He was already launched on his magnificent eighteen-year swan song, directing the National Broadcasting Company Symphony in its interpretations of the world's masterpieces. It must be remembered that Toscanini was one of the all-time absolutes in classic music. His will was paramount; his interpretations—even for singers (whom he normally disliked intensely) molding their phrases and directing their emotions—were recognized as the final word in any performance. It was said that he knew the intention of the composer better than the composer himself in his intuitional responses to the score—drawing, as he did, upon his vast memory and passion for perfection which was part of his personality.

Yet I could never feel the veneration that most of my fellow singers felt for Toscanini. Of his consummate artistry there was little doubt. But I had never had a god before. I refused to start with the little maestro—and I believe he liked me better for it. On one occasion he wanted me to perform a phrase in a certain way. I objected, saying I felt it was better suited to me if it were done differently. He flew into a rage; I sat quietly until he was done. Then I said I was perfectly willing to do it any way he wanted. The spry, white-haired conductor instantly calmed.

"We will try it my way and try it your way," he said. Forthwith, we ran over it together. After he had heard it "my way," Toscanini sat for a long moment staring into space. His mouth crinkled up and he turned and patted me on the cheek.

"Your way is better," he said. "We will do it your way, eh?"

I worked three times with Toscanini—"worked" in the sense of singing. He was a great taskmaster—the *bête noire* of some—but to me he was a perfectionist who matched my own ideals. The first time we had a session of our own was a rehearsal at NBC. I arrived early. The maestro was there first, pacing up and down, his hands under his coattails. He saw me and greeted me with the courtesy and respect that he always said he reserved for genius. A dapper little ladies' man, with waxed mustache, boutonnière, and tiny feet, he refused to wear glasses despite his failing sight. He depended upon his gigantic memory and his unfailing intuition to supply what his nearsightedness took from him.

We went directly to the piano. He commenced to play a scene from *Die Walküre*. I was amazed at his touch; I am sure that Toscanini could have been a great pianist if he had wished. I sang it through with him, he folded the music and put it aside. "Do you have any suggestions?" I asked.

"No, no!" he exclaimed. *"Magnifico!* Let us go on!"

We sang a scene from *Die Götterdämmerung*. Again I asked and received the same answer. "Maestro," I told him carefully, "you're not helping me!" He frowned. "When I feel something wrong, I will tell you," he retorted.

We started the Immolation scene and I went through it like a buck through hot ashes. Toscanini turned to me. "Now I have something to tell you," he said. "Will you allow me?"

"Of course," I said. I must explain that in one spot here Brünnhilde sings: "Everything, I know!" which in Wagner's tortured German means "I know everything!" It reads "Everything, everything, everything I know!" Toscanini wanted me to hit that first *alles* as hard as I could; I wanted to build up to the third one and end on a sob, as if, knowing everything, Brünnhilde still had nowhere to go. Toscanini frowned again. He got up and paced the studio. He came back and asked me to sing the phrase again. He meditated. Then a broad smile came over his face. He swung to me: *"Cara,"* he said softly, "you are right and the old man, he is wrong!"

At the end of our first concert a few days later he took me aside and held my hands, looking up at me and saying in an ecstatic whisper: "You are the greatest voice in the world!" He then reached up with one hand, as he often did, and gently caressed my throat.

The second time we worked together—each time entailing a half-dozen or more rehearsals—was the recording of the famous Immolation scene. Again he repeated his opinion and touched my throat. I think he worshiped sound—despite his contempt for most singers—as much as I did. I have no idea what specific talent he had that no other conductor ever showed me besides this total immersion in his art. Long before hi-fi, Toscanini had his home filled with loud-speakers, forever blaring out music in which he swam from room to room. Toscanini had a quality that somehow brought out the best in those who worked with him. Call it an inspiration that was as contagious as measles, an idealism that infected those around him joyously and truly. This is not to say that Toscanini in his own ego and his other life away from music was not an entirely different man. All I know is the pure side he showed me when we worked together.

I recall he directed Lauritz and me in one selection where Lauritz liked to indulge himself by holding a note for something like twenty bars. It was supposed to be held for less than half that time. Not for Toscanini: he was on Wagner's side. As Lauritz started to hold his note, Toscanini in front of him brought his little baton swishing across, ending it. It was a throat-cutting gesture. Lauritz, who was prepared to hold the note all night, shut it off and went purple.

Toscanini himself was often deceived by those around him who feared both the wrath and the fame of the conductor. Bill was once standing in the rear of the auditorium listening to a rehearsal of my singing the "Liebestod" from *Tristan und Isolde*. He was next to another conductor who turned to him and muttered: "The old man is overpowering Helen!" At that moment Toscanini turned on the podium and called back: "William, the balance, how is it?"

"Perfect!" shouted the conductor next to Bill. "Just perfect!"

It was Toscanini who paid me the highest compliment of my recording career. After I had completed the Immolation scene and he had heard it, he turned to me and said solemnly: *"Cara, that is the finest recording ever made in the history of music!"*

I had often heard Toscanini described as a monster that would make his singers rehearse to the vocal death—making them go over the score again and again, five or six times, with full voice. Since I never feared this, it was never demanded of me by Toscanini, who also apparently felt I needed less rehearsal than some of the others. I recall one occasion when I visited him to try out an aria that he sat down and heard me sing with the piano. As I finished, he leaped up with his customary exuberance, crying: *"Magnifico!* I will meet you at Carnegie Hall!"

"No more rehearsal?" I asked him, surprised. Toscanini's eyes twinkled. He came close to me, looking up at me.

"For you, no," he said slyly, "but for me, if you want, yes?"

He and I had a genuine rapport. He hated pretense, society, and sham—all the many parasites that still hang onto the world of music. As I did, he loathed the clichés of the often-repeated classics. Nor was he half so irascible as he may have seemed to others—nor was he as godlike and free from faults. I had often been told that Toscanini was impeccable in his tempi. As a matter of fact, he was far from it. His renditions were never of the same length; sometimes he played them slowly, sometimes fast. This was especially evident in recording, where it often took ten to a dozen replayings of a score to get it to mesh with the unvarying mechanical requirements. Once, when this had happened so often as to make it absurd, I asked the technicians to tell him about it. They recoiled in horror. "We'd be fired on the spot," said one feelingly. I went down to the podium and told Toscanini that he would have to speed the tempo of the music if it was to fit the record. He nodded gratefully. "Then we'll put it up," he said mildly, and proceeded to make it with one more take.

I have been informed in no uncertain terms—and have replied in the same fashion—that I was the only person ever begged by Toscanini to make a record with him who refused to do so. It was after I had recorded the whole of *Die Götterdämmerung* with him and Toscanini requested me to do one aria I had performed before very satisfactorily. I refused. The maestro demanded: "It is I, Toscanini, who ask you to do this!" I said: "No." I pointed out as clearly as I could that I had done this selection, *"Dich Teure Halle,"* once for a friend and that it had no flaws I could detect. I could see no reason for doing it over—especially as it was just for filling out the sixth side of the set of *Die Götterdämmerung.* My God! It has just occurred to me: was this the reason the whole recording was eventually botched? Ah, well, those tempestuous days are over.

I believe it was Charles O'Connell, then for a dozen years head of the Red Seal records for RCA and three years with Columbia Master Works, who was originally responsible for my meeting and working with Toscanini. He was one of my earliest and most enthusiastic boosters. He had happened to tune in to my first Ford radio broadcast in 1939 that Fritz Reiner had conducted and called immediately afterward to sign me up. I told him then —and I meant it—that making Red Seal records, those black-disc treasuries of wonderful music which had entranced me when I was young, was more of an ambition for me than was singing for the Met.

In 1940 I was singing for Victor—at a rate of 10 per cent of the royalties on the records and no guarantee. This was the usual contract given a first signer. In a couple of years I got a sizable guarantee deductible from that same 10 per cent royalty. I should add that in 1948 Goddard Leiberson, vice-president of Columbia Records, estimated that my records sold "more than those of any other classical singer in the world." These sales at that time, together with opera, radio, and concerts, usually were put at a gross figure of between two hundred and fifty thousand dollars and three hundred thousand dollars a year. Today, with television adding another dimension to the earning power of any artist, this income has been estimated even higher. It has been guessed by the statisticians of music that my voice will gross a total of five million dollars before it creates its last chord.

But in those days I was still working on my first million—of which I was always lucky to get even 10 per cent. O'Connell knew that his bosses at RCA were eager to get Flagstad and had little use for a country-grown girl from Missouri. He knew that Toscanini, up to that time, had never recorded with a woman soloist because he did not like the caliber of their voices. For example, it was well known that he disliked Flagstad's voice. O'Connell took him one of my records. He played it for him. "This is the voice you've been looking for," he kept repeating. "This is the voice you want!"

Toscanini, nodding to the sound, agreed: "This one, she is great! We shall record her!"

A concert with Toscanini was arranged in Carnegie Hall in 1942. I had no idea of the tooth gnashing it created at the time. O'Connell, in his memoirs published in 1947, where he gave the back of his hand to a great many other singers, puts it this way: "I failed with Traubel; failed to overcome the ignorance, the stupidity, the dull lack of imagination, the indifference and inertia, the wicked malice, envy, and jealousy.... There is a curious similarity between her recording career and her concert career while it was managed by another RCA agency, the NBC Artists Bureau.... During her relationship with this bureau, I understand, Helen was guaranteed ten thousand dollars annually; and having grown a bit cynical after so many years in the music racket, I have often wondered if this was what in other and equally murderous rackets was called 'hush money.' Helen did not get, through the NBC Artists Bureau, anywhere near enough engagements to justify such a payment, though she did sing on a few sustaining broadcasts. The bureau had at the same time a great singer named Flagstad under its management. Logic, if not ethics, would have suggested the suppression of competition. Flagstad was having an unprecedented success; why introduce a competitive factor? At any rate, the name of Traubel, as a candidate for Red Seal records, was never presented to me."

I have no means of knowing whether the flaming defense by O'Connell was needed. Then and now, it is difficult to believe that musical talent, whatever its source, would be deliberately handicapped by the people supposed to develop it.

Fortunately, the whole silly feud evaporated back into the thin air out of which it had been concocted. Fate stepped in. In June 1941 Flagstad, who had starred at the Met for six years and had been threatening to return to Norway for two of those, finally left for her own country—not to return until 1951 when the issue of who was queen was academic. Worse, that same summer fate struck down with infantile paralysis a lovely newcomer who might have risen to the heights, the Australian soprano Marjorie Lawrence. I was to be left alone on my teetery pedestal, not particularly enjoying my eminence. The next five years were to prove that music not only had its charms but also it emoluments.

By 1946 it was to be estimated that I accepted about seventy engagements a season for an average annual income of one hundred and fifty thousand dollars, including a minimum of ten to fifteen Metropolitan appearances at a thousand dollars per opera. I might do five to ten more opera assignments in San Francisco and Mexico for about twenty-five hundred dollars apiece, forty concerts with fees varying from two thousand to thirty-five hundred, depending on the size of the house, and radio guest shots at thirty-five hundred each—the total winding up at about seventy a year.

But at that time, five years before, I was singing: that was enough for me. I went about my business of preparing for my appearance with the maestro. I knew he was a very famous man but I did not think that his followers worshiped him on the other side of idolatry.

The concert—the Immolation scene—went off very well. O'Connell had cannily used the concert itself as a rehearsal for the recording. The next morning we went into the recording session and worked out the half-dozen sides (at 78 rpm in those days) in a minimum of time and money. It was this recording, I was told, that made history. It is probably the most famous single recording of Wagner—and of the Immolation—ever to exist in music. One prominent critic, who can never be accused of being one of my partisans, Irving Kolodin, is on record as saying awefully that it "is without parallel in the recorded literature of Wagner"—strong words of praise from one who used to like to kick me right in my pizzicato.

O'Connell said that the twenty-odd minutes of the scene were "the closest to perfection we shall ever know"—but they did not appear in a genuine, unadulterated form. Toscanini, though he unofficially loved them and had not criticized a single note of my performance, refused to release them officially. We shared the right of approval. He wanted the orchestra to be "fortified" artificially by complicated re-recording devices. This was done. When the music finally did appear, it had gained a good deal of background noise as well as losing brilliance and clarity. But the maestro had exercised his privilege and had his way.

Thus far my recordings cover a wide range. I estimated that I have made more than three hundred records—perhaps nine tenths long-hair—opera and lieder—and the rest popular. They run the whole gamut from classical to two pop records with Jimmy Durante, "A Real Piano Player" and "The Song's Got to Come from the Heart." On the other side there are recordings with the Victor Symphony Orchestra in the Philadelphia Academy of Music and the New York Philharmonic at Carnegie Hall and the NBC Symphony; such selections as *"Im Treibhaus,"*

"Schmerzen," and *"Träume"* with the electric backing of Stokowski and the Philadelphia Orchestra.

Speaking of conductors, I had more trouble with Leopold Stokowski than I had with Toscanini. I have always considered Stokowski one of the great colorists of music. His ability to use music as a painter uses a palette was unsurpassed. He was capable of putting sensuality into the most forbidding passages of any composer even though they might be as bleak as Bartók. I sang with him for years, starting in 1942. More than once I refused to continue because he wanted me to do literally impossible things with my voice. Knowing I had unusual breath and tone control, he tried to use this in our renditions of Bach and Handel to produce unheard-of continuity of sound. After turning blue in the face on several occasions, I said loudly: "The hell with it, Stoky!" His attitude toward spending money also offended me. He would rehearse and rehearse for minute perfections unlike Toscanini's search for divine rightness. My blood would commence to boil.

"You're spending so much money, Stoky," I would expostulate. And he, who could speak perfect English one moment and broken Polish the next, replied: "Eet ees our beezness only to make bootiful music!"

I remember when I sang the "St. Louis Blues" in a hotel night club in St. Louis in 1954. I finished and heard a roar of *bravas* in the audience. I saw Stoky at the table in the spotlight applauding, his long white hair waving, his graceful hands flickering like summer lightning.

Eugene Ormandy, the little "jeep" of classical music, who deservedly rose from conducting in a movie theater to the head of possibly the most distinguished musical organization in this country, was another trial of mine. He used to come to our house, plop down, and say in a loud voice: "Helen, I've seen you sing with Jimmy Durante on the television and it is absolutely disgusting!"

"I had fun when I was singing with your group," I would say mildly, "and I had fun when I was singing on TV. So, quiet, please!"

Ormandy was wrong to think that merely entertaining was something alien to me. My grandfather Stuhr had founded, owned, and directed the Apollo Theatre in St. Louis, the first German dramatic theater of its kind west of the Mississippi. Here it was that classic German plays were presented—in their own language—for the delectation of the city's big German population. I had grown and thrived on my ambition to do something of the same sort.

Ormandy, in my opinion, was for years much more of a conductor than he was an ordinary human being. He had to work terribly hard to achieve what he did. Everyone kept giving the credit to his predecessor at the Philadelphia Symphony. As the years went on and the organization changed personnel entirely and still maintained its superb quality, Ormandy had to be credited with both taste and genius. A man who is either profoundly modest or immensely vain, depending on his mood, Ormandy is still an enchanting man. He is at his best when he is working his magical art of dovetailing the human voice into the intricacies of an orchestral score.

I began to become acquainted with all these conductors in the early years of my singing. A few of them became close friends. Some, who have had various eccentricities, deserted our fireside for valid reasons. One, who suddenly became enamored of my secretary and tried to make love to her in our hall closet, is no longer with us. Another, who made a habit of having secret assignations with a pretty member of his orchestra, found out too late that her husband was one of the local musical bigwigs, and only an impassioned denial that there had been anything between them except musical solos got him a reprieve to go on and become one of the deans of American music.

With all of them, without exception, I sang Wagner again and again.

Not a few people have asked me why I chose to be a singer of Wagner. There are scores of other great composers, of course; the Wagner operas form only a small percentage of those written. Wagner's music is sometimes overwhelming: it constitutes an aesthetic experience of the first rank to hear it—or to sing it. The sustaining of such a catharsis is by itself an effort.

The answer is that the music chose me; I did not choose it. I loved the music and I was physically capable of presenting it. The quality and power of my voice had much to do with it. Most of all, perhaps, I was interested in the durability of a career. I wanted to sing music that was eternal. The great danger in musical cycles is that one kind of rendition becomes popular and fades while another comes to the fore. I discovered that Richard Wagner was timeless.

Music has two lives in the classical sense: opera and concert. All else—records, popular tunes, musical vogues—derives from these. Only Puccini, Verdi, and Mozart rival Wagner in the perennial popularity of their works. My voice, though capable in such composers' themes, is not always given its full latitude. It has to explode rather than shimmer. Wagner's operas may not always be popular, but his music is forever fresh in the concert hall. His music opens up more emotions, is more dramatic, and its sheer, colorful narrative is unexcelled by any other composer. It reaches up to the sky and down into hell for its themes: it is as constant and immediate as human nature.

By attaching whatever talents I possess to Wagner, I was insuring myself a future. Once I had scaled the heights of this tremendous music I could safely descend and make my way among the peaks of less taxing composers—and enjoy myself with the tunes of the day and the rhythms of my time. I enjoy life as much as I do music—and that is saying a great deal. I want to achieve what I believe to be the ultimate in each. One goal has been achieved; now I seek for the other.

Each of Wagner's compositions is both a spring and a river. Each grows out of the other and overflows into the ear. Wagner was aware, I think, of the supreme drama inherent in music itself which none before him had fully realized. It did not appear in the ridiculous libretto nor in the tortured phrasing of the words, but in the juxtaposition of scenes and the conflict inherent in each one of them. Wagner had only disdain for stage conventions, but his music made everything seem plausible. Where else in all literature do you have a set of stage directions such as ends the opera *Die Götterdämmerung?*

As Brünnhilde leaps into the burning pyre on the stage, "the flames immediately blaze up so that they fill the whole space in front of the building itself. The terrified men and women press as far to the front as possible. When the whole stage appears to be filled with fire, the glow gradually fades, so that there is soon nothing left but a cloud of smoke that drifts toward the back and hangs there as a dark bank of cloud.

"At the same time the Rhine overflows and the flood rolls up over the fire. The three Rhine maidens swim forward on the waves and now appear over the spot where the fire was. Hagen, who since the incident of the Ring has been watching Brünnhilde's behavior with growing anxiety, is much alarmed by the sight of the Rhine maidens. He throws away his spear, shield, and helmet and dashes into the flood as if mad, crying out, 'Back from the Ring!' Woglinde and Wellgunde fling their arms around his neck and swimming away draw him down with them into the depths. Flosshilde, swimming ahead of the others toward the back, joyously holds up the recovered Ring. Through the bank of cloud on the horizon a red glow of increasing brightness breaks forth, and, illumined by this light, the Rhine maidens are seen merrily circling about and playing with the Ring on the calmer waters of the Rhine, which has gradually retired to its natural bed.

"From the ruins of the fallen hall the men and women watch in great agitation the growing gleam of fire in the heavens. When this is at its brightest the hall of Walhall is seen, in which the gods and heroes sit assembled as described by Waltraute in the first act. Bright flames seem to seize on the hall of the gods. When the gods are completely hidden by the flames, the curtain falls."

Not many, even of the Wagner devotees, have ever read those directions. They are magnificent nonsense, of course: any stage director will tell you that the only place to literally present such a scene is in a lunatic asylum located in the Coliseum of Rome. What Wagner is describing is, literally, the end of the world— which to him was evidently a very natural thing. Yet absurd though the conception is, the music actually matches his soaring thoughts. I have always imagined that on the day the world *does* end, it will collapse on the wings of Wagner's marvelous chords.

16

A Blow for Liberty

DURING my years at the Met and on the concert stage I often longed for the little specially-built twenty-gauge shotgun my father made for me. Somewhere, moving about from apartment to apartment and hotel to hotel, it had become lost. But as a child I had known how to shoot ducks with it. I was sure that in later years I could have picked off a critic or two as he flapped into his aisle seat.

But time has softened my feeling about those who sat on their macduffs and cried: "Lay on!" As I swash through these pages, hip deep in fact and anecdote, I like to think that the opinions of both friends and foes were valuable to me. Perhaps the best way to plumb the sea around me is to hand out some measuring sticks. To give some idea of what was said over a span of seven years, allow me to select a few reviews from 1941 to 1948.

I think one of the nicest I ever had came in Baltimore in October, 1941. It was written in the *Sun* by Weldon Wallace:

"If Helen Traubel was disappointed in the two hands full of people that came to the Lyric last night to hear her, she gave no evidence of that fact, but then this singer seems to have the kind of personality in which there is no room for ill will of any kind.

"She gave obvious evidence of her pleasure in the response of that audience and the applause proved that under the spell of such a voice, even two hands full of people can make an acceptable demonstration.

"Though interpretively the program was not all of equal interest, the vocal production was consistently ideal, with the exception of a metallic, over-resonance in high fortissimo passages, though this may have been accentuated by the large empty spaces in the auditorium. The only thing one can do in attempting to convey the qualities of this voice is merely to list a few of its distinctions: A very wide range, with a scale in which there is not a flaw; breath control of a kind that makes one forget either the existence or the necessity for breath; *messa di voce* (the swell of volume from pianissimo to forte and back again) that defies description."

He said other nice things, too, but those are enough. It was as warm a review as the one that had been written about me sixteen years before, in 1925, by the critic of my home town St. Louis *Courier-Journal:* "Miss Traubel has youth, beauty, and a gorgeous soprano voice—rich, warm, and vibrant."

Such a welcome gave my first real concert season, starting late in September 1941 and running through the middle of May 1942, a remarkable demand for my services as a singer. The available dates were 100 per cent snapped up by the end of August—more than fifty dates at a minimum of two thousand dollars each. Our income had burgeoned by more than ten times our original NBC contract price.

On the other hand, Kolodin of the now-defunct New York *Sun* was always solicitous about me and my talents. I can quote from one of his reviews in 1941: "This will be remembered as an occasion when Miss Traubel truly approximated the magnificent potentialities of her voice with the musical fervor of her conceptions. The most obvious manifestation was in the final scene of *Götterdämmerung* which concluded the program in a riot of dramatic intensity and tonal sumptuousness. In the interests of her future, Miss Traubel should be more careful of the strain she imposes on her voice in flinging forth the top tones of such a scene." Happily, I have never had to hold back except as the composer demanded. My voice has withstood for twenty years the ravages that were feared by Kolodin. Other critics went the other way. One in the *Herald Tribune* that year declared:

"Miss Traubel, as everyone knows, is the possessor of one of the finest dramatic soprano voices now to be heard. It is a huge voice and Miss Traubel revels in the sheer volume of tone she is capable of producing."

So much for the first years of my singing. At the end of the first decade (if 1937 is counted as my "debut") the opinions had changed subtly—as if to indicate that I had arrived at a maturity they had not suspected possible. They did not comprehend that for me music was an operation of continuous education—that I learned all I could from every source about how to sing and sing better.

In 1947 one of the heads of the recording field described me as "musically, artistically, the most important member of the Metropolitan Opera Company, the joy of the song-loving public in eighty or ninety American cities each season, the darling of the local concert manager, the most sought-after singer for the least undignified, least vulgar, and probably most remunerative of broadcasts." I was grateful for such unstinting support in my field. I have always tried to live up to the standards imposed on me by my friends—but more than that, to the standards imposed upon me by the ideals of the music I sang.

As a measure of how far the critics thought I had—or had not —come in 1948 in my singing of the *Tristan und Isolde* opera, against the memory of Flagstad, the New York *Times* said: "Miss Traubel's interpretation right through was of the highest intelligence on the loftiest plane. It was dignified and noble, perfectly paced, acted, and sung with complete comprehension.

Texturally, it was an achievement for the treatment of the text and the coloring of every tone to clothe the emotional import of that word.

"The first act was certainly the supreme problem of the Isolde role. We could not see that she missed one of its salient points or subtle nuances, but she was sensible enough not to try to make the high C's in the second act, lost the audience nothing of essential importance, and contributed to her own security and quality of tone. More voice would have helped her at the last, but with less voice she would have profoundly moved her listeners by a dramatic verity, depth of meaning, and consonant musicianship."

This was a long jump from the time when people had complained about my relegating high C's to their proper place in the singing of the role. I felt when I read this review that I had at last gained a convert to my ideas.

As for the portrayal of my role of Brünnhilde in *Die Götterdämmerung* the same year, I may quote from the *Herald Tribune* of December 3, 1948:

"This was one of those all too rare occasions when every important role is faultlessly cast and the interpreters of those roles are in their best vocalist state. As Brünnhilde, Madame Traubel reached the peak of her career on the stage, investing her enormously taxing music with unfolding tonal splendor in its most dramatic pages and bringing to its tenderer, more intimate moments appositely colored tones of ravishing texture. Her vocalism was throughout the evening of the utmost expressivity and profoundly affecting. Dramatically, too, she disclosed considerable growth in her portrayal, acting with uncommon intensity, yet always with telling economy of gesture."

I recognized in those days—after ten years of work at it—I had become a bearcat for thoroughly memorizing roles. I missed not being able to work at a new challenge. Horizons of music outside those of Wagner were commencing to show themselves to me: the beauties of tones like pastel colors, the inaudible gradations of beauty that moved behind the music itself. Thus, after *Lohengrin* had not been presented for a year, I was gratified when the Met brought Wagner's work back in 1944 for me, with myself in the title role of Elsa of Brabant. It was not a perfect vehicle for me by any means but it was a welcome change. Again I ran head on into the special predilections of the critics.

"It was the familiar production in settings, cast, and costumes," sourly wrote the New York *Sun* critic, "save for the first-time Elsa of Helen Traubel and her strangely inappropriate gowns." Remember what I said about the critics versus my costumes? He went on: "Her attire has remained out of the period in other Wagner essayals. Perhaps it is too much, therefore, to expect her now to conform to ordinary operatic dictates in her costuming of Elsa," just perhaps as it would have been too much for me to expect this critic to indulge in good English in his "essayals." He also lit into poor Lauritz, saying that he "swished about in his specially designed stylistic monstrosities." After these broadsides against fashion, his musical comments came as an anticlimax. He said I was "painstaking in singing and impersonation" and that my voice was "generally of beautiful quality" but that I was "slightly below pitch" and that I "barely touched" two high notes, whatever that meant.

His most revealing comment came when he claimed that I did not that night have the voice "for the high tessitura of the role." That single incredible word gave him away. Opera, like any other art, has its special cult and its special meaningless vocabulary. I had a friend who, sitting in on a meeting of the high brass of a famous orchestra to discuss budget, spoke out against a proposed cut in a certain sector. "What," he said blandly with a straight face, "will happen to the tessitura?" The directors looked blankly at each other. "Oh, well," said one at last, "in that case we had better not cut it down." The item remained.

Even in definition, *tessitura* remains almost without meaning.

Here is the official dictionary translation of this Italian term and I defy anyone to explain it fully: "The general range or 'lie' of a melody or voice part; that part of the compass in which most of the tones of a melody or voice part lie." I hope that is quite clear. Opera has many terms similar to this, most of them coined by the critics a half century or more ago and dug up and reused by the usually uninformed critics of today. One example is the use of the word "transversal." A critic may say: "Her transversal of the aria was adequate." I do not know what he means. It is a sort of pseudo-cultural double talk which is heard nowhere else. The equivalent of the audience double talk is to call a certain portrayal of a role "divine"—which may mean anything from excellent to odorous. Gatti-Casazza used to be famous for his own method of dealing with this nonsense. Whatever he said, it was safe to assume the opposite. If a singer came offstage and was congratulated heartily by the maestro, for example, the singer trembled in his boots. It meant he would probably be fired in the morning.

I was an iconoclast—the bull in the china shop of the Met—by necessity rather than choice. It was necessary for my career that I expand somewhere or bust a gusset. I was aware that styles change in singing. Like clothes, they are variations on the basic equipment. It used to be the fashion to sing with a "dead" voice, one without vibrato. I do not mean tremolo: that is a hole in a voice that the singer tries to disguise with a wobble. I mean that resonance within a tone that gives it life and expression. I was aware as well that Elsa, noble as the part was, did not give me the room for the nuances of vocal expression which I felt necessary for continued development. At about this time, among my omnivorous reading, I came across a description of opera in the late nineteenth century by Mark Twain in his *A Tramp Abroad* that made me shake the house with laughter.

He commented rather fully on a performance of *Lohengrin* as follows: "I went to see a shivaree—otherwise an opera—the one called *Lohengrin*. The banging and slamming and booming and crashing were something beyond belief. The racking and pitiless pain of it remains in my memory alongside the memory of the day that I had my teeth fixed. There were circumstances which made it necessary for me to stay through the four hours to the end . . . yet at times the pain was so exquisite I could hardly keep the tears back. At those times, as the howlings and wailings and shriekings of the singers and the ragings and roarings and explosions of the vast orchestra rose higher and higher and wilder and wilder and fiercer and fiercer, I could have cried. . . .

"It was a curious sort of a play. In the matter of costumes and scenery it was fine and showy enough; but there was not much action. That is to say, there was not much really done, it was only talked about; and always violently. It was what one might call a narrative play. Everybody had a narrative and a grievance and none were reasonable about it but all in an offensive and ungovernable state. . . . Each sang his indictive narrative in turn, accompanied by the whole orchestra of instruments, and when this had continued for some time and one was hoping they might come to an understanding and modify the noise, a great chorus composed entirely of maniacs would suddenly break forth and then during two minutes and sometimes three, I lived over again all that I had suffered the time the orphan asylum burned down."

Mr. Twain did like the Wedding Chorus, saying that it was "almost divine music," but he declared that opera "deals so largely in pain that its scattered delights are prodigiously augmented by the contrasts. A pretty air in an opera is prettier there than it could be anywhere else, I suppose, just as an honest man in politics shines more than he would elsewhere."

However his personal tastes may have differed from mine, I was in accord with what he said about opera goers. "One in fifty of those who attend our operas likes it already, perhaps, but I think a good many of the other forty-nine go in order to learn to like it and the rest in order to be able to talk knowingly about it. The latter usually hum the airs while they are being sung, so that their neighbors may perceive they have been to operas before. The funerals of these do not occur often enough."

The reviews of my performance in *Die Götterdämmerung* in December 1944 had long ago betrayed the fact that the critics were now wavering in favor of my Isolde where before they had applauded the Brünnhilde. One said, "Miss Traubel's Brünnhilde is not yet so wholly satisfying in achievement as Isolde." He went on to give me my customary whacks in the costume department, saying, "If Miss Traubel could be persuaded to discard her unfortunate costume with its surplus yardage, which serves only to unnecessarily enlarge her figure, her conception would profit greatly from the dramatic point of view." (This comment about how drama could be improved by what I might wear has always puzzled me.)

By the end of 1944 I was hoping that I could do something besides Wagner—perhaps Beethoven—but I was forced to keep on with my usual repertoire, including such flavorless parts as Elsa. At this point I was beginning to be asked questions about whether my "distinguished" portrayals would continue as they had been. To these friendly inquiries I always replied, "I just sing a role. I study the music and sing it as I feel it—and of course that will be my way, I suppose, as distinguished from anybody else's. I always think of myself as simply a part of the picture, of the over-all—and that of course is Wagner. I study the music of the whole work and fit my part into it, always considering it as part of the whole. I try to get everything out of the music that is in it; I try to wring it dry. How in the world anyone can say: 'This is my part, I will stand out through the whole and above the others,' I simply can't see."

It was highly ironic, of course, that I was forced to defend a composer for whom I had nothing but the greatest veneration, but whose works I was on the verge of abandoning because I felt they could not give me the total projection that I demanded within myself. It was even more ironic that my performances in other roles were achieving the summit of critical applause—even for roles where they had once classified me as second to Flagstad.

I felt I had done Sieglinde to a turn. My three Brünnhilde renditions seemed to be maturing into a state of being that at least satisfied my own artistic standards. I could not agree with those who praised my Isolde so highly so early. It was to be two more years—in 1946—before I could claim that I had sung Isolde about thirty-five times in the United States and South America and was really beginning to feel part of it, to know all the nuances of the role. To one reporter who asked me if I thought I was singing better, I said, "I am just beginning to scratch the surface of Isolde, and when I itch, I scratch—hard."

During that winter of public success and personal discontent I could truthfully say that my two most satisfactory moments were in amateur performances. The opportunity for the first came one night in a servicemen's canteen in Chicago. I had dropped in there to offer my services to the USO. They had accepted them. I was introduced (and by this time my disguise of "Mrs. Bass" was no longer of any use) and got the usual perfunctory applause. I walked over toward the piano. As I did, I passed a sailor who emitted a groan I was not meant to hear. I heard him whisper to his companion, "Oh, no! Not more of that long-hair stuff!"

In that moment I made up my mind. I leaned over and whispered to my accompanist and then turned to face the audience. To them I said: "I shall begin with a song by a composer who has made the peasants of my home town famous among music lovers all over the world."

With that I proceeded to blast them as loud as I could with a torch singer's technique—in the "St. Louis Blues." The cheers and whistles thrilled me as no opening-night applause had ever done. I was beginning to see my way into the future.

The second occasion arrived when I was lunching at a small

French restaurant in New York. There was a soldier's wedding party going on at the next table. I love to see weddings. They make me feel so very warm inside. On this occasion I overheard the bride say to a friend wistfully: "This is a nice wedding, but I've always wanted the kind where someone sings 'Oh, Promise Me'." I do not know what prompted me, but I got to my feet and crossed to her. I offered my services. They were accepted with some surprise. I sang the tune and walked back to my table with the silence loud in my ears—one of the most spontaneous and affecting tributes I have ever had. The wet eyes of the bride and the intensity of the stammered thanks of the groom made me aware that I had taken yet another step into the role for which I had always believed my voice had been designed.

17

L'Affaire Margaret

NO one who has not attempted to teach the daughter of a United States president to sing can understand what it is to be a Republican. It was an adventure into both politics and polyphony, in which I, as a veteran of the backstaging of the Met, took the only course I could. As I had once said grimly to Bill concerning an uppity tenor who was trying to upstage me one night during a performance, "No one gets away with that with me—even if I have to go so far back that I push my rear right through the scenery!" That was about how it turned out.

By 1948 I was as firmly established in my niche of singing fame as it was possible to be. My role as a prima donna never impressed me too much; nor did it really get home to Bill. I can remember when he began calling me "my little prima donkey." He described my vacations as "turning me out to pasture."

I can always say of Bill, however, that he has never misquoted me. Even when he described me as of "so even a temperament that no one can tell if she's dumb or just lethargic," he was on his own. I often shot off my mouth to the reporters and was startled by the echo that came back. On one occasion I was not going to sing Wagner—and the reporter added "any more." What I had meant was that I had not included any Wagner selections in that particular concert; what the public got was the impression that I hated Wagner's guts. It was a good deal like the time when Sergei Rachmaninoff, the great pianist and composer, was interviewed and the reporter rushed to the telephone and sent through a smash story saying that he was "retiring." The next morning Rachmaninoff cleared up the impression. "I merely said," he protested, "that I was going to bed."

Despite this attitude, the honors kept rolling in. One that I appreciated more than most was an honorary doctorate of music awarded by the University of Missouri. Thus I became in June 1948 the first woman ever to be given such an honor. The president, a fine figure of a man named Middlebush, gave it to me at the commencement exercises at Columbia, Missouri. His citation said I was "America's pre-eminent Wagnerian soprano of the Metropolitan Opera Association, born and educated in Missouri." He went on to say: "In you our state and nation have produced for the first time a native-born American-trained soprano who excels in the mighty roles of Isolde and Brünnhilde. Your golden voice is now the possession of the world and of posterity. In recognition of your superb artistry, and in appreciation of your glorious song, the university of your native state honors you today."

The only other woman ever to be so honored in the history of the University of Missouri up to that time with an honorary degree was Louise Stanley of the United States Department of Agriculture. She got a doctor of laws degree in 1940. Perhaps it can be said that Miss Stanley, a teacher at the university for a dozen years, had taught the students how to raise the corn. I had showed them how to sing it. (At the 1947 commencement exercises at the University of Southern California I had received an honorary doctorate of music.)

The very fact that I had been connected so long with the Met was in itself an accolade. With its world reputation, intensive repertoire (twenty-four weeks and twenty-four works) that played one hundred and fifty performances a year to about six hundred thousand people—not counting the radio audience—and appeared to about half that number in sixty performances on tour, it was an institution that honored its members by its very existence. I had helped it through its crisis of 1940 when it raised a million from the public, the stockholders, and the radio audience. Queen of the German Wing was my onstage title. I was the one who shook hands with the stagehands before each performance for luck, who loved the sound of an orchestra tuning up as a fire horse loved the sound of the tocsin—or, if you wish to keep on going, as a brewery horse in St. Louis would love the thud of a beer barrel.

At any rate, it must have been something like these qualifications that attracted notice in the highest spot in the nation. It was 1948 when I first became acquainted with the ideas and ambitions of Margaret Truman, the only child and apple of the eye of both Harry and Bess Truman. The occasion came that spring. I was asked to sing (after accepting the "feeling out" invitation) at the White House. We went down to Washington. I stood up in the wonderful Blue Room with its special piano with five golden eagles for legs and delivered Schubert, Richard Strauss, Beethoven, and a couple of arias to the assembled multitude. It was a cabinet dinner, full of full dress and folderol with judges of the Supreme Court, generals and admirals, ambassadors, socialites—something like an exquisite miniature of a Met opening. I was tremendously impressed, open-mouthed most of the time and not altogether from singing.

After the concert and the dinner there is not really much to do at the White House. The joint folds up. But Margaret Truman, I noticed, amid the congratulations, was talking animatedly to Bill in the hall. She was a tall, pretty blonde who could be very persuasive. She asked Bill if I would talk to her about music. He said I would if she happened to be in New York. Sure enough, in the next few days Margaret appeared at our apartment on Park Avenue. She talked excitedly about what she wanted to do. She had ambitions to sing and wanted to start immediately.

I hate to talk theory or ideas. I have learned long ago that the only way to test something out is to do it. So I said to Margaret: "Come over to the piano and let's hear what we've been chatting about." She came with me. I ran off some scales. As I expected, her voice was inexperienced and really rather bad. But it had an appealing quality, one that I thought might very well be developed in the future to give her a respectable series of concerts at home. "It's a small voice but it could be worked on," I told her. "It will take at least five years—perhaps ten—of hard work before you could possibly expect to give even a minor concert in public."

"I don't mind the work at all," Margaret said eagerly. "To me, it will be just the career I want." To her credit, she always worked as hard as she knew how; not even I, an old and grim taskmaster, could complain about the hours she put in. She was dedicated to becoming a great singer. Unfortunately, she never had the equipment. I warned her from the beginning.

What I did not know was that Margaret was going to dedicate me, as well, to her voice. My time, my efforts, and a section of my own career became involved. First and last, the three years I spent with Margaret Truman cost me considerably in lost concert fees, an incredible amount of sweat and disappointment—and, finally, a loss in the eyes of the musical world for ever having my name connected with such a musical aspirant. Let me make it clear, Margaret was never a "protégée" of mine; nor was she ever my pupil. Nor did I intend—though that was not the way it ended up —to do more than be a background adviser. Unfortunately, though I was candid from the first note that Margaret sang, I never had the courage to break off until years later. I had never faced such a situation before. How does one tell the daughter of a United States president that she is not a good singer?

Unhappily, not long after she started her career, Margaret agreed to sign with her agent for a series of concerts. As the daughter of Truman, she could expect high fees and a succession of appearances. I discovered this fact and talked with the manager. He and Margaret said she would not appear in public for at least five years. I never charged a nickel for my services. I recommended Margaret to my own accompanist, Cooney, to help develop her vocal cords. I may add here that I had rarely before given an audition to an aspiring voice student. Such auditions—unless the child is an outstanding genius—are always cruel. Nine hundred and ninety-nine times out of a thousand there is no voice. The once-out-of-a-thousandth time the voice is handicapped by other factors that make failure almost a foregone conclusion. Other singers get a considerable income from holding "auditions" for fifty or one hundred dollars in small towns, praising the neophyte and then fleeing the premises. I had been taught a lesson when a dear friend of mine brought in a niece who had been assured that she was a second Galli-Curci. I was hog-tied. I listened, drew a deep breath, and delivered myself: "My dear, you may take lessons for amusement, yes, if you like. But not for a career. It is tough enough to become a singer if you are superb—which you are not."

I said much the same thing to Margaret. It bounced off her eagerness. I suppose I was to blame for falling in with her capacity for hard work and her dedication; perhaps at times I even felt she had a chance to succeed, against my better judgment. At any rate, Margaret moved to New York. She appeared morning, noon, and evening at our apartment. She spent weekends with us. She went on trips with us and turned up early in the morning and late at night. She was importunate and driving. Before I knew it I was one of the team. I rearranged schedules, turned down broadcasting and concert dates, spending two to four hours a day away from my own rehearsing. Though I had stipulated that no publicity should come out about us two Missouri girls working together, the leaks commenced to appear. "It happened like ham and eggs," Bill said ruefully later. "Margaret just took us over."

It was a change-up pitch for me, the kind we used to call a "fooler" on the St. Louis back lots. Just as Harry Truman persuaded a lot of people that he was a good piano player, so Margaret persuaded people into thinking she had a voice. Bess Truman never kidded anyone: she was a good, solid, honest woman who ran the family and she said she hated every minute she was in the White House. In those early days of 1948 I saw a Truman I respected a great deal. He was a man without much education, a haberdasher and a political judge, a member of one of the most aggressive political crowds that ever existed in this country. But he was humble, eager to learn, conscious of the greatness of his position, and still under the shadow of Franklin Delano Roosevelt. The women of the family disliked the Roosevelts. Margaret could not stand any of the Roosevelt boys. She used to tell me FDR had treated her father "terribly shabbily." I do not think in the days of FDR the president and vice-president ever met socially. Truman had been the Throttlebottom of the Roosevelt administration, as far as I could make out.

His reputation was so far gone in Washington that, when the news that I was "coaching" Margaret got out, people used to say: "Why are you wasting your time? Don't you know that after November Truman will disappear into the wilds of Missouri and never appear again?" To this my response was that my concern was not with the father but with the daughter. I had made an agreement. Come what might I would stick with it until circumstances made it impossible. I would not break my word, nor did I; it was Margaret who finally made our parting inevitable. "And after all is said," I would conclude, "this girl has a tremendous drive toward an ambition and she is willing to work. How many people with far more talent than hers are willing to do that?"

At election time virtually the whole of the nation was against Truman—the press, the radio, the commentators, the pundits had already buried him. Nobody was for him, evidently, except the voters. They made him president in his own right. It was an admirable feat, something done almost singlehanded by a man fighting back alone against all the forces that could be summoned against him. It made Truman a hero overnight. Unhappily it also brought out some of his less admirable characteristics. We, as frequent visitors to the White House (or Blair House, since the White House was being repaired during most of our acquaintance with the Trumans), could see it clearly.

Truman became stubborn and opinionated. His always-prominent trait of being loyal to his friends became almost an obsession. He was often vehement on subjects which he knew very little about. I can even recall some of his discussions with me on the subject of classical music. Now he felt he was on his own and had earned the right to step out. At the same time he had great candor. On one occasion, after he had written his famous note to the music critic who had dared say that Margaret had little talent, he confided to me: "I should never have written that letter. But now it's written, I'll stand by it!"

What mattered to me was not so much the political end of events as the musical. As Harry Truman changed after his election, so did Margaret. She, too, acquired extra convictions. Except that, in her case, they concerned her voice rather than the national welfare. The first intimation I had of this was a note in the clipping services. It said that she and the manager I had recommended for Margaret—my own manager at the time—had concluded an agreement for a tour of eight to ten concerts with a southern bureau. This particular bureau had an excellent reputation. I knew it had no illusions about Margaret's voice. The whole point of such an engagement was only the money to be made on the concert platform. The publicity which I had so long avoided now broke around my head like a thunderstorm. I was pelted with *drang und dreck* for having taken on such a "pupil." It was made to appear that Margaret was my protégée, who might take my place at the Met, who was totally endorsed by me—all of which was totally false. It was true that Margaret depended heavily on me: my presence seemed to give her courage to sing. She would watch me all through the concert or rehearsal. Believe me, I sang each one of her notes twice as hard as she did and ten times as hard as *I* ever did! Every time she got up, my knees commenced to shake. I sang silently, harder and with more agony in my seat than I had ever sung on the stage. I can say here that my first, greatest, and unconquerable difficulty with her voice was simply keeping her on key.

I called her in and the manager with her. We had a stormy session. When the scene was over, I had made another mistake: I had agreed not only to accept the inevitable but Margaret had also persuaded me to accompany her on the trips. I was hooked. All on the basis that this would be the first and last time. Bill and I embarked on a two-week trip where I did nothing but play backstop to Margaret. With accompanist and maid it amounted to about $200 × 14 × whatever engagement I refused so far as out-of-pocket expenses were concerned. Nor was this chicken feed at the time. In October 1949 it was reported that from about twenty-five performances in the Met roles each season plus approximately sixty concert engagements, television, and recordings for Columbia, I was earning twice the salary of the president of the United States each year, very roughly two hundred and fifty thousand dollars.

We left Margaret to her own devices in St. Louis after the concert, the last stop of our tour, unable to face the opinion of that home-town reception. Truman, who had attended his daughter's original debut in Constitution Hall in Washington and told a friend that he "almost tore up two programs in my excitement," had a different reaction to the cool criticisms from the big town in Missouri. I felt the trial was over. I hoped Margaret would settle down to simply training her voice. I was disillusioned: her manager informed me she was booked for concerts in the Lewisohn Stadium at New York and the Philadelphia Dell—where tens of thousands instead of hundreds were to hear her.

This was too much. I told Margaret that she would have to call off the concerts. She refused. I told her there was no other way as far as I was concerned that I could work with her. It ended with all of us taking it to court—down to Washington to see Daddy Truman in Blair House. We saw him in the study.

"Mr. President," I told him, "when I agreed to help Margaret, I said she should study and not sing in public for five years. You know that."

"Yes," he said.

"I know you want Margaret to stand on her own two feet and not on anything that you have done. I don't want her singing to be based on her father's reputation as a president." At this point Margaret rushed out of the room.

"Yes!" cried Truman. He smacked his desk with his fist. "That's exactly what I want!"

"Then," I said, "she will have to call off these concerts she has booked."

Truman thought it over. He called Margaret back into the room. He told her to telephone her manager and cancel the concerts. Truman was not angry with her. On the contrary, he was very gentle but very firm.

"But I have contracts with these people!" she protested. "How can I get out of them?"

"That's your job," her father told her. "You got into this, now get yourself out."

That was the formula for the whole affair. The concerts were never held. But I was not yet free to do what was needed and what Margaret really deserved. The next thing that turned up was that Margaret (and her manager) had planned and contracted for a series of radio appearances.

This was the last straw. If it was not proper for her to appear before hundreds, it was less proper before thousands. But what could you say to the ambition of a girl who, untrained and musically unknown, wanted to appear before millions? At this point I guess I felt I was fighting not so much to develop Margaret as a singer as I was fighting to uphold the national honor. She would be singing in direct comparison with some of the finest artists of opera and concert. It would have been, I felt, a personal disaster of the first magnitude for me to be connected with it.

I would describe Margaret's voice as a lyric soprano with a very sweet quality. If she had studied five years—better, ten—she would have had an adequate singing ability. If the TV and radio personalities of today are any example—something I would never have dreamed of in those days—she might have had an acceptable career on the air. But using any standards, there simply was not enough of everything—or anything—to make her really a concert and light opera singer. She did not have the right temperament, though she was a glutton for work. The meaning of the song always escaped her. Her physical build was promising but she lacked emotional understanding of what the tone and the projection of the music meant.

While Bill and I—Bill eventually got most of the blame for these shenanigans—were stewing over this, the news came that Margaret's manager had scheduled a concert at Carnegie Hall.

This time it was impossible for me to stop her. I did not yet have the sense to cut everything short and publicly step out. I thought something might be salvaged from the girl's desire to be a singer, from her really genuine need to work at something. I was wrong once more: I consented to go to the concert. I thought it would be a debacle. I was wrong—it was a catastrophe.

It was so bad, almost from the first note, that I spent all of the evening for the first time in my life hiding behind the curtains of my box. Mrs. Roosevelt sat in the box next to me and we chatted, but both of us studiously avoided the subject of Margaret as a singer. What the former First Lady felt about it I never discovered. I left long before it was over, trying to escape from the memory of those wavering, off-key notes that were made even worse by the impeccable stage presence that Margaret always had. Nothing could dint her self-confidence. At least nothing I could do. That function was reserved for her father alone.

A few days later we had the climactic scene. My experiment in teaching was nearly at its end. Margaret came to our house and had a conference with Bill and me. This time I was firm.

"You can't go on the radio," I said. "That's out."

"We're all ready to go!"

"I don't care. You haven't the training, the knowledge—you haven't anything to back you up."

"The contracts are signed and I have ten appearances at more than five thousand dollars each!"

"Not under any circumstances."

At this point Bill ventured a word. "I don't think it's the best course of action," he said.

Margaret whirled on him. "You keep out of this!" she flared. "You've always tried to turn Helen against me!"

That was the beginning of the end. Whatever decisions I had made were purely my own, on the basis of my intimate knowledge of Margaret's capability. Bill retired. Margaret and I kept at it, hammer and tongs, raising our soprano voices—trained and un-trained—at each other until the welkin and the neighbors rang. I rarely indulge in such antics but, as a krautgirl from old St. Louis with a *schimpflexikon* of my own, I am certainly capable of hold-ing my own. It ended with me on exactly the same spot. The radio negotiations were called off the next day.

In all fairness to Margaret, during the time that she worked with me she did show tremendous improvement. Even her father said so. She learned not to "sing in the cracks," as we call singing off key in the trade—except when she got excited. I think her great fault was that she could not hear herself sing. She never knew what a real amateur she was—an honorable designation in any way of life.

As I said to Bill when I quit: "I feel as if the horses had stopped running away with me."

I had once said that she was "a darling girl with plenty of personality and drive," and I never regretted it. I had also said that I had "confidence in her," and I did. In the fall of 1951—all these events had spanned a couple of years—I delivered my valedictory on the whole thing for the press. I said: "I didn't think she was ready for all these appearances. The offers just kept coming in. I even went down to Washington to see her daddy. I told him I couldn't go on if she accepted the offers. Well, it's too bad. Most young singers just don't realize how much they have to study. The funny thing is that Margaret Truman really has a nice voice— nothing great—but good enough."

I gave orders to everyone that I would be out when Margaret called. I did not even want to be told that she had come to the house. Disappointment and chagrin were joined inside me. In some ways I regretted the inevitable break with Margaret. From our association late in 1948 to our parting in June 1950 we exchanged many tokens of regard. She used to write me that "the concert went well . . . the critics on this trip have been nicer than ever before." She would listen to my broadcasts, sending me wires that I was "closest to the mike with the mostest" or tell me that "we were together on the front page of the *News,* a tabloid, and very clear." Once she told me that my tutelage was "the difference between success and a total flop for me"—which I am afraid it never could be. Bess Truman sent Christmas presents and the president added his thanks with a note "to a lovely, kindly lady whose patience I appreciate."

In early 1950 Margaret thanked me again for "all the hours you spent trying to instill a modicum of singing into my head," but when the final break came, she wrote that she would not be able to see me again but that she was still grateful for my time and efforts. Rumors came flying to me—all of them untrue—that her father had written me a scorching letter comparable to the remarkable one he had scribbled to the Washington *Post* critic. I was grateful that he had not. But the parting Bill and I had with the president himself was quite different though not less dramatic.

It made me a little unhappy to forego what the White House had meant. I was very much impressed with the glitter and ceremony. Bill and I loved being piped aboard the *Williamsburg*, the presidential yacht. That super-duper launch was really an experience for me. We enjoyed the couple of dozen times we ate at Blair House. Bill enjoyed going to the football game with Truman on the special train (while I had to stay home and work with Margaret). The receptions and the attention given the presidential party—we sometimes appeared at three or four functions before dinner—were all very glamorous and exciting. As an old movie fan I used to adore Truman running pictures in the little theater that Roosevelt built where the wall practically melted away to make room for a screen. We could see the latest or the earliest of pictures just by calling up.

There is little more to be told. One small anecdote will serve to show the temper in which *l'affaire Margaret* wound up. I asked Bill to do the feat that I could not summon courage to do: I asked him to call the White House and tell Truman that the deal was off. Bill agreed. He got on the list of appointment calls and one evening was put through to the President.

"I'm afraid, Mr. President," Bill said, "that Helen feels she can't go along with Margaret any longer the way things are."

"Why not?" demanded Truman. Bill recited the long list of our complaints and disappointments.

"Well," said the President at last in his nasal, brittle voice, "I'm afraid that whatever Margaret decides, that's the way it'll have to be."

Bill delivered the *coup de grâce*. He was a little angry, too. "No, Mr. President," he said quietly. "If it isn't done the way Helen wants, it won't be done at all."

As a reply, he got the crash of a telephone receiver slammed down in the White House.

18

Bing, Bang, and Bangkok

I USED to come back to our apartment at a quarter of one in the morning after a stretched-out performance of Wagner and find Bill half asleep. He would rouse himself and mumble his opinion of my performance: "If I had to marry an operatic soprano, why wasn't she an Italian? She could have sung those short, jolly little works where everyone gets stabbed or married in the last act and everyone would get home early."

I saw his point. Opera was not nearly so serious to us as it was to its devotees. We were beginning to feel that life had a good deal more to offer than a high note held *in excelsis* or the heroine worship of the society-teenage clique that was then becoming popular at the Met. That side of my life—the opera and concert part—went along swimmingly, immersed in the lushness of the music.

On March 21, 1950, I sang the role of Kundry in Wagner's *Parsifal* for the first time. The New York *World-Telegram* said: "Among those singing in *Parsifal* for the first time, Helen Traubel easily walked off with first honors as Kundry. Her interpretation of that strange divided personality is worthy of her other roles. Vocally, it was a Kundry of power and glow and, if the acting

217

missed the demonic frenzy that points up the conflict, it was at least in the tradition of studied intensity."

In January 1951 I sang the role of the Marschallin in Philadelphia as part of Richard Strauss's opera *Der Rosenkavalier*. The reviewer said: "The outstanding voice and vocalism of the evening were Madame Traubel's. Slimmed down considerably since last season, the American soprano presented a dignified and majestic princess. However, it was not in her mild and restrained histrionics that Madame Traubel made her mark but in the ineffable beauty of much of her singing which was silvery in tone and distinguished at all times."

By way of evidence that I was not in a decline at the Metropolitan, it would be enough to quote the New York *Times* on my *Götterdämmerung* singing in 1951: "Miss Traubel seems to grow in the Brünnhilde role with every season that passes. She interpreted the role throughout the two acts with a noble fire and pathos."

In November 1952 a critic in Miami said: "The striking success of last night's Wagnerian banquet is due to two things—the orchestra's remarkable mastery of the music and the strong climax of Miss Traubel's thrilling 'Liebestod.' The 'Liebestod' in *Tristan und Isolde* is pure gold, vocally and artistically, and we personally have never heard Miss Traubel sing so well. Of course she has been a distinguished and finished artist for many years, but we venture to deduce from last night's experience that she is still growing in artistry and has grown much since we last heard her in ability to generally move and enthrall listeners in addition to awing and overwhelming them." I would give something to know what this friendly critic meant by saying I was a "finished artist."

I also wrote a mystery novel with a ghost writer. It was called *Murder at the Opera*. My husband dutifully read it through to the end and remarked: "It certainly is murder at the opera. This is so bad that people will really believe you wrote it." (On the other hand, I treasure a small dedication written in another book of mine called *A House Is Not a Home*. It reads: "For Helen Traubel, a lady who has talent, from a lady who knows talent. Polly Adler." This tribute from one of the most famous madams in New York is an antidote to my secret literary life.)

In my own library, though, I have only two or three books that deal with opera. Most of my reading is confined to three types: fairy tales, mysteries, and cookbooks. I am an authority on the faraway and never-never, the fantastic and fabulous. I have, for example, one of the best and almost unknown collections of fairy stories edited by the famous writer and historian, Andrew Lang, that comprises yarns from every country in the world. As for cookbooks, I buy them by the dozen whenever they come out. I do like to cook—or fool around in the kitchen. I can knock out a loaf of bread or a digestible sauerbraten before your mouth can water three times.

My sports addiction began to bloom into a publicity flower. I have always loved sports of every kind since my tomboy childhood, but the newspapers greatly exaggerated it. Let me say here and now that I am no authority on baseball. I cannot decide a bet on who was the second substitute pitcher for the Baltimore Orioles in the third game of the 1908 season. I love the game chiefly because I get an aesthetic thrill out of watching or imagining it. I think the coordination of a fine fielding play or synchronizing a bat to meet a fast ball is simply incredible. It is like great ballet— an expression of art. I can gyrate like a pitcher myself, but I cannot pitch nor do I know the finer points of the game. I just like to watch and yell. I really never care who wins a game; nor do I care who wins a sulky race, my second greatest sports passion. Third and fourth, I guess, for my own relaxation are crocheting and ironing, but those long, rhythmic muscles on the ballplayers and the horses are first for me!

I had spent the 1940 World Series weeks—when the St. Louis Cardinals lost—hanging over a radio with, as one witness explained it, "one hand over her mouth to prevent thousands of dollars of high notes from degenerating into squeals, the other held in her husband's soothing grip." In sports columns my greatest reputation was as the "most musical rooter in the stands of the St. Louis baseball teams."

A Missouri editorial said about me, "Probably the worst Helen Traubel's critics say about her is that she is only one of the greatest instead of the greatest Wagnerian soprano of all times. Probably the worst the critics of the St. Louis Browns say about that unhappy ball club couldn't be printed. The best that can be said is that they did emerge gloriously from their habitual worm's eye view of the baseball world at least twice in modern times. Yet Madame Traubel wants the Browns and only the Browns.

"There is something wholesome and democratic about all this. It is a bit of evidence, too, that Americans have come of age. Gone are the days when fine artists from Pittsburgh or Phelps Corners had to acquire a European past before they could win an American present. Helen Traubel can go back to her home town in the heart of her home country, buy a chunk of its sorriest civic advertisement, and still pack 'em in at the Met."

I love those St. Louis Browns. I bought an interest in them in 1950—I can confess it was only a few shares—for sentimental reasons. My first recollection of baseball or of any sport at all is of watching the Browns in action. Every day in the summer that they played from the time I was seven years old I went to see them with my father. We had seats right above the dugout. My father explained to me what the game was about. I can never forget the exciting days of 1944 when they were in the pennant race and actually won. I admit that once I was actually made the mascot of the Cardinals (and the New York Yankees). I was crazy about that man Pepper Martin, the Dean brothers, and Joe Medwick. But the Browns always seemed to need my encouragement more than the Cardinals did. The Browns represented not only my first recollections of baseball but also the first men I adored in my life

—George Sisler and Urban Shocker, stars of the 1922 Browns which lost the pennant to the New York Yankees by only one game.

I have always wanted to meet Joe DiMaggio of the great Yankee team but I will always remember 1946 as the year of my greatest baseball thrill. In that year I met a charming widow in San Francisco. She said to me: "My husband was always such a fan of yours. He would go and hear you whenever he could. He never told any of the fellows on the team because he was afraid they would think he was sissy." This man, believe it or not, was one of the two most famous of the Yankees—their all-time iron man Lou Gehrig.

I was finding pleasure in places that were far away from the customary haunts of opera singers. Life became as unpredictable as the time when, late for singing the most exalted aria of Wagner's operas, I rushed in late with my feet wet—to have my cape taken off and instantly pushed onto the stage. I began to take my life as it came.

There was the moment when a wealthy St. Louis industrialist came to me and begged me to see his wife. She had been in a mental institution in the East for years. One of her obsessions was that I was her mother. She had accused him of keeping her from seeing me, her "mother." The psychiatrist in charge thought it might help rid her of this delusion if she could talk with me. Ordinarily, such requests must be denied, but this one came from a dear mutual friend. We set up a meeting in a hotel dining room. It was to appear as a casual affair and I was to chat informally with the poor woman. Bill, of course, was as nervous as a hen with chicks. He surrounded the joint with plain-clothes men.

At the appointed time I crossed to the table where the woman was having lunch with her husband. He introduced me, then left us. We had a long chat. I was fifty at the time and she was about forty-five. "I understand that you believe I may be your mother," I said. "I don't think this is possible, do you, now that we've met?"

"Why do you try to conceal it?" she asked me tearfully. "Are you ashamed of me?"

"Not at all," I said. "But I would have had to be about five years old when I had you as a daughter."

It resulted in a pleasant luncheon conversation, but I got absolutely nowhere as an amateur psychoanalyst. Probably the same woman still believes she is my "daughter."

My friends bought me a chromium horn for my limousine that went "Hi-yo-to-yo!" in the best Brünnhildian tradition. In the winter of 1949 Lauritz, taking his first safari in South Africa, got hold of two lion cubs. He thought of me and sent me both of them as a Valentine present. I, in turn, transshipped them to the St. Louis Zoo. The director promised to give them a good home and name them Helen and Lauritz.

During the last season of my singing at the Met my relationship with the management was turning into something less than gold. From 1939 to 1950 Eddie Johnson and I had come to know each other's idiosyncrasies very well. From an elegant tenor with well-turned calves he had changed into a highly competent impresario. It might be said I had turned from a song-struck girl into a diva. Whatever the arrangement we had, it worked.

My widely publicized "break" with the Met—not really a rupture of relations, rather a musical growing up—consisted of two crises. Both can be explained in two sentences. Johnson left the Met in 1950 to be replaced by Rudolf Bing. Bing disliked Richard Wagner. It was so simple and so complicated.

Bing was a thin man with piercing eyes who came from Vienna and Scotland. I had little knowledge of his musical background. He had a connection with the Edinburgh crowd in Scotland and the Glyndebourne Opera. That was all I knew. When his appointment was announced there was a good deal of screwing-up of foreheads and scratching of brows. The common question was: "Where did he come from, what did he do?" Like Johnson, Bing has matured during his tenure at the Met. At the time he was an unknown quantity to me.

During my years in grand opera it was the custom for Johnson,

Bill, and me to meet at lunch and talk over the arrangements for the coming opera season. I would have many engagements that would have to be built around my appearances in concert halls and recordings. Signing of the contracts was a mere formality. Usually we would let them lie around the house and one day Bill or I would get absent-minded and sign them. But I always knew where I stood with Johnson. He knew he could depend on me. My standing at the Met was unquestioned.

Bing came in as head of the Met. I knew nothing of it. I was busy setting up my concerts; I expected my usual conference at lunch in the spring. But the months passed. I had no communication whatsoever from Bing. I realized a new impresario had much to do, but I also thought I was entitled to at least an introduction. Finally time caught up with us. "I'll have to set my concert dates," I said to Bill in the spring of 1950. "I can't wait." Bill asked: "What about the Met arrangements?" I pondered that one. "I'll have to say that the time is so late that I can't wait any longer," I said. "I'll have to say that I assume I will not appear this season." We wrote a letter saying that and, in addition, that I would be now unable to accept a contract which was tantamount, of course, to my resignation. So it was done. The letter was posted and simultaneously released to the press.

Somewhat to our astonishment, it became a nationwide *cause célèbre* headlined on the front pages. A feud between myself and Bing—whom I had never met—was instantly drummed up. And, unconsciously, I really had done him a wrong. The same day as I wrote my letter—which Bing complained was "rather unsporting"—he had written one to me. They had crossed in the mails. He called me apologetically on the telephone. We agreed to meet.

Meanwhile, Flagstad had returned from her self-exile in Norway. Her voice was not so full and lovely as it had been but it was still a marvelous medium. Bing had engaged her for the season. This irked my ego, not because he had engaged her but because she had been signed before I was. I felt, since I had been the star at the Met for the past nine years, that I deserved that courtesy. But Flagstad's popularity, oddly, had also risen in the eyes of the operagoers. During the war she had been unjustly accused of being pro-Nazi; now she was acclaimed as a pure artist who had nothing to do with politics. Both charges, of course, were nonsense, but a strong minority group in the Met was in her favor. This was spurred by the fact that I was considered aloof and temperamental. Bill and I had never kowtowed to the society crowd. We had been equally cool to the squalling youngsters who had invaded the Met. We had refused, for example, to go on the Met tours around the country except when these engagements happened to come near each other. I was interested in art; I was also interested in money. The Met gave me the former (at one thousand dollars a throw) and we had to cash in on it in our own way.

The lunch with Bing at an off-Fifth Avenue restaurant was a revelation to me. He was very pleasant. We were completely in agreement until the manager crossed to our table. He whispered that the press was outside. Bill turned to Bing. "How does it happen that the press knows about this meeting?" he demanded. Bing shrugged and spread his fingers. "I'm sure I don't know," he said—a statement which was slightly in error since we discovered afterward that the Met press department had alerted the newspapers. I suppose Bing was having his revenge for my having released my letter to the press. I thought it as unsporting as he did. At any rate, the pressure on him had been tremendous. I was trapped into having my picture taken with him in a smiling "reconciliation scene."

Bing said some revealing things to Bill and me at that lunch. "Personally," he declared, "I dislike Wagner. He does nothing for me." A little later he leaned over and said confidentially: "How do you feel about Flagstad? I have engaged her, of course, but actually I have never heard her sing."

Our agreement—with which I was perfectly in accord, though

I might have insisted otherwise—was to split the whole opera season right down the middle between myself and Flagstad. She was going to do a non-Wagnerian opera, *Alceste*. I was offered my choice of a similar work. I knew no other roles than those of Wagner but I accepted a leading role in *Der Rosenkavalier*. I also made up my mind never to comment upon anyone like Flagstad in public. I adopted a noncommittal phrase which appeared again and again: "She can stand on her own record." It meant whatever the hearer meant it to mean.

Bing explained his actions by saying that he assumed "that Miss Traubel was permanently a part of the Met." I accepted that statement at its face value. How much he considered me a part of the company was revealed when later that year he came to my dressing room and asked me to perform with the touring company in Cleveland. I pointed out that my commitments would not allow it.

"I demand that you appear in Cleveland!" he said haughtily.

I chuckled. "Here, Mr. Bing," I said, "we never use such words as 'must' or 'demand.' "

"I didn't mean it that way," he said quickly. "What I meant was that the performance will be far below its standard unless you appear." The upshot was that I did not appear.

During the next two years the singing of Wagner's works noticeably decreased. It was plain that Bing intended (as he later did) to drop them from the repertoire of the Met in favor of the lighter, more popular Italian and French works. By the roll around of the contract time in 1953 I was no longer under any illusions about the Met.

When the fuss and feathers had died down in the press from the first argument with Bing in 1951, somehow my thoughts had taken on a much bigger idea of the future. It was not so much that I knew there were millions of people who had not heard me sing. It was that I, who loved to watch my audiences, had not seen millions of people and sung to them. So when an impresario named Strock who had heard me in opera came backstage to talk about a tour of the Orient—especially Japan—he met with a more cordial reception than he might have expected.

"The Japanese love Western music," he said enthusiastically.

"I know that," I agreed. "But what would I do?" That was the eternal question. What I had was merely a voice, not an act—and so often an act was needed.

Strock was impatient. "Are you afraid you will not be a success?" he demanded.

"Yes, I am," I said. "Don't forget I don't sing in Japanese. I only sing in English, German, and Italian."

Strock sprang up and clapped his hands. "I guarantee you will be a sensation!" he cried.

That was not exactly how we arranged it—I talked to Bill and my concert bureau about it for several days—but it was the beginning of the temptation to which I finally succumbed. The tour was guaranteed by the *Asahi-Shimbun,* one of the top Japanese newspapers.

My first two concerts in April 1952 were in Hawaii. The land enchanted us. The people were my ideal of friendliness. The food was exotic. The only disappointment came from the famous flower leis. The juices of one that was put around my neck ruined a fifteen-hundred-dollar lace-and-satin dress. From Hawaii we flew directly to Tokyo. In Japan I sang twenty-six concerts in all three islands, in a dozen cities, eight of them in the capital. It was a grand experience—and one of the most exhausting I ever went through. No matter where I sang, waves of enthusiasm, demands for encores seemed to pour over the platform. There had been a death in the imperial family. I was requested by Crown Prince Akihito to sing Brahms' "Lullaby." The ecstatic management wanted me to announce from the stage that he had requested it, but I demurred. "I'll sing it," I said sympathetically. "He'll know I'm singing it for him." I even learned a Japanese song by memorizing it phonetically, one called "The Lotus

Flower Song," a charming lyrical composition. The fervor of the people to hear a Western artist—less than eight years after the bombing of Hiroshima and Nagasaki—was phenomenal. They would run alongside the car, just to touch it; they would try to kiss my hand; they sent vases, silks, brocades, mats—all kinds of presents.

I had been warned before I left the United States that the Japanese did not particularly like singers—they preferred instrumentalists to vocalists. I was warned that they would not particularly cheer for Wagner's imagery in music. To those friendly admonitions I replied that I could only do my best and that if I could throw my voice the way Mickey Mantle could throw a ball into the home plate from the outfield, I was positive the Japanese would catch it. I must say with gratification that the Japanese fielded every high note as if they had been born to do nothing but listen to Wagner. One critic was kind enough to say that "Miss Traubel's wonderful voice has helped to heal the wound of seven unpleasant years." Another critic, a rather diminutive man, said to his friends: "Ah, this Miss Traubel, she is so big and broad. She is such a wonderful sight up there." The finest compliment I got was one from a Japanese opera singer who rushed up to thank me after the performance and was courteous enough to say to me: "Now I know what singing is. Hereafter I shall devote my time to painting."

It was at Hiroshima that I continued the custom I had started in Tokyo—a custom that finally spread to every city in Japan. It was the planting of what might be called a "penitential" rose garden. Years before one of the largest nurseries in California, owned by an opera enthusiast, John A. Armstrong, had been kind enough to name a large, pale apricot-pink rose after me. I distributed six hundred of these rosebushes, ceremoniously planting them in every city where I sang. (The rest were sent out afterward by the newspaper.) The first of these were planted in the spot where the Japanese reckoned the very epicenter of the first atomic bomb explosion. At the same spot I received the most treasured gift of the whole trip. The mayor of Hiroshima gave me an elegant little wooden box filled with cotton on which rested a tiny bit of fused rock and metal—part of the atomic bomb, he claimed. On this object, smaller than a small marble, was engraved: "In appreciation, to Helen Traubel."

I sang fifteen to twenty songs a concert. My repertoire lengthened as I went until finally it included more than one hundred and fifty songs of various kinds, including operatic arias. I even sang with two excellent Japanese symphony orchestras and I gave my all until—in the Philippines—I came a cropper over mangoes. I must say here that mangoes are (or were) my favorite fruit. I love that juicy spurt, the delectable orange-peach-banana flavor, and the texture. I had eaten bushels of mangoes, one after the other, in South America. I repeated the process in the Far East. Suddenly one morning I found myself puffing up as if I were an inflating balloon. It became so bad that my eyes were swollen shut. It was an education in pain to put on a dress—even when it would fit me. One doctor said it was caused by the chemical atabrin used to fight malaria; the others had no idea. Bill and I never really did find out until months later. It was that I was allergic to Asian mangoes—but not to South American ones. This, I think, enters the sweepstakes as the queerest allergy of all time.

I had the appearance of a poisoned pup for weeks. This was made all the more embarrassing by my schedules of concerts. The trip, now coming under the aegis of the American State Department, assumed the aspect of a pouter-pigeon triumphal march. At every stop we were met by the officials of the embassy or the consulate. They would bring long lists of things to do and not to do—and I honestly tried to cooperate as long as protocol did not get in the way of the music. This occasionally happened—as in the case of Singapore.

We arrived there after my single concert in Manila and two in the highly hoity-toity—but delightful—atmosphere of Hong Kong.

I am sure that there will always be an England in Hong Kong long after the original England has vanished. The ceremony, long-tailed coats, and society discipline were marvelous to see: evening dress and white tie, escorts, timetables, limousines, yachts, charts of table seatings, solemn processions hither and yon, and stiff upper lips scattered all over the place. I skidded on a few of the latter, as I shall relate, but I regained my balance.

The man who skidded with me was Malcolm MacDonald, the Commissioner General in Southeast Asia. Get this protocol: he ranked the governor of Singapore, and so as not to embarrass the latter, MacDonald lived outside the city. He had a real fairy palace, one built by a sultan friend, that with its airy minarets, pools, marbles, and landscaping was a dream of real estate in the midst of the jungles of Johore. We were invited out there for lunch. Both Bill and I strenuously objected. We were tired, in that dreadful heat and humidity, of dressing up to the ears and then sweating it off. There seemed to be no real comfort to be had in all the British Commonwealth.

Nevertheless, Bill persuaded me that in the interest of international amity I should appear. We rode the thirty-odd miles out into the jungle and turned into the spectacular drive. Standing there was a big man in white pants and white open-collared shirt. "Boy, I bet he'll get fired when the boss sees him!" I ejaculated.

Our car came to a stop. The casual bystander strolled up and introduced himself as Mal MacDonald. He looked at Bill being garroted by his tie and suggested: "Why don't you take that thing off?" From that time on we were fast friends. We had a fine, leisurely lunch, inspected our host's remarkable collection of oriental ceramics, and, in general, got along like crazy. At the end of the afternoon, MacDonald mentioned that he was coming to my concert in Singapore the next evening. He added thoughtfully: "Isn't this heat bloody awful?"

"Yes," I said. MacDonald grinned at me. "Isn't it awful to see men sopping wet in stiff collars and dinner jackets?" he asked.

"Yes," I said.

MacDonald went on: "Would you mind terribly if I cause a fuss?"

"No," I said.

"I'll just turn up in a white shirt and a cummerbund. Pants, of course."

That was how it happened that the horrified official report on the conduct of MacDonald was heard round the world. It made front pages in the most obscure towns in the most out-of-the-way nations. England and the United States especially reveled in it, though in different ways. It seemed that the most widely known habit of the English was their pukka psychosis. MacDonald had dealt it a dreadful blow. When he turned up at the concert—ranking the others as he did—there was a general shucking off of coats and putting on of black looks. If you have ever seen a kind of glittering coating over a simmering boil when you make jelly, that is the way it was that evening. Four days later, when Bill and I flew out of Singapore, the newspapers were still carrying headlines about it, highly indignant ones. Editorials and letters bawled MacDonald out in purple prose. One called his coatlessness a "shameful display before a great woman," and another demanded hotly, "What is to become of the British Empire if this keeps on?" I suppose the ordinary Englishman feels really naked on such occasions. Bill and I, however, were highly amused by it and applauded MacDonald's calm reply that he had asked my permission beforehand.

From thence to Bangkok, where we bounced around the city in a jeep and had our first respite from singing. On to Calcutta, where I caught a handsome cold and puffed up once more. I was supposed to sing, but I was flat on my back in bed. I did manage to rise for a concert in New Delhi, however, and met with the approval and earnest attention of the daughter of Pandit Nehru.

That was the last concert of our trip. We had been asked to extend our tour this far as a favor to our country, the State Department in India being kind enough to cable Washington that our appearances constituted "the best kind of public relations." From then on I kept my mouth shut and my eyes open. We visited the lovely Vale of Kashmir, came back to Bombay and Basra and Dhahran in Saudi Arabia, then to Istanbul. I think, next to New York, this is my favorite city of all time. I am overwhelmed by its history, its gilding, its mysterious inscriptions, its flood of life and its awareness, the new against the old, the vast extent of its past and the glimpses of its future. To live in Istanbul, even for a little time, is to have a whole advanced course in history pass before your eyes. It is impossible to see it without being fascinated. I was as charmed by it as a rabbit by a cobra. I said to Bill: "I want to stay here. I'm tired of traveling. I don't even want to move another inch."

But we had to leave, and we spent a few weeks in Rome and Paris. We had gone so far around the bulge of the world that we felt we might as well go all the way. We shot up north to Copenhagen and Stockholm, taking a long and majestic trip through the famous fjords. This was Wagner country, the land of the Scandinavian gods. I could see for myself where the inspiration for the Ring operas had come. I could understand, deeply, for the first time, the tradition and the legends and the frozen emotions that when melted came rolling down in such avalanches of chords. All that country was music to me. From there, of course, any stopover would have been anticlimax. We flew to London and on to New York and home to California.

19

The Last of the Met

PRESUMING that I was pooped when Bill and I checked into California from our first trip around the world, I thought I would never again stir out of the confines of oranges, smog, and sunshine. You may imagine my surprise, then, when my old thirst for travel gripped me by the throat. Bill and I set off on our circumnavigations once more. Nor did we go in any direction other than the one we had already taken. Like the man who used to hit himself on the head with the hammer because it felt so good when he stopped, we were daffy with the travel bug.

Galli-Curci had been the first coloratura soprano to tour around the world; I suppose I was the first dramatic soprano to do it—twice. But this record was not our prime objective. Bill and I had missed a stop we should have made before: the battlefields of Korea.

Bill and I left New York December 1, 1952. I was to make fifty-three appearances on the stages of a dozen countries. I was to sing thirty times in a jam-packed week's tour of Korea, nearly three fifths of my total appearances, before I came back home in February 1953. I can truthfully say still, as I said then, that those thirty were one of the highlights of my entire career as a singer.

The thirty were given in five days—the heaviest and most delightful schedule of singing I had ever had. In one theater I automatically turned around to locate a draft that was blowing across my chest, as I generally did in the Metropolitan. I found that in my particular "concert hall" the roof was gone. I was actually singing under the stars and had forgotten all about it. I always tried to wear the standard recital costume, an off-the-shoulder evening gown. I did this because I felt that although I was no movie star, the boys there would like it better. They seemed to. They whistled and cheered and laughed until the glow that I felt more than compensated for the cold of those nights. I saw one of the soldiers near the platform whistling his teeth out. I stepped down and said: "I had a kid brother who could whistle like you. I've been trying ever since to whistle that way." I tried it, there on the platform, two fingers and my front teeth. The audience broke up and he gave up. His buddies pulled his hat down over his eyes and slapped him on the back until he lost his breath. I guess he never knew that I ranked him.

While visiting in the area I had a card with my fingerprints, and under the line *Assimilated Grade, Rate of Rank,* the words: "Major through Colonel." Whatever this may have meant, very few people in Korea called me anything but "General."

I tried to give as many of my recitals as I could on Christmas Day to provide them with a home feeling, some sort of contact with what they dreamed of. I even got a Christmas present myself. It was a silver medal ordered struck for me by General James A. Van Fleet, then head of the Far East Command. On one side it read "Far East Command" with a headquarters flag; on the other it had an inscription: "In appreciation for contributing to the entertainment of our United Nations Armed Forces Personnel in Korea." Flying between the little towns of Korea, I rode in a plane equipped with the aluminum bucket seats that accommodated perhaps one tenth of my rear end. They were highly uncomfortable but not so much so as the gigantic parachute harness I wore. When they buckled it on I asked what it was for. They told me: "Well, you know there might be a little trouble." "A little trouble?" I said. "What do I do then?" They said, "Don't you worry, honey. We'll be back to let you know." Luckily for me, nothing happened. I am sure that that parachute never would have held me, going down to the ground through that thin air.

I sang and visited everywhere I could. Sometimes I could not quite twist a note around the lump in my throat—as in the case of the hospital ships at Inchon. There were helicopters, loaded with wounded, arriving almost every five minutes. In the wards I tailored my songs to what they asked for. Once in a while I said no more than a few words and tiptoed out. I sang for the Korean soldiers; for a reception of the Van Fleets; for Syngman Rhee at the Korean presidential palace. Rhee gave me a three-foot-high Korean doll, a fabulously dressed and ancient ritual toy. I lunched with the majors and brigadier generals of the Air Force who were almost too young to shave—who used to say "Pardon me" and disappear for about forty minutes, coming back in to sit down and talk. I inquired about these casual, repeated disappearances—where some did not return. I was told that they had just hopped into a jet and made a reconnaissance trip up to the Yalu River! Seoul, Pusan, Taegu—then back to Tokyo where I had already done five concerts. Bill and I spent some time there and saw the roses we had planted in full bloom. We got a new Spanish accompanist who had taught at the University of Manila. I sang in the Philippines and then we took off for another visit to Hong Kong and on to Macao.

At the latter spot, the local headman paid all our expenses—about six thousand dollars—for me to sing at his seventeenth-century, Portuguese-built private theater. We had a very formal lunch. I discovered he had built a special recording booth for me to sing a special song. Bill investigated this and came back with his eyes popping. "He's no better than a billionaire racketeer," he said. "What's worse, he's an amateur composer. It's *his* song he wants you to sing!" I canceled it from the program and went on to the recital. We discovered that the little dictator of Macao was so enraged by my refusal that he stayed home from the concert.

We went back to Hong Kong, then flew straight to Karachi, in Pakistan. Having arrived, we were immediately confronted with the usual protocol procedure. Bill and I, for the first time, rebelled. He told the American consul that I could not attend his reception because I was ill. Our excuse was taken, we gleefully stripped down to as few clothes as possible, and went down into the cool garden. We wanted to enjoy an enormous lunch together with our first iced beer in days.

In the midst of our feasting Bill wailed: "Oh, my God!" I looked where he indicated. I saw a couple of members of the American consulate making their way toward our table. Bill seized all the food and pulled it in front of him—including four bottles of beer. He grinned inanely at our visitors. "I have to eat for two, you know," he said, "now that Helen is ill."

"It's a pity," said one of the representatives of our country sternly, "that she is ill."

"I do feel wretched," I said.

"Perhaps your husband can come," he said to me. "It's a Pakistani custom." I rejoiced to find such an easy way out. "Of course!" I cried, and slapped Bill on the back. "You go ahead and tell them everything about me! Sing if they can stand it!"

Bill groaned and got to his feet. I was afraid to look him in the face. I was already pulling the beer back toward me. I heard afterward, despite his bitter reproaches, that he had done an excellent job representing me and my country.

A return visit to Istanbul—which is not at all like St. Louis but just as precious—and over to Athens (where I must confess the cultural atmosphere did not impress me; I would have been a Persian, not a Greek in bygone ages), and a few weeks in Rome.

After that we went north to Amsterdam, Oslo, Stockholm, and Helsinki. I was supposed to sing in each city but in the last two a virus rained me out. I managed to get up in time to hit London and enjoy a technical victory over the advice of Cooney long ago.

Remember it was the first time in my life—at the age of fifty— that I had sung in Europe, traditionally the catbird seat of culture. Cooney had warned me how finicky the people were in London. He had pointed out to me that I could never sing there unless a whole orchestra went along. "Wagner will not be accepted just with a piano," he declared.

"Why not?" I demanded.

"Because it won't," he persisted. "It's not good musical taste. You must sing songs, lieder, not opera, with the piano."

"I've broken precedent before," I said doggedly, "and I'll do it again."

"Not in London you won't," Cooney said tranquilly. "They won't stand for it."

I guess it was his urbane firmness that made me pigheadedly decide to do what I wanted. "I'm going to be myself in London," I said. I sang my operatic medley as scheduled and waited for the boos and hisses. To my gratification, there was the tremendous sound of applause. They gave me an ovation and tossed flowers. I had won my bet. I picked up my psychological nickels and walked out. Cooney, for one of the very few times in his career, was wrong. The impresario later wanted me to do two more concerts of all-Wagner simply with the piano.

Other problems, less picturesque but more complex, were coming up to have their turn at bat in our lives. They reminded me of an attitude I had taken long ago and which now had to be reaffirmed. Once, in the days when I commenced training my voice in New York, I was interviewed by a teacher who had some personal theories on sound. "I will tell you how to focus your voice," she said. "Think of it as a train going through a tunnel."

"Uh-huh," I said. "What about the voice inside your throat?"

"Think of that as smoke coming out of a chimney," she said. "I wish you would sit down at the piano and show me how to make my voice rise like smoke and come out like a train going through a tunnel," I said. She never did. I never had her as a teacher. But if I felt advice was sincere and had its source in the heart, I usually took it. Among my most treasured memories is the early counsel given me by that gorgeous singer Madame Schumann-Heink. She heard me sing in my teens and I imagine what she told me must have influenced me more than I thought. Her advice was: "Promise me you will stay near your mother and your home for a few years more." Another occasion of this sort came the night I was singing on an NBC program. I thought I was doing too much, a kind of all-Traubel affair. I wanted to give some of the songs to other artists. But it was Arturo Toscanini who came to me and said, "I, Arturo Toscanini, beg you to please sing the whole program for me." So I sang that time for him alone on his "advice."

I have never had any interest in kidding myself or being kidded by others. It was this habit of a lifetime that led me to choose to step into another and, for me, more dramatic and interesting role. I did not have to pretend any longer that I was a love-lorn Irish or German princess or an Italian waif or an American sweetheart—I could be myself. Years before the final judgments had been pronounced on my equipment. Three years earlier one critic had expressed himself about me: "Her voice is still without a peer among its kind, if a shade less peerless than it was in her absolute prime." I was never sure when I was passing my prime, or in it, or coming back to it. But I did know that in 1951 the grand-opera commentators had been appalled that my contract with the Met had been "delayed." I was enough of a fixture for the staid editorial columns of the *Musical Courier* to say that I "was singing beautifully—her young Brünnhilde was ecstatic and tender; the *Götterdämmerung* Brünnhilde was regally glorious." I had seen Harry T. Burleigh, the famous little gray-haired composer, in the wings listening to me singing his versions of "Deep River" and "Swing Low, Sweet Chariot." I had come off the stage to hear him say in a trembling tone with tears on his cheeks: "Helen sings spirtuals as well as anyone I have ever heard—more than that, better." The one to whom he was speaking was no other than that great singer, Marian Anderson.

These were extraordinary compliments. But in any career, in any art, one is suddenly aware of a plateau, a spot in life where everything is flat and dull without warning. The only remedy is to start climbing again, to rise above oneself into the rarefied air above. That was what happened to me only a decade after I had joined the Met as a soloist, only shortly after I had been acclaimed as the world's leading Wagnerian soprano. That may seem a long time to some, to be stuck on one high note, but it is short in the Met, where the singing and the posturing seem to go on forever.

I felt that somehow I was missing the heart of music itself. I was in too strange an atmosphere. I kept thinking of the informal song fests we had enjoyed at home in St. Louis; of the vocal jam sessions in New York and Korea; of the receptions in Tokyo, in India, London, and a hundred other spots. Perhaps my trips around the world had put a magic salve on my eyes: they seemed to be opened for the first time. There was, I believed, an immense audience that waited patiently for some kind of music outside the specialized circle of opera lovers.

I had become cursed—or blessed—with a double nature. I do not mean that I am schizophrenic; far from it. The life I live with Bill is so normal that when I make hot potato salad the smell of it alone puts three pounds on him. I mean that my artistic and personal life seemed to be divorced. I recall that one critic, talking about my first appearance as Kundry, said: "Madame Traubel was as distant and unapproachable as the statue on top of Grant's Tomb." This wounded me. Nothing could be more untrue about me in my own life: I try to hold myself back from nothing that is genuinely friendly, warm, and interesting. The realization of the fact that my public appearances might overtake my private life—that such adjectives as "majestic" and "regal" and "aloof" were becoming alarmingly frequent in my reviews—was forcing me to seek out another road for expression in music. I had always been taught in St. Louis to include my audience with my presentation; at the Met, I was asked to sing as if the audience did not exist. It seemed an impossible situation.

Perhaps I should have taken warning from what had happened four years before. I like jokes, practical and otherwise. In 1949 Bill and I had a lot of fun kidding in public about a fifty-five-hundred-word novelette, "The Ptomaine Canary," which in turn kidded the mystery-writing business. I had announced a second called "The Post-Mortem of Mortimer Post." I said I would bind twenty-five copies of the first in limp leather for friends. I wrote my own reviews for the volume, saying that *Pravda* would call it "upper-class propaganda." The story itself (on which I had what you might call professional help) concerned a party when Bill invited all the top mystery writers to our house and a trained canary knocked them cold. My detective was named Sam Quentin. The heroine was Brünnhilde Wagner. I claimed I wrote the end first and then wrote the beginning later. Bill told one reporter: "What really happened to Helen is that she used to be able to guess who done it early in the book. She hasn't been such a smarty pants lately and she wrote this one so she could figure out what happened before she read it."

I simply felt that the detective world was getting too complicated for my tastes. I do not care for murders by rare poisons or mysterious hypodermics. I like plain old guns and clubs and lots of gore. I like characters who just kill because they like it, not because of a psychological mixup. So I wrote my own, just like a cowboy rolls his own. The "Metropolitan Opera Murders" was a much more prosaic book—which is probably why it sold not nearly so well as "Ptomaine" which was syndicated in two hundred newspapers and went over quite well.

This kind of extravagant practical joke—which really paid off—could have been a warning to me that I was heading in a different direction. I was punchy with too much opera singing. This literary spoofing was one way of relieving my inner tensions.

Other symptoms were evident. A never-reproduced record of mine had a roar in my voice in the midst of a Wagner high point: "Get that goddamned fly away from the microphone!" My interest in baseball—I later sold my stock to Bill Veeck, that too-canny manager—had boomeranged into editorials all across the country. I had been voted the "woman of the year in music" for a couple of times by the Associated Press and had not felt too much elation; the tag of being the "greatest singer, male or female, in the world today" did not cause me a case of goose pimples. It did not rouse me when I heard that Margaret Truman had done nearly seventy concerts at fifteen hundred dollars a throw and was being offered radio and TV contracts. In short, to me the world was a state of mild ennui—or as near to it as I could get temperamentally. It is only a newspaper canard that the night of my Metropolitan debut I had spent the time just before curtain call sitting in my dressing room happily playing the unique records of that pianist Alec Templeton—the favorite being a burlesque called "Through Wagner's Ring Cycle in Three Minutes"—and guffawing about it. I did do this in my dressing room from time to time, certainly, but it came at this period.

It occurred to me repeatedly that I had little in common with the stuffy side. I realized that my career as a singer reached its zenith for me personally on some of those first appearances as a girl when I literally soared out atop the orchestra and felt like yelling at the top of my voice: "Bring on another hundred musicians! We're marching through!" I recalled that the people I liked best were those musical iconoclasts such as Sir Thomas

Beecham who used to grunt and squall and march up and down pulling up his pants while I was singing. (I had a special pair of red suspenders made for him.) His facial contortions, his little beard wagging up and down, nearly made me burst with laughter more than once during the solemn performances which he conducted.

I remembered the time I sang on the same radio program with John McCormack, the fabled Irish tenor. When I had breathlessly listened to him, I went on and did my own stint. When I came off, he was holding his head with an expression I could not analyze. I thought: "Murder, what have I done now?" After my bows, I returned to the wings and he seized me. "What did you say your name was, my dear? How did you ever get a voice like that in your throat? I can't believe what I hear, it's not possible." But both Beecham and McCormack were looked down upon by many of the highbrow music lovers.

Maybe my thoughts were drifting back to the *gemütlich* spirit of the old German *bierstubes* and the joy they produced in their patrons. Perhaps I was tired of the old routines. I have no full explanation of what firmed up my final decision but I can guess at one.

I brought back home with me from Korea a secret chore. I started to telephone personally the hundreds of wives and mothers of the servicemen I had met on that battleground. They were scattered from one end of the country to the other. It took months and a few concert tours before I accomplished my objective. Now I realize that a selfish reason stirred me to do it. This was never publicized, but I was testing myself to see if getting close to people everywhere was what I wanted. It was precisely what I wanted.

I decided to accept an offer to sing at the Chez Paree, a very well-known night club in Chicago. This precipitated another storm which I had not anticipated. After my appearance there—which lasted three weeks—I received a curious letter from Bing.

He declared that to him my *doppelgänging* of popular singing and operatic singing did not seem "to mix very well. Perhaps you would prefer to give the Metropolitan a 'miss' for a year or so until you may possibly feel you want again to change back to the more serious aspects of your art." He then added in an abrupt postscript: "I would definitely consider it highly undesirable for any night club publicity to appear before, during, or immediately after your work at the Metropolitan. May I have your assurance on that point?"

To this I retorted: "To assert that art can be found at the Metropolitan Opera House but not in a night club is rank snobbery that underrates both the taste of the American public and the talents of its composers." I added that I loved the songs of George Gershwin, W. C. Handy, Cole Porter, Jerome Kern, Irving Berlin, Richard Rodgers, and many others. I was glad to be able to sing them. I went on: "Since I cannot sing them at the Metropolitan, I am singing them at night clubs. I am happy to have found that night-club audiences are enthusiastically accepting me on their own terms." I added: "Artistic dignity is not a matter of where one sings. It is not the environment that categorizes the performance. The artist of integrity who refuses to compromise his standard is able to endure whatever place he appears in with his own dignity." I returned the signed Met contract that they had previously sent me—unsigned by me. The upshot of all this, of course, was that I left the Metropolitan Opera permanently. I have not been back since my final letter to Bing.

Bing again accused me of "poor taste" in making public his request. "If she doesn't want to sing with us, it is just too bad," he said. He defended his position by saying he was within his rights to suggest that I refrain from night-club appearances while singing at the Met. "I don't feel that opera and folk music mix," he declared.

I felt then—and now—that Skinny should have shinnied on his own side. He had no idea who he was wrestling with: I was the gal who used to dry sheets in our little New York apartment that had no outside windows. Wash them in the tub, wring them out by sheer muscle, and hang them up to the electric-light fixtures. I was the gal who had sung and listened and sung and listened and sung and listened to myself until the sound of my own voice nearly drove me nuts. I was tough enough to know what I had and where I should go and what I should do. I had learned as a child that the window dressing was not enough to do a job.

One of my earliest ambitions, in addition to singing, was to be a harpist. I had seen the graceful gestures of the harpist in an orchestra recital with my family. I was smitten with the ambition to be "just like that." My family told me that if I went to a party I probably would not be able to play. I demanded why. They explained I would have to say, "I didn't bring my harp," whereas I would always have my voice handy. I quit that ambition in a hurry. Ever since I felt I could handle myself anywhere I could take my voice.

One great gamble *was* taken by Bill and myself. We were never sure just what the night-club people wanted: Met prestige, cheesecake, or myself. After a few appearances—about three years later—we were confirmed in our belief that I was the salable article, a desirable popular performer in my own right. As I remarked at lunch one day to Elsa Maxwell, another rather fully developed woman, I may look like a bag of meal when I am well fed and contented but I would rather accept that and be able to sing. The mirror is always a psychological hazard to women. I have long ago learned to ignore it as far as my figure is concerned. When I put on the final touches as Brünnhilde and prepared to dash out for my barbecuing in the magic fire in the last act of *Die Walküre,* I never looked back at myself.

The first and biggest night-club problem—one which melted away—was to take the hurdle of public acceptance as an all-American phenomenon. More than once people have taken me for a foreign-born and -trained singer even after the long years of publicity. I recall that in Seattle a woman told Bill in surprise: "Why, your wife speaks almost perfect English! How long has she been in this country?" To which Bill replied: "All her life. And if I told you how long that is, she would shoot me first and divorce me later." The second—which was also quickly dissipated —was that people used to tell me that singing in night clubs was "unhealthy." Bing talked about singing in smoke-filled rooms being bad for the voice. My answer to that got to be that most of the clubs in which I performed were air-conditioned and in much better odor than the Met itself.

One of the cartoons a national magazine ran soon after gave me more chuckles—and still does—than anything I had seen for a long time. It showed an opera performance with the whole cast, as usual, rigged up in their absurd Wagnerian costumes. Front and center in the picture was a huge piano, even the accompanist being in costume. Lying down on it was this big fat gal, the star—I couldn't imagine who she might be—also in costume. Her mouth was twisted all out of shape. The caption below read: "They say she sang in too many night clubs!"

20

Night Clubs, Movies, Television

I OPENED my unheard-of (and unheard) night-club career at the Chez Paree in Chicago in September 1953. It was a brave new field. I had no idea of what it might mean to my future. No other opera star, certainly never one who had been called "queen at the Met" for more than a decade, had ever done such a thing. My friends called it everything from "undignified" to "disgusting." I just thought it was fun.

I had never thought of myself as this kind of entertainer. Subconsciously, I must have wanted it. I had had a taste of what it was. In 1949 my sponsors on the radio had persuaded me to devote part of my broadcasts to telecasts. In those days the camera work was highly amateurish. When I saw myself I shrieked in horror. There are some singers who look better when the camera fattens them up. I am not one of them, and there is no bigger bore than to keep seeing the tonsils of a singer in depth. Television left nothing to the imagination. I thought it stripped me naked. I swore never to do it again.

A year later, as so often happens, other leaven started working. One of Jimmy Durante's pals had heard me laughing on a Duffy's Tavern broadcast with Ed Gardner. He spotted me for future reference. He went to his boss, perhaps one of the greatest entertainers America has ever produced, with his overwhelming humor, his simple magnificent humanity. Durante, I understand, was as frightened and baffled by the proposition as I was. "Sure, I know she can sing," he said. "What I wanna know, can she strut? Everybody around me hasta strut!"

When I heard of this, it piqued my curiosity. I watched the program to find out what a strut was. I practiced it in private in my bedroom. I guess Durante was practicing his role of Siegfried while I was growling the blues. We were finally brought together and eyed each other with mutual suspicion. Finally Durante went over to the piano and commenced to play and sing. I followed him. We worked out a hilarious act which resulted in that first historic telecast late in 1950. It was followed by half-a-dozen more appearances with Jimmy.

Durante, of course, used to break me up as much as he did the audience. The first time I strode on in full Brünnhilde armor he gasped: "Holy smoke, she's been drafted!" His efforts to pin a corsage somewhere on my amply defended person (ending up with tacking it onto my skirt) sent me into hysterics. I think my laugh broke him up more than a little, too. Altogether, it was a highly satisfying combination. The show was deemed the top of the season despite the sniffs of my more rarefied friends. "Theatrically speaking," said one critic, "I hope Traubel and Durante team up for life."

After the first Durante show, fan mail came in bags. Thousands of letters fluttered down and few mentioned my voice. They said I was a wonderful girl, that I had brought them happiness, they still chuckled over my appearance (in the burlesque Walküre episode), and most of them said something like "we love to see you and hear you laugh."

This kind of sentiment was a revelation to me. I was being appreciated for myself for almost the first time. Others had cared for me because of my voice, which I had always felt as a treasure given to me to take care of and develop. But never before had I felt this vast affection for me alone and the hell with my voice.

It was a wonderful feeling. I secretly determined to do all I could to keep it. There seemed to be no way to further it except by spot appearances on TV programs. I had long ago become bored with radio and its invisible audience. I was getting top fees of five thousand dollars and more for my concert appearances. I was approaching a surfeit at the Met. What new horizons were left to me, it seemed, depended almost entirely on my appeal to this huge audience that so far had been outside my knowledge.

So when Durante came back to our house one day and stammered a request for me to appear at a Las Vegas night club, I was dumfounded. "What would I do?" I said. Durante scowled. "Ya do the same t'ing ya done wit' me!" he cried. He said he had been asked by some of his friends there to get me to appear. "Da boys t'ink you're sensational!" he told me.

His opinion gave me a good deal of thought. There were other facts, as well. Within a month I had received offers to appear in various ways that would have netted me about half a million dollars in the next year. I had already been accused of sniffing out opportunities for cashing in, insinuations which, under the tax structure that Bill and I already enjoyed, were totally silly. It did mean that I was wanted, even needed, to sing and entertain in other spots.

I had to turn down Las Vegas. I felt I was not ready to face the critical appraisals of the club habitués after they had seen so many other excellent acts. I thought I might be willing to accept a three-week stint at the Chez Paree, a place my agents cunningly described as "a little old night club in Chicago." As I found out afterward, the Chez and the Copacabana in New York were actually the zenith for any night-club act.

I blandly went on to toss myself to the wolves at ringside. I put together a program of Viennese music, semi-classical selections, operatic medleys, and modern tunes. I was fortunate enough to secure the services of a couple of superb young writers, Lawrence and Lee, later to become famous in their own right for a play called "Inherit the Wind" and the musical adaptation of the classic *Auntie Mame,* to scribble chatter for me. They coined what seemed to my humor to be a deathless line to introduce the "St. Louis Blues": "Now I will sing for you a folk ballad made famous by the peasants of my native village." They refused any pay for their work, so I sneaked them a couple of good wrist watches, suitably engraved. As I recall, the musical arrangements were worked out on the plane en route to Chicago. The arranger was still scribbling in our suite as we arrived.

I appeared, and was a success, much to my relief. "It's always the same when Helen appears," said a friend to Bill after opening night. "Always the same?" demanded Bill, bristling. "Yes," sighed the other, "always cataclysmic."

The best compliment I received after the opening was a very serious request from one of the four bosses who owned the Chez Paree. As a backer of that swank, rococo place, he came up to me, a big, lowering man, and growled: "Any time anybody bothers you anywhere in the States, you tell me."

After our engagement at the Chez we went on to New York. There I had my head-on collision with Bing and then went down to Washington. We had an amazing press conference that looked as if I were a spy come to assassinate the President. They had TV and newsreel cameras, reporters and critics, editors and leg women—I had never seen such a crowd. They backed me into a corner in my suite where Bill was patiently trying to listen to the World Series. Reporters kept pushing their fingers in my face and hollering: "You did it for money!" And I'd holler back: "What else?" It got to be a joke after a while to everyone but Bill.

I was the object of some pointed questioning by the music critics of that city. Among them was Paul Hume of the Washington *Post* who became famous as the first newspaperman to be personally threatened by a president of the United States. Hume wanted to know if I really thought the "St. Louis Blues" was as good music as Wagner. I said: "Sure, W. C. Handy is just as good—in his own field." The quizzing about taking money for singing continued as if I had betrayed my country. "No, I didn't," I said, "but if I did, would it be such a terrible tragedy?"

"Wasn't it really the idea of big money coming in?" inquired another reporter.

"No," I said. "It was really that I feel closer to my audience on a cabaret floor than I do on the Met stage."

There it rested. For the record, I must add that I have never regretted the decision. I should have taken the step much earlier. I cannot agree that singing is sacred to any place or any persons. It is a gift to as many as will accept it.

My roasting by the newspapermen, all in the spirit of good dirty digs, kept us from hearing the rest of the World Series. The fact that I would get paid—actually *get* good money—for appearing in night clubs seemed a crime to the long hairs. The argument swept across the country. The involuntary publicity was remarkable. I was booked for as many more night-club appearances as I could accept. Riding on the wave of highbrow versus lowbrow, I was able to coast quite a way into the beach of public favor. I went on to appear in such places as Las Vegas, Cuba, New York, Chicago, Dallas, Florida, Hollywood—at prices ranging from five thousand dollars up to twenty-five thousand dollars a week. My last appearance, as a matter of fact, was in September 1958. I intend to hit the road again whenever the inclination strikes me.

There is something about meeting people face to face, in feeling the elation of giving them what they want, watching their faces as they take it in, which has no equal in my experience. I never got used to the microphone—that little ball of metal that keeps coming between me and those outside the spotlight. I tried to disregard it. If I had let out my voice full against the electronic equipment, I probably would have blown a fuse. I used to retreat and almost whisper songs to the people. It reminded me of what it must have been in the days of the gold rush when the finest entertainers in the world had a habit of rushing West in order to spread their wares for an entirely new audience. It was up to me, an interloper, to get and hold their attention in their own milieu. I am happy to say that most of the time I did it.

A generous appraisal of my night-club appearance at the New York Copacabana, as famous and as top of the heap as the Met itself in its own field, was written by music critic Mary Craig:

"The pleasant, harmless comedian meandered through the joke book; the long line of Copacabana beauties undulated off the floor to brisk music; and the ringside observers tensed for Traubel to make her descent from Valhalla to the haunts of the celebrants of night hours and bright lights. Heaven alone knows what the cash customers expected. Possibly a leaping entrance with a ringing 'Hi yo to ho,' or a bemused, draped figure clutching the fatal cup of Isolde (to clink with the martinis on her left), or perchance a wild rider on Grane to shiver the champagne glasses.

"Then she entered—lately first Valkyr, beloved of the All-father and first lady of opera's German Wing, moving out of Nordic gloom and grandeur into the carrousel of midnight gaiety. To the suddenly unleashed storm of greeting stately Traubel paced sedately, but with a little lilt in her step; once secure in the niche of the piano, her glorious voice silenced the chatterers, the revelers, the bibulous curiosity peerers, and the general comment.

"Her night-club program was rather a strange one. She sang ditties from operetta, unimportant songs just off the Hit Parade (the ones we are acclimated to hearing gasped, growled, and wailed in voices evidently suffering from excruciating injuries), and with her cathedral-organ tones she made each and every one sound like a rare gem. She dipped into opera, permissibly with 'Un Bel Di' and 'Ritorna Vincitor,' but one feels that the diva was pleasing herself even more than catering to the tastes of her rapt audience when she ventured into the 'Toreador Song' and 'Vesti la Giubba.' (All sopranos want to sing the tenor and/or baritone airs!) Nevertheless, the listeners took it eagerly and yelled for more. When the soprano's clarion tones rang the chandeliers in 'an ancient folk tune that peasants in my little home village love to sing,' and it turned out to be the 'St. Louis Blues' (as Handy never dreamed of hearing it), with orchestra brass blaring and drums going wild, she took over not only the Copacabana but the entire night-club circuit. She did a lot of other numbers—'No Other Love,' the good-humored Jimmy Durante piano selection, and at the end an eerie, whispered singing of Brahms' 'Lullaby' which had the customers crying large, copious tears, sobbing into their teacups."

As a Metropolitan Opera star, one news account reported, I had been "knocking off some two hundred fifty thousand a year before taxes. In the year after she left the Met, according to educated guesses, she doubled her income." Of one of my first night-club "concerts," in 1954 in New York, one of the night-club critics said: "Traubel is neither a moppet nor a streamlined sylph, but a portly female who doesn't list her age in *Who's Who*. She is solidly constructed along super-dreadnought lines as befits a top-ranking diva. But when she gets out on the floor recently graced by Martin and Lewis, Durante, and Joe E. Lewis, she puts on a supper club act that is wonderful and thrilling and every super adjective in Roget's *Thesaurus*. Half the customers have tears in their eyes— from happiness.

"Now wait a minute, don't get me wrong. I don't pretend to be a music critic (thank heaven). I suppose any third-rate opera thrush with a big voice could sing well enough to send me into a pickle-factory aisle, especially after a few glasses of bubbles. But Traubel sells not only a divine voice, but plenty of show-business savvy and enough good humor and wisecracks to put her into the top rank of comics if she ever loses her larynx."

Early in 1954 a review in *The New Yorker* began this way:
"Having startled myself several times in a row by repeating the
simple but somewhat preposterous sentence, 'Helen Traubel is at
the Copacabana' to myself, I now find myself able to confront the
situation squarely. Miss Traubel then, having forsaken the Wagner crowd at the Met—for the season at least—in favor of night-
club audiences, can presently be discovered singing indiscreetly
unbending in the midst of the rigid palms and . . . young ladies at
the—yes, the Copacabana. She is nothing short of wonderful.
Gracefully sweeping onto the floor in a simple black velvet gown,
this delightful woman proceeded to captivate everyone in the
room. Singing with a beauty of tone and artistry not often encountered in opera houses let alone night clubs, Miss Traubel—
she used a microphone by the way—gave the customers an
enormously varied program."

I got so I respected the critics of the entertainment world more
than I did those of the upper crust. I can easily illustrate what I
mean when I say that I could respect the critics of night clubs and
TV. At least they talked their own lingo and threw their own
conclusions. They had some unanimity on what they saw. I never
expected to be praised all over the place on an opera performance
but I was surprised at the remarkable splits that sometimes came
about. One review, in the *Herald Tribune* for December 2, 1950,
went as follows: "As Isolde, Madame Traubel was in poor form.
More and more the higher passages of the music of the role are
overtaxing her resources. It is not only that she is forced to omit
the topmost tones; but even her attempts at the B's of the first-act
narrative and the love duet were in vain and the upper part of her
soprano voice sounded almost consistently strident. There were
some expressively sung passages in the middle register; but her
lower tones were as often as not barely audible and much of her
singing was wobbly." Wow! I might just as well have stayed home
that night and sent a bent tin whistle to appear in my place.

In a chastened mood, I turned to the New York *Times* for the same date. It read: "Miss Traubel has sung Isolde here many times before but it may be doubted that she has ever done so with more musicianship and depth. There was no forcing. She had no need to force. She seemed to have acquired a new mastery of nuance. Her soft singing was remarkable in quality, floating effortlessly over an orchestra that Mr. Reiner held in firm control. And in climactic moments her voice had a stirring impact."

Well, in the famous baseball phrase, who remains on first? I wish I knew. The point is, of course, that music is what the hearer-critic makes it—the singer has to decide her standards for herself. And in night clubs I did just that.

A long-standing beef of mine has been that culture does not have the *décor* and comfort of a night club. All culture has is hard seats. I know it may be to keep some awake. I have seen old ladies knitting at my concerts, but I have always tried to keep the manager from stopping them. It is wrong to make good music so hard on the posterior. If I can't stop the knitting in concerts or the chatter in the clubs by my singing I am sure the manager will not be able to do it simply by talking to the culprits.

There were a couple of intervals between 1953 and 1958, however, when I did not appear on the road. The first was when I quit in September 1955 to rehearse for the Rodgers and Hammerstein musical, *Pipedream,* a show that ran until July 1956. The second was a break of three and a half months in the summer of 1957. Bill and I broke loose for a vacation in London, Monte Carlo, and Paris—with me singing only once and that at a charity fete. The third time was in 1954. I spent twelve weeks making a movie for Metro-Goldwyn-Mayer.

I was very happy to do that movie. I had had offers before—none of them very elegant, and not in sufficient quantity to say that I had been besieged—but this one appealed to me. I knew that movies could do wonders with music—*Red Shoes,* for example, the English ballet picture, was good enough for me so that I sat through it nine times. *Deep in My Heart* started mainly because Roger Edens, one of the gifted movie musical producers in Hollywood, had heard me in opera and had seen me in night clubs. He had long ago suggested that I would be ideal for a special role on the screen. I was as happy to have his opinion as I was surprised. I think it was 1948 when the first movie proposition was made to me—a period when I was just nestling in at the Met. When, finally, some time in 1953, the idea of my being involved in doing the life of Sigmund Romberg, the famous Viennese popular composer, came to Metro-Goldwyn-Mayer, it was an inspiration of Edens.

To those who ask me how I could play a musical fluff I respond with dignity: "I was no fluff. I was the lady that Sig was seen with night after night." I was Romberg's great friend and adviser, a broad-beamed woman who ran a Vienna café—the stars in the picture were José Ferrer, Merle Oberon, myself, and a huge list of great actors. I found that the picture became a smash, made crocks of money, and I—for my first and only appearance on the screen—got the *Look* magazine award for the best "newcomer" of the year. This was a prime chortle to me, since I had been "newcoming" ever since 1939, about fifteen years before. The publicity was amazing—everything from articles to editorials. Newspaper editors seem to like to talk about me from the mountaintop—I guess it is because they cannot see through me. At any rate, as Bill said: "You have to pay attention to those awards. In Hollywood, people go to bed with things like that."

I was happier with the fact that MGM offered me a three-year, no-option contract. It would have grossed more than five hundred thousand dollars in three years if I had accepted it. We never did. Bill and I were cold stupid. We wrangled over script approval, since I was a little leery over my experience with scripts on other occasions. We did get MGM to say they would present three scripts for me and I could choose one. But no one went any further, and negotiations were broken off.

"You should get with us," said one movie executive reproachfully. "You've got what nobody else has."

"What's that?" I demanded suspiciously.

"You're non-cheesecake and still dynamite," he said. I missed on my first roundhouse swing but I was glad I did. I still have the same assets and I laugh louder.

I did meet José Ferrer. That was an education in a number of ways. Ferrer is the one-and-only talent who can mount a bull and gallop off in all directions simultaneously. I have no idea if he is a genius or what: I was so breathless following what he did—in business, directing, producing, acting, writing, singing, composing, editing, and just generally kineticizing—that I never found out. He liked what I did on the screen. As someone told me, I was a good reactor rather than an actor. "People in the audience don't act but they do react," one director told me. "That way they get identified with you. They love you for it."

I certainly reacted to Ferrer—and his wife, the singer Rosemary Clooney, who is his greatest booster as proved by the number of children she has had by him. I never heard Rosey—who is herself one of the nicest people alive—say a word about her husband that was not pure adoration. It was nothing for Ferrer to spend until two in the morning discussing business—and this one-man-band used to do all the talking, too. He was a guy who buried a bone under every tree in the park—and personally dug it up.

I never could quite understand Oberon. She did a good job in the picture but she was far away from me. She was of the old school of glamor. She insisted on being the last person on the set every day. Once Ferrer and I planned to spike her guns. We set spies to tell us when she arrived. We hid outside. The time came, she marched in, we got the flash and came in after her—and you know what? She licked us again. She saw us, made one of the most intricate excuses I had ever heard, was escorted out, and then came in with another glamorous entrance.

I imagine I disrupted some of the MGM routines. In their enormous commissary I used to sit next to a table where the old-timers such as Louis Calhern and Walter Pidgeon would sit and tell stories and laugh uproariously. I used to cock my ear at its best angle, but I never could hear what they were saying. Finally, I stood up and tramped over the aisle to them and said impressively: "Gentlemen, either stop telling such funny jokes or tell them louder so that I can hear—or invite me to have lunch with you!" After that I was part of the table. The first thing Pidgeon said to me was: "Miss Traubel, I have all your records. You've cost me a lot of money." I was glad I was able to reply: "So have you me. For all the movie tickets I've bought to see you."

My penchant for laughter probably accounted for a good percentage of the estimated two million five hundred thousand dollars *Deep in My Heart* cost. One of the actors was Jim Backus, a man who has a thousand funny faces and stories and can tear them off one after the other. At one point Ferrer and I were supposed to enter through the café doors. Backus was yarning away outside as the director shrieked at us. Perhaps it was because I was laughing and blasting the sound equipment that nothing happened. At any rate, it cost ten precious minutes of their time to get the set calmed down. When I did come in, the scene had to be cut. I had been laughing so hard that my make-up—and especially my mascara—was in grotesque arroyos down my face. I had to have a whole new face painted in. I got over my chuckle jag while it was going on.

All of this *segued* naturally into my doing the stage musical, *Pipedream,* for Richard Rodgers and Oscar Hammerstein, II. When I had sung my first big New York night-club date at the Copacabana, Hammerstein's bearlike bulk had come backstage. He was, as always, a wonderful guy. He wagged a finger at me and said, "You realize, young lady, you are headed straight for Broadway, don't you?" The evening ended in a spray of compliments and I went on out to Hollywood to begin *Deep in My Heart.*

There I found that R and H were producing the movie version

of *Oklahoma* at MGM. Hammerstein visited me again and we talked once more. This time he had a definite idea in mind. He told me they were thinking about doing a book of John Steinbeck's. "It's got just the role for you," he told me. I wanted to know what it was. His eyes twinkled. "It's the wholesome madam of a house," he said.

Rodgers came to Las Vegas during another engagement of mine there and inspected me as a performer for three or four days. We talked about the role and I became very intrigued with it. R and H prepared a thumbnail sketch of my character and it seemed just right for me.

Not long after I signed the contract with Dick Rodgers and Oscar Hammerstein for their show. I did not realize that the announcement of their newest musical would bring on a rush of advance sale of tickets estimated by the newspapers at one million two hundred and fifty thousand dollars, a record for that particular time. That meant the show would have a long run—win, lose, or draw. At that time Bill and I were living in an ocean-front house in Laguna Beach, California, having the sand-and-barbecue time of our lives. We moved back to our Park Avenue apartment in New York.

As things progressed on *Pipedream,* I became slowly aware that I was accepting money under quietly false pretenses. I had met John Steinbeck, on whose book, *Sweet Thursday,* the whole musical was predicated. I liked his earthy madam who ran a house in Monterrey, I loved the original scenes that had made her such a human being—salty, tough, and forthright. Steinbeck used to use his bushy eyebrows as a sort of semaphore and I could usually tell what he was thinking by the way they went up and down. As the revisions of the musical proceeded, they went down and down. He told me he was very unhappy with the way the play was being cleaned up—to the point of innocuousness. "Why don't you speak up?" I demanded. He said he would. But he did not.

On the other hand, I did speak out. I think everyone was

shocked—including Harold Clurman, the director doing his first musical, who is one of the most distinguished talents on Broadway but perhaps overwhelmed by the magnificent R and H record of musical hits. Clurman tried to have his own way only for a little. I had a scene in the show where a little guy wanted to dance with me and I grabbed him, hollering obscenities, and proceeded to shake him up and down until his ears flapped. This became a cutie-pie "oh-gosh" bit instead of broad comedy; everything became steadily emasculated. It was so apparent finally that I wrote a long letter to the pair of R and H, outlining all that I thought wrong with my songs in the show. It would have been impertinent of me to criticize any other element. They dictated an equally long letter back to me. They disagreed with all that I had said and pointed out that each of my songs was a "gem." Rodgers, the musician, and Hammerstein, the lyricist, had never gone over the music and words with me before the show contracts were signed. At one of our first luncheons a year before Rodgers had said to me: "Of course, Miss Traubel, you'll take the music for granted," and I had replied: "Mr. Rodgers, I can't even take Beethoven for granted." I meant only that my voice was suited to certain ways of singing and I would like it to be framed properly. Beethoven is a great composer, of course, but not everything he wrote is right for me. So Rodgers played the score for Bill and me one evening. We were delighted with it, hearing Rodgers play it on the piano as Hammerstein read the lyrics. But we had never yet heard the lyrics *sung* to the tunes!

This was what upset the applecart, I suppose. In opera, no one understands most of the words. Even if you do understand them, they do not make much sense. It is the music that matters. It is so tremendous that it sweeps all wordiness away. In musical comedy the words are very important. Neither Bill nor I knew this. We discovered, as we went along, that the words changed my actions, my expression, my very attitude—and even the particular singing of a note.

The result was that my character onstage became the opposite of what I was in real life. I became a footlight namby-pamby. Since I have never claimed to be much of an actress anyway, this put me at a real disadvantage. I used to groan to Bill that all my songs were "down songs." I would demonstrate that all of the R and H great hits had been "up songs." I was right: not one of the songs I sang ever became a hit. While writing the score Rodgers discovered he had cancer of the jaw. He was operated on and was back at rehearsals in two weeks, despite his pain and personal distress. It was a very gallant display of courage. It was impossible to bring up such minor matters as a song or two against a man who had shown his guts in such a fashion. Art or no art, no matter how I felt, I determined I was going to give R and H all I could.

I had the title song (in the book sense) of *Sweet Thursday*—which I told them I hated and I did hate it. I also had a Mozartian song of very clever wording when I and my gaggle of whores on-stage have a sentimental time talking about Christmas cards. (I suppose it was at this point that Polly Adler became enamored of my character.) The promises of revision made in New Haven and Boston never came through. I plunged ahead. I had one number that stopped the show—but not because of my singing. It was because a bunch of the guys in the flophouse gathered around and were able to lift me up for the finale of the scene.

So myself caught up to myself in spite of myself. During the November-to-June run of the play I became ill with a bad throat —possibly only a psychosomatic ailment from feeling sad and wretched about my role. I tried to sing; it was impossible. I was out for weeks. I tried to get R and H to let me out of the show. They refused until they got a replacement that suited them— which happened only a few weeks before it closed. "The trouble is," the critics said solemnly, "Miss Traubel is too much of a lady and it shows through."

At least a partial proof of the pudding we have been talking about can be derived from the opinion of the newspapers. Here is a consensus of the reviews in Boston, New York, and Hollywood on *Pipedream* and my part in it. They all concerned November and December in 1955 when the show opened and the early part of 1956. I can string them together in a series of quotes:

"The vast vocal resources of Miss Traubel did not find satisfactory employment. A wicked waste of a superb organ (Boston). . . . Her voice is a formidable instrument. Here it is as frustrated as a Diesel pulling a hand truck (New York). . . . The songs she has make only the faintest use of her vocal talents (New York). . . . Miss Traubel is given small, folksy songs. She is an illustrious Wagnerian who can belt an aria clear across Times Square (New York). . . . Helen Traubel never sings an opera-sized note (New York). . . . None of her numbers amount to much (*The New Yorker*). . . . Richard Rodgers' score gave so little scope for display of her glorious voice (New York). . . . Helen Traubel sings beautifully within the very modest limits of the small numbers she is given. She never gets a chance to bounce any notes off the far wall of the theater and stampede an audience (*Variety*)." One New York paper credited me with as much influence in creating the original sell out as it did the famous Rodgers and Hammerstein. Early in the game it declared: "The reputation of Rodgers and Hammerstein, with the box-office power of Helen Traubel, pulled a million-dollar advance sale," an accolade I take with a grain of salt.

Outside that astounding presale of tickets *Pipedream* was a failure in every sense. It was one of the few failures for the team of R and H. It was also my first genuine failure in any medium.

21

The End of a Beginning

TO conclude a memoir at my age is a little like cheating. It took me thirty-six years—until 1939—to get where I dreamed of getting in the world of music. I figure I must live an active life in the profession at least that much longer. So my swan song is not due until I am a minimum of seventy-two—until 1975.

Nevertheless, what I have said serves a purpose—for myself and, I hope, for everyone who has had the patience and the sheer gumption to read this far. I have exposed myself to the life of sound and melody deliberately. Here I have given myself away as much as I could. Not completely: I must save the best part of me for my own memories. But there is enough in the foregoing pages to make some critics ask if possibly I have not been too frank about myself.

What I have written was never meant to be a confession. I reserve that, too, for my prayers. It was meant to be a revelation of joy and happiness, the two qualities that have impressed me most about life. I have been lucky enough and have had enough hard sense to make myself come to terms with reality. I was fortunate enough and fey enough to give myself an escape through music.

Perhaps it is significant—symbolic of my career—that I now

have a dozen long shelves packed with fairy tales from all over the world. For years I have collected the doings of never-never land with the same devotion that a miser might count his gold. I enjoy reading them over and over, smiling at their pleasure, and feeling my eyes moisten at their disasters. The adventures of the children, dwarfs, kings, and princes, swans and geese, heroes and cowherds, giants and elves—these, I find, are not unreal at all. They seem to me to be more genuine than many of the happenings in real life. In the best sense my own life has been a fairy tale. Not because of its success in terms of money earned and spent nor in terms of magic worked because of a voice. I know enough of every fantasy in every language to realize that such stories are more often than not grim, bloody, and blunt. They meet life on its most terrible terms—and solve its problems in the shortest and most obvious ways.

I have done the same. Many of the things that have happened to me I might have avoided. But where I might have skirted a disaster, I would also have missed a joy. Where I dodged an enemy, I might also have lost a friend. Besides, it was not in my nature to avoid: I always wanted to meet the world head on.

Because I believe in fairy tales and their inner meanings as devoutly as I do anything in the world, my dreams have come true. If I had three wishes, I could put them all into one: "Let me have my life over as I had it—with all the sorrow, despair, exaltation, and rejoicing!" Or is this too much pride in merely living?

What have I enjoyed? Singing, most of all: floating away on that sea of sound that rises from an orchestra, contributing to it myself and yet being part of it. Love: the devotion of a man and learning to match it with my own love and loyalty. These two are foremost of all the delights that have come my way. There are others that are by the way. Conversation: the long talks over the table with friends, the evening lying in bed and discussing the day's events. Good food: the hot and cold, the sweet and sour, the crisp and creamy, the simple hamburger and the rich cake. The sensation of swimming, so much like that of singing with the harmony of the strokes and the freed muscles that obey the will without thought. These will last me as long as thought lasts, as long as memory can work its own spells. I have no desire for anything beyond what I have had—I am, you see, of the earth earthy and heaven will have to resemble my life here if it is to be satisfying. Is it not true that when anyone, in any land, imagines heaven it is always with music and with laughter and with the fulfilment of freedom? I had almost forgotten what makes all these things possible: work. I cannot recall when I did not cherish and train my voice, when I did not work at it every hour possible. Even in my sleep, I thought I was still doing scales for Lulu, learning the notes of a song, and indulging in the ecstatic swoop up to a high note like a bird reaching the highest twig on a tree. Life has been work to me; I expect no less of heaven.

Music today is in an era of transition. Not only opera and concerts but also popular music. I was fortunate enough to enter the Metropolitan, for example, shortly after the end of one era—the glittering and fabulous formal one ruled over by Gatti-Casazza. The time I spent there marked another era, one of transition to that of Bing, the more modern era of opera. I can say that I regretted being tail-end Helen of the first era—I like a little swank and show as much as anyone—and that perhaps Bing and myself have more in common than we acknowledge. He has set his face steadfastly toward the forward look in opera—and I applaud him for it. I cannot share all of his tastes but I do go along with his continuing plans for modernizing the Met.

Thus I can stand at the crossroads of a career and look both ways—a privilege that is not accorded to many people. I have seen music struggle to escape from the strait jackets of the past and go into a certain insanity in the present. But I believe that there is now greater freedom of art and personal interpretation than ever before. It is pleasant to be received equally well by the traditional-ists and the *avant-garde*.

The present fluid shift of musical times—the hydrodynamic drive of the present, so to speak—is of great importance. For the first time I see tremendous hope for the consolidation of all musical tastes from the highest to the lowest. I can see signs of opera being accepted in circles where it would have been a stranger ten years ago. I have seen jazz being accepted as a basic American contribution to music international. This is owing largely to mechanical devices: television, radio, recordings, and the piping of music everywhere. Music is now realized to be what I instinctively knew it to be all my days: a vital, essential part of living. A beautiful sound is the basis of the health of the body, mind, and spirit—and the proofs are being advanced every day by science.

Strangely enough, in my time I have not seen one single step backward in musical taste. I may disagree with my neighbor as to what may constitute the best, but I find him constantly seeking it. Classical music is now pirated so widely by motion-picture scores, TV renditions, popular songs, and popular composers that even in the so-called "hick" towns the musical tastes of today are incomparably higher than they were when I was a girl. Music that would have been booed in St. Louis years ago is now a commonplace in the night clubs and bars. Despite the old canards to the contrary, if an artist goes into such spots with what is called a "cheap" program—of tired clichés out of his repertoire—it is very likely that the audience will not accept it. An audience nowadays is far better informed than ever before about music. I have always felt that any audience would understand and appreciate anything sincerely sung to them and selected with taste. I have proved it on battle fronts, in small towns, in foreign cities, before audiences of radio, television, and movies—before the great and the unknown. It is always true: music is the common denominator of the world. It transcends thought and deed. To me it is the purest and most lasting of all emotions.

Moreover, people all across this country of ours can now pick and choose their music. Television gives them this first standard. They are no longer pushed by social pressures—"What does Mrs. Jones like, dear? See what she likes"—but by their own secret longings and needs. There is more tolerance from both ends of the stick toward a music middle, a universal medium if you like. Such items as opera on the radio, TV, and records give the hidden public a chance to sit and enjoy and to let loose their willingness to understand. They need no words. They can understand the eternity of sound that never changes in such musicians as Bach, Wagner, Mozart, Beethoven.

Music surrounds me, music supports me, music gives me the will and inspiration to live. I see such feats as that of André Kostelanetz, the husband of Lily Pons, the last of the great coloratura sopranos, taking the heart of an opera—binding together the wonderful and familiar melodies and using the unfamiliar passages as a bridge. This, together with the orchestrations that are miracles of dexterity, produces in me the hope that someday we will learn to relish music with our hearts rather than our minds.

If I were trusted with the job of telling someone how to appreciate music, I would first beg off. If I were whipped to the task, I would advise my victim to pay only a little attention to what I said and all possible attention to the way he himself felt on hearing a certain conglomeration of sounds. Artists tend to disdain someone who defies their esoteric standards and bluntly says: "I know what I like." I applaud such people: let them know what they like and improve it, passing on not to different standards but to bigger and richer standards. No one should set a limitation on what he wants to hear or should hear. My sole rule would be: make a sandwich of your likes and dislikes. Hearing a record or a recital, make sure it is first something you like; then something you may not like; and lastly something you like. In this way ultimate understanding comes. It is like eating olives: no one thinks of making a meal of them but by using them as hors d'oeuvres one gradually comes to relish the taste.

Yet in all my thoughts of the music of the future I find a saddening note. In the young singers, even among those who have fine technique and mastery of their art, I have yet to hear a sound that I genuinely admire. To achieve this with the lungs and the throat as the instrument requires God-given equipment. It also requires years of work. Perhaps the microphone, that hunk of wires that has always stood between me and my audience, that has always been my *bête noire*, is responsible. It makes small voices large, it distorts big voices. It destroys true tone. No mechanical device can supply the true, pure tone of a voice launched directly at the ear. I do not know any artist that really enjoys mechanical reproduction. I remember I sat next to Jascha Heifetz, undoubtedly one of the world's finest and most experienced violinists, at a New York concert in which we were both to appear. We were taping broadcasts for the armed forces. That evil thing, the microphone, was on the stage and had to be sung to. I turned to Jascha. Before I could speak, he split his impassive face and whispered to me: "Feel my hands!" I did. They were cold as ice and trembling a little, starting to sweat. I managed a nervous giggle. "I can't have you feel the inside of my throat," I said, "but it's the same way." Jascha nodded. "I'm terribly nervous," he said. I almost clapped my hands. "You, too," I said, "you, too!" I thought I was the only scaredy-cat in the business but Jascha had the same dread of the mike as I.

The mechanical developments—the so-called "high fidelity" among them—demand a whole new and more critical way of listening for the audience. They also make the greatest demands on the young artists coming into their own: they must learn to listen to themselves. More than ever this is mandatory. They must pay attention to the sound they make and heed nothing and no one else. This is the first and most important principle of great singing—indeed, of any great music.

It is possible for me now to confess candidly that the top tones of a woman's voice have always been unpleasing to me. I have never heard a dramatic high C—including my own—which achieved that resonance and fullness that it deserves. After a dramatic soprano hits a high A or thereabouts, everything else has the faintest tinge of being forced. It was this feeling for sound that made me curb my own inclinations to hit the high C's in Wagner. Flagstad, who possessed the only other "big" voice that has been compared to mine, always had a cold and stretched range in this regard. In my case, I gradually commenced to develop a psychological block about singing high C's. I honestly felt at first that they were unnecessary to the portrayal of a role and often detracted from it. As I ceased to sing them, the feeling crept over me that my whole attitude might be solely because I *could* not sing them well enough. I confess that in the later years at the Met this was a serious hazard in my singing. At home, at informal concerts, almost anywhere else, my high C was true and occasionally unstrained—at least, listening with my ear that has nothing to do with my ego, I liked it better than any I had heard. I could not say the same onstage. Flagstad was better than I in the high register in several ways; I think I can take the honors from her in the over-all performance of warmth and dramatic intensity.

My own comfort in singing has always been twofold. I myself wanted to enjoy my sound and make sure of its purity and strength; then I wanted to share it with the public. I spent all those years making positive that my voice was dependable; I never wanted to burden an audience with it otherwise. There are many effects that can be created with the human voice—from the Bugs Bunny squawl to a sergeant's yoohoo. But how many of these are consistently beautiful?

I repeat that my goal was always the most beautiful sound possible from my own equipment. If I would retrace my life and work out some of the many mistakes I have made, the greatest in a musical sense would be to iron out the quirk in my mind that finally made me afraid to attempt a high C. A singer who aspires to be a great singer—and there are more of them, many more, than there were in my time—must have the following:

1. *The Equipment.* He or she must be physically able to stand the rigors of singing which, I assure you, are more demanding than professional football. More, each must have the actual build and potential of voice. Without such a foundation, nothing can be erected.

2. *The Deep Pleasure.* This means that the singer must find in the production of sound a great happiness—not an ego, but a happiness in the sight of faces reacting to her, growing and increasing. She must be able to make old friends in a single performance.

3. *The Hard Ear.* Such aspirants must be able to listen to themselves until they nearly go out of their heads—but not for one moment must they allow conceit or any other consideration other than the impartial appraisal of their voice values to sway their consideration.

4. *The Great Moment.* These must be prepared for—such as I had singing with Toscanini or singing with the Philadelphia Orchestra with Ormandy. This is the frightening thing about singing well—sometimes you come face to face with naked greatness, as in the case of Toscanini as an individual or the Philadelphia group and Ormandy as an organization. Then panic is liable to seize you—if you are not prepared.

After one has said all this, what else is there in life to recount? As one gets older, the size of things diminish; as they fade on the horizon, they assume the same color and aspect. Everything is much on the identical order of magnitude—small as well as large. I take as much pleasure from the minute events of my life now as I did from the great. I like to know that a rose as well as a prize-winning gladiolus has my name. I remember that one of the finest dishes at the Plaza Hotel used to be *Capon à la Traubel,* a marvelous dish of baked chicken with exquisite sauce.

Pleasure for me comes in partnership, too. Being married has never handicapped me; on the contrary, it has set me free as I never believed possible before. Nor do Bill and I have to contend with the ordinary hazards of such a life. We believe in letting each other alone when it is obviously necessary; we believe in a common ground that can always be reached by common sense.

I think of Bill as an excellent husband. Whenever he is asked to describe my faults, he says they are normal American female faults. His chief complaint about me is that I continually mess up the anecdotes I tell—as I may have messed up this book in spots. He says, "She starts laughing before she comes to the point, and by the time she gets there her laugh is so loud that everyone else is laughing and they never hear the joke." His complaints are largely now limited to my driving. He thinks it is very good if I keep my eyes on the road—which I rarely do. His second complaint is that he thinks my hats are too big and flowery. I have finally fixed him on this question. When I go out to buy a hat I make him go along with me. He must express his opinion on the spot, which naturally puts *him* on the spot—sufficiently, at least, to let me make my own choice.

We have always felt that what was good for art—simplicity and good taste—was a good recipe for life. Bill and I have always made it a point as far as possible to own as few possessions as we can—including house, furniture, automobiles, and jewelry. This, of course, has been less possible of late years, but we have tried to keep things down to a minimum.

Sometimes the amount of money that an American favorite can earn—not only in his own country but anywhere in the world—tends to throw the whole picture of life out of proportion. I have been in the top-salary brackets for much of my earning years. I have never seen much good come out of having so much income. Without Bill it would have been a source of worry and positive lunacy, I am sure. Everything gets distorted, as it does in the depths of a pool. You are never quite sure where you are going or where you will wind up. All you know is that you are in the midst of that delicious golden shower and you want to wash thoroughly while it is coming down. It is very hard to step out and get dry and sane at last.

Merely dropping names is a poor tribute to anyone. I was at a party with one disdainful Hollywood actor who had become a star and was fond of pointing out that fact. On one occasion another lesser-known star passed by and he leaned over to Bill and said: "There, but for the grace of God, go I!" Bill turned to me with a straight face and said: "He's a name dropper." But I have so many memories of my days in singing—memories that are still living realities as my career goes on—that the thought of them can warm me like a fireside in winter. Conductors: how many of them have stood before me with their batons to escort me through a score! I remember George Szell, one who could take an orchestra at the Met and give it his own inimitable driving force, sweeping everything else before it in a performance, going through the audience like a hurricane through a forest. I recall the marching form of Sir Thomas Beecham, making faces at me, grimacing out his heart for a performance, formulating his witty asides that we would hear later. There were the two Fritzes—Fritz Reiner and Fritz Busch—the first of whom was a man of great depth and feeling for a musical passage, a conductor who could take a score and back of a singer as if she were standing within the security of a palace of sound; the second, a man of outstanding gentleness, who made chords flow like a river, a great conductor in the realm of emotional, colorful music. Towering among them all is Bruno Walter, a conductor who stands out in my mind not only for his clean-cut musicianship but for the fact that he begged me on a dozen occasions to learn the leading part in *Fidelio,* Beethoven's only opera. This I always refused to do—not that I honored myself less but Ludwig more. You see, the heroine of that particular opera wore tights. Not only that, she also wore a short coat. I admit that her boots were long, but there was that certain interval in between which, in my case, nothing could disguise.

Risë Stevens, who could sing such a role and be perfect for it, was one of those performers who besides having a beautiful voice was a delightful person in her own right. Artur Rubinstein, one of the finest living pianists, who has a slight resemblance to an upside-down turnip when he plays, is another person whose range is far beyond that of his extraordinary talents. I have sat next to him at many a dinner table and been dazzled not only with his ability at telling slightly off-color stories but with his absolute authority and knowledge in many fields. I have already mentioned blond-haired Eugene Ormandy, the one symbiotic conductor whose greatest art depends on his Philadelphia group just as theirs depends largely on him; I must include Artur Rodzinski, a sound conductor though a trifle unpredictable.

Lotte Lehmann, that remarkably sweet singer, comes to me in a remembrance of her silently wringing her hands before her entrance in the opera, the symbol of nervousness that possessed all of us under such circumstances (though I concealed it better than some)—and her superlative performances the instant she set foot on the stage. Erich Leinsdorf, who will not mind if I designate him as a man putting solid workmanship into his conducting rather than the showiness of some others—and, of course, Toscanini. Toscanini, Stokowski, and Ormandy—with this trio I have enjoyed the highest possible moments of my musical career. If I had years to retrace my steps, I would prefer to go note by note over the performances with these three.

Lawrence Tibbett, one of our close friends, showed me the way long before we knew him, the way of an American blazing a fresh trail through the jungles of music that were so long a European colony. His voice has always been one of the most exciting to me—just as among the women that of Rosa Ponselle was one of the greatest of all times. To me she was an idol; and I cannot forget one night at a recital in Baltimore when I found her waiting silently in the wings for me. "I have become a fan of yours," she said simply—the cycle had run its course. Still, if anyone asks me who had the most beautiful voice I have ever heard, I am sorry I cannot attribute it to any of my competitors. In my own secret heart of hearts I believe that my mother had the most exciting and thrillingly beautiful soprano voice I have ever heard. She never had a career because she never had any professional interest in it, but if she had wanted to, I am sure she would have surpassed all of us.

There are others in my life whom I remember fondly. Cole Porter, who threatened to write music for me; Ed Gardner, whose stories have me speechless with laughter most of the time, on or off the air; Red Skelton, whose immense skill at comedy has always had me openmouthed, and who said to me once: "I'm really bad off. You've got talent but all I've got is guts." Lionel Barrymore has a special place in my recollections because of his love for music—he was a good composer himself—and the time we appeared in a magazine double spread that was entitled "$60,-000,000 Worth of Talent!" with every star at MGM staring straight into the camera except him and myself. We were discussing a new way to make apple strudel and had missed the cameraman's instructions. Major Donald Neville-Willing of the Café de Paris, London, is still another inhabitant of my memory—the man who is possibly the last of the classic impresarios in his field. He used to make it his personal business to see that everything was ideal for his performers and ran the smartest and most exclusive night club in England. He was so English that when he spoke his English had to be interpreted by the English for the English. I never did understand much of what he said beyond his impeccable manners and declamatory gestures and the glitter on his monocle.

I think of Sophie Tucker, for whom I have the greatest admiration for her talent and endurance; I remember my sessions on TV with Arthur Godfrey, the redheaded genius of sales and easy does it. I never had such a relaxing experience even under the hands of a masseuse. On my preliminary talks, we dispensed with any writers and just chatted on the air, flitting from cloud to cloud of conversation. And I must not forget Jerry Lewis, one of the great comedians of our generation with a real wit and feeling for his art—whose talent is as sensitive about fine music as it is about a belly laugh.

There are a thousand others, from the beginning to this point, that I might include. But they all know my flighty mind and my capricious memory, and they know, too, that they are included in the spirit if not in the letter of the text. I am very fond of the friends who have made the life I have had possible.

That is the end of the fairy story until this very moment. The princess is out of her castle and fleeing from the villain, the hero by her side. She is still in the middle of her escape. The way she travels is lovely and enchanted. There is always the danger that the wicked witch will pop up and turn her into a frog or a clod. She is willing to take the chance. She has some inherited magic in an old vocal reticule with which she can still cast her own charms.

Best of all, the princess knows that no fairy story can end—unless it pronounces the most charming and magical words ever invented: "And they lived happily ever after."

Appendix

METROPOLITAN OPERA, CONCERT, TELEVISION,
RADIO, STAGE, RECORDINGS, NIGHT-CLUB,
AND MOTION-PICTURE PERFORMANCES

OF

HELEN TRAUBEL

NOTE: The following includes only a partial list of tour performances with the Metropolitan Opera Company at Boston, Philadelphia, Baltimore, Rochester, Cleveland, Chicago, St. Louis, Dallas, and Los Angeles as well as appearances with the San Francisco Opera Company, the Chicago Opera Company, and the Detroit Opera Company, and European concert appearances.

METROPOLITAN OPERA APPEARANCES

SEASON	DATE	ROLE	OPERA
Spring '37	May 12, 17, 22, 1937	Mary Rutledge	*The Man Without a Country*
1937–38	Feb. 17, 1938	Mary Rutledge	*The Man Without a Country*

1939–40	Dec. 28, 1939	Sieglinde	*Die Walküre*
	Jan. 29, 1940	Sieglinde	*Die Walküre*
	Feb. 15, 1940	Elisabeth	*Tannhäuser*
	March 2, 1940	Sieglinde	*Die Walküre*
1940–41	Dec. 4, 16, 1940	Sieglinde	*Die Walküre*
	Jan. 22, 1940	Elisabeth	*Tannhäuser*
1941–42	Dec. 1, 1941	Elisabeth	*Tannhäuser*
	Dec. 6, 1941	Brünnhilde	*Die Walküre*
	Feb. 12, 23, 1942	Brünnhilde	*Götterdämmerung*
1942–43	Nov. 25, 1942	Brünnhilde	*Götterdämmerung*
	Dec. 4, 1942	Isolde	*Tristan und Isolde*
	Dec. 10, 1942	Brünnhilde	*Götterdämmerung*
	Dec. 14, 1942	Isolde	*Tristan und Isolde*
	Dec. 19, 1942	Elisabeth	*Tannhäuser*
	Feb. 6, 1943	Isolde	*Tristan und Isolde*
	Feb. 16, 20, 27, 1943	Brünnhilde	*Die Walküre*
	March 2, 1943	Brünnhilde	*Siegfried*
	March 9, 1943	Brünnhilde	*Götterdämmerung*
1943–44	Nov. 24, 1943	Isolde	*Tristan und Isolde*
	Dec. 2, 1943	Brünnhilde	*Die Walküre*
	Dec. 11, 1943	Isolde	*Tristan und Isolde*
	Dec. 13, 1943	Brünnhilde	*Die Walküre*
	Dec. 18, 1943	Elisabeth	*Tannhäuser*
	Jan. 7, 17, 1944	Isolde	*Tristan und Isolde*
	Feb. 15, 1944	Brünnhilde	*Die Walküre*
	Feb. 22, 1944	Brünnhilde	*Siegried*
	Feb. 29, 1944	Brünnhilde	*Götterdämmerung*
	March 4, 1944	Isolde	*Tristan und Isolde*
	March 25, 1944	Brünnhilde	*Die Walküre*
	April 1, 1944	Brünnhilde	*Siegfried*
	April 8, 1944	Brünnhilde	*Götterdämmerung*
1944–45	Dec. 2, 1944	Brünnhilde	*Die Walküre*
	Dec. 4, 1944	Isolde	*Tristan und Isolde*
	Dec. 8, 1944	Brünnhilde	*Götterdämmerung*

METROPOLITAN OPERA APPEARANCES (Cont.)

Season	Date	Role	Opera
1944–45	Dec. 14, 1944	Brünnhilde	Die Walküre
	Dec. 20, 1944	Elsa	Lohengrin
	Dec. 23, 1944	Isolde	Tristan und Isolde
	Feb. 6, 1945	Brünnhilde	Die Walküre
	Feb. 13, 1945	Brünnhilde	Siegfried
	Feb. 20, 1945	Brünnhilde	Götterdämmerung
	March 15, 1945	Elsa	Lohengrin
	March 17, 1945	Brünnhilde	Die Walküre
	March 21, 1945	Isolde	Tristan und Isolde
	March 24, 1945	Brünnhilde	Siegfried
	March 31, 1945	Brünnhilde	Götterdämmerung
1945–46	Nov. 26, 1945	Elsa	Lohengrin
	Dec. 8, 1945	Elsa	Lohengrin
	Dec. 14, 1945	Elisabeth	Tannhäuser
	Jan. 21, 1946	Elisabeth	Tannhäuser
	Jan. 25, 1946	Brünnhilde	Die Walküre
	Feb. 2, 1946	Isolde	Tristan und Isolde
	Feb. 11, 1946	Brünnhilde	Götterdämmerung
	Feb. 14, 1946	Isolde	Tristan und Isolde
	March 14, 1946	Brünnhilde	Götterdämmerung
	March 18, 1946	Isolde	Tristan und Isolde
	March 27, 1946	Brünnhilde	Götterdämmerung
	March 30, 1946	Brünnhilde	Die Walküre
1946–47	Nov. 15, 1946	Brünnhilde	Siegfried
	Nov. 20, 30, 1946	Isolde	Tristan und Isolde
	Dec. 5, 1946	Brünnhilde	Die Walküre
	Dec. 13, 1946	Isolde	Tristan und Isolde
	Dec. 16, 1946	Brünnhilde	Siegfried
	Dec. 21, 1946	Brünnhilde	Die Walküre
	Jan. 14, 1947	Elsa	Lohengrin
	Jan. 17, 1947	Brünnhilde	Die Walküre
	Jan. 22, 1947	Brünnhilde	Siegfried
	Jan. 25, 1947	Elsa	Lohengrin
	Jan. 30, 1947	Isolde	Tristan und Isolde
	Feb. 3, 1947	Brünnhilde	Die Walküre
	March 1, 1947	Elsa	Lohengrin
1947–48	Jan. 3, 1948	Isolde	Tristan und Isolde
	Jan. 13, 1948	Brünnhilde	Die Walküre
	Jan. 21, 1948	Brünnhilde	Siegfried
	Jan. 24, 1948	Brünnhilde	Die Walküre
	Jan. 29, 1948	Brünnhilde	Götterdämmerung
	Feb. 2, 1948	Isolde	Tristan und Isolde
	Feb. 10, 1948	Brünnhilde	Die Walküre

METROPOLITAN OPERA APPEARANCES (Cont.)

	Feb. 18, 1948	Brünnhilde	*Siegfried*
	Feb. 24, 1948	Brünnhilde	*Götterdämmerung*
	Feb. 27, 1948	Elisabeth	*Tannhäuser*
	March 6, 1948	Elisabeth	*Tannhäuser*
	March 13, 1948	Isolde	*Tristan und Isolde*
1948–49	Dec. 2, 1948	Brünnhilde	*Götterdämmerung*
	Dec. 11, 17, 1948	Isolde	*Tristan und Isolde*
	Dec. 20, 1948	Brünnhilde	*Götterdämmerung*
	Dec. 29, 1948	Brünnhilde	*Die Walküre*
	Jan. 6, 1949	Isolde	*Tristan und Isolde*
	Jan. 10, 1949	Brünnhilde	*Die Walküre*
	Jan. 14, 1949	Brünnhilde	*Siegfried*
	Jan. 19, 1949	Brünnhilde	*Götterdämmerung*
	Jan. 27, 1949	Brünnhilde	*Siegfried*
	Jan. 29, 1949	Brünnhilde	*Die Walküre*
	Feb. 7, 1949	Isolde	*Tristan und Isolde*
	Feb. 17, 1949	Brünnhilde	*Die Walküre*
	Feb. 23, 1949	Isolde	*Tristan und Isolde*
	March 4, 1949	Brünnhilde	*Götterdämmerung*
1949–50	Dec. 1, 1949	Isolde	*Tristan und Isolde*
	Dec. 12, 1949	Brünnhilde	*Die Walküre*
	Dec. 17, 1949	Isolde	*Tristan und Isolde*
	Jan. 2, 1950	Isolde	*Tristan und Isolde*
	Jan. 7, 1950	Elsa	*Lohengrin*
	Jan. 14, 1950	Brünnhilde	*Die Walküre*
	Feb. 2, 1950	Elsa	*Lohengrin*
	Feb. 10, 1950	Brünnhilde	*Die Walküre*
	Feb. 13, 1950	Elsa	*Lohengrin*
	March 18, 1950	Brünnhilde	*Die Walküre*
	March 21, 1950	Kundry	*Parsifal*
	April 7, 1950	Kundry	*Parsifal*
1950–51	Dec. 1, 9, 16, 1950	Isolde	*Tristan und Isolde*
	Jan. 5, 11, 16, 1951	Princess von Werdenberg	*Der Rosenkavalier*
	Feb. 1, 1951	Brünnhilde	*Die Walküre*
	Feb. 10, 1951	Brünnhilde	*Siegfried*
	Feb. 17, 1951	Brünnhilde	*Götterdämmerung*
1951–52	Dec. 13, 1951	Brünnhilde	*Götterdämmerung*
	Jan. 5, 1952	Brünnhilde	*Götterdämmerung*
1952–53	March 11, 21, 1953	Isolde	*Tristan und Isolde*

TELEVISION APPEARANCES

YEAR	DATE	PROGRAM
1950	November 29	Jimmy Durante
1951	January 24	Jimmy Durante
	October 6	Jimmy Durante
	October 7	Celebrity Time
	December 29	Jimmy Durante
1953	April 11	Jimmy Durante
1954	February 28	What's My Line?
	March 13	Godfrey Friends
	August 7	Bob Crosby (tape)
	August 25	Red Skelton
	October 12	Red Skelton
	November 10	Arthur Godfrey
1956	March 25	Ed Sullivan
	April 15	Ed Sullivan
	September 23	Ed Sullivan
	November 27	Herb Shriner
1957	January 26	Perry Como
	December 28	Perry Como
1958	January 9	Perry Como
	February 11	George Gobel
	April 17	Jerry Lewis
	October 18	Jerry Lewis
	November 26	Milton Berle
	December 16	Garry Moore

NIGHT-CLUB PERFORMANCES

YEAR	STARTING DATE		
1953	September 11	Chez Paree	Chicago
	October 2	Statler Hotel	Washington, D.C.
	November 28	Statler Hotel	Detroit
	December 15	Clover Club	Miami
	December 31	Statler Hotel	Cleveland
1954	January 15	Chase Hotel	St. Louis
	January 29	Chez Paree	Chicago
	February 25	Copacabana	New York
	July 15	Mapes Hotel	Reno
	August 31	Hotel Sahara	Las Vegas
	September 23	Statler Hotel	Los Angeles
1955	February 25	Fontainebleau Hotel	Miami Beach
	April 19	Royal Nevada Hotel	Las Vegas
	June 23	Cal Vada Lodge	Lake Tahoe
1956	August 30	Riverside Casino	Reno
	September 10	Statler Hotel	Detroit
	September 24	Statler Hotel	Cleveland
	October 9	Moulin Rouge	Hollywood
	November 7	Chase Hotel	St. Louis
	November 29	Statler Hotel	Dallas
	December 27	Palmer House	Chicago
1957	February 14	Sans Souci	Havana
	March 7	Flamingo Hotel	Las Vegas
	May 10	Beverly Hills Country Club	Newport, Ky.
	September 5	Mapes Hotel	Reno
	October 24	Edna Gladney Ball, Shamrock Hotel	Houston
	October 26	Yale Club of Tulsa	Tulsa
1958	September 12	Beverly Hills Country Club	Newport, Ky.

MOTION-PICTURE PERFORMANCE

1954   *Deep in My Heart*

STAGE PERFORMANCE

1955   *Pipedream*

RECORDINGS

DOT

"Because," single release; "Trees," single release; "Because," album.

COLUMBIA

Wagner: The Bridal Chamber Scene, *Lohengrin;* American Songs; Sacred Songs; Wagner: *Die Walküre,* Duet and Act III; Negro Spirituals, Popular Ballads; Italian Operatic Arias; Brahms: Ernestegesang, Brahms Recital; Beethoven Settings of Irish and Scotch Songs.

VICTOR

Old Vienna; Traubel Sings Wagner; Beloved Religious Songs; The Gay Nineties with Helen Traubel; Helen Traubel Sings Italian Operatic Arias; Helen Traubel Sings Folk Songs and Ballads; "Silent Night, Holy Night"; "Adeste Fideles"; "Abide with Me"; "The Lord's Prayer"; *Tannhäuser:* Introduction and Dich, teure Halle (Act 2); *Alceste* (Gluck): Divinités du Styx; Frauenliebe und Leben (Schumann); Wagnerian Songs (Three Deathless Songs); Helen Traubel Sings Wagner; *Die Götter-dämmerung*—Act III: Brünnhilde's Immolation; *Pipedream* (Rodgers and Hammerstein); Ten Sopranos-Ten Arias: *Die Walküre,* Act II, Du bist der Lenz.

CONCERTS

Season 1939–40

Date	City	Type of Engagement
October 8	New York	Town Hall recital
October 15	Detroit	radio (Ford Hour)
October 22	New York	soloist with New York Philharmonic

Season 1940–41

June 21	Bedford, N. Y.	recital
August 11	Washington, D. C.	soloist with National Symphony
October 4	New York	Town Hall recital
October 16	Austin	recital
October 21	Boise	recital
October 25	Seattle	recital
October 29	Fresno	recital
October 31	Hollywood	radio broadcast
November 4	Tucson	recital
November 7	Cincinnati	recital
November 14	Roanoke	recital
November 16	New York	recital
November 22	Kitchener, Ont.	recital
November 26	Bryn Mawr	recital
November 29	Baltimore	recital
December 5	Toronto	recital
December 7	Toronto	recital
December 9	New York	recital at Waldorf-Astoria
December 18	New York	recital
January 19	Detroit	radio (Ford Sunday Evening Hour)
January 31	St. Louis	soloist with St. Louis Orchestra
February 1	St. Louis	soloist with St. Louis Orchestra
February 4	Galveston	recital
February 9	Chicago	radio
February 14	Pittsburgh	soloist with Pittsburgh Symphony
February 16	Pittsburgh	soloist with Pittsburgh Symphony
February 18	Kalamazoo	recital
February 22	New York	soloist with NBC Symphony
February 27	Saginaw	recital
March 6	Allentown	recital
March 10	Philadelphia	soloist with Philadelphia Orchestra
March 11	New York	soloist with Philadelphia Orchestra
March 13	Worcester	recital
March 16	New Bedford	recital
March 20	Harrisburg	soloist with Harrisburg Symphony
March 23	Bridgeport	soloist with chorus and orchestra

Date	City	Type of Engagement
March 25	Omaha	recital
April 1	Kansas City, Mo.	recital
April 6	Detroit	radio (Ford Sunday Evening Hour)
April 13	New York	soloist with Philharmonic
April 17	Ogden, Utah	recital
April 21	Reno	recital
April 22	Oakland	recital
April 25	Los Angeles	recital
April 29	San Francisco	recital

Season 1941–42

Date	City	Type of Engagement
July 27	New York	radio (Coca-Cola Hour)
August 6	New York	soloist with orchestra, Lewisohn Stadium
August 9, 10	Chicago	soloist with orchestra
August 17	San Rafael	recital
August 28	Los Angeles	soloist with orchestra, Hollywood Bowl
August 30	Santa Barbara, Cal.	soloist with orchestra
September 4	Hollywood	radio (Kraft Music Hall)
September 30	West Chester, Pa.	recital
October 2	Scranton	recital
October 6	Nashua, N. H.	recital
October 7	Providence	recital
October 9	Utica	recital
October 11	Grand Rapids	recital
October 14	Buffalo	recital
October 16	Wellesley	recital
October 20	Pittsfield	recital
October 22	New London	recital
October 24	Troy	recital
October 28	Detroit	radio (Ford Broadcast)
October 30	Baltimore	recital
November 1	Norfolk	recital
November 3	Durham	recital
November 5	Bristol	recital
November 7	Knoxville	recital
November 10	Atlanta	recital
November 12	Macon	recital
November 14	Greensboro	recital
November 17	Louisville	recital
November 22	New York	radio (Coca-Cola Hour)
November 25	Philadelphia	Metropolitan Opera
December 3	Boston	recital
December 16	Lansing	recital
December 18	Detroit	soloist with Detroit Symphony Orchestra

DATE	CITY	TYPE OF ENGAGEMENT
January 2	Havana	recital
January 5	Miami	recital
January 8	Philadelphia	recital
January 11	Norwalk	recital
January 15	New York	recital
January 16, 18	Pittsburgh	soloist with Pittsburgh Symphony
January 25	Boston	recital
February 1	Detroit	radio (Ford Broadcast)
February 3	Baltimore	soloist with National Symphony
February 4	Washington, D. C.	soloist with National Symphony
February 27	Northampton	recital
March 1	Hartford, Conn.	recital
March 5, 6	New Orleans	recital
March 8, 9	Dallas	soloist with Dallas Symphony Orchestra
March 12	Baton Rouge	recital
March 14	Houston	recital
March 16, 17	Tulsa	soloist with Oklahoma State Symphony
March 20	Birmingham, Ala.	recital
March 23	Toledo	soloist with Toledo Symphony
March 24	Milwaukee, Wis.	recital
March 26	Cedar Rapids	recital
March 30	Topeka	recital
April 2	Salt Lake City	recital
April 7	Claremont	recital
April 9	Pasadena	recital
April 12	San Francisco	recital
April 14	Los Angeles	recital
April 16	Stockton	recital
April 28	Vancouver	recital
April 29	Tacoma	recital
May 1	Seattle	recital
May 4	Lawrence, Kansas	recital
May 8	Ann Arbor	soloist with orchestra
May 11	Charleston, W. Va.	recital

METROPOLITAN ENGAGEMENTS

November 25	Philadelphia
December 1	New York
December 6	New York
January 28	New York
February 12	New York
February 17	Philadelphia
February 23	New York

Season 1942–43

DATE	CITY	TYPE OF ENGAGEMENT
August 24	New York	radio (The Telephone Hour)
October 8	Toronto	recital
October 12	St. John, N. B.	recital
October 14	Bangor, Maine	recital
October 16, 17	Philadelphia	soloist with Philadelphia Orchestra
October 20	Schenectady	recital
October 22	Lancaster	recital
October 26	Philadelphia	soloist with Philadelphia Orchestra
October 29	Hamilton, Ontario	recital
November 1	Davenport, Iowa	soloist with orchestra
November 10	New York	soloist with Philadelphia Orchestra
November 16	Pittsburgh	recital
November 18	Boston	recital
December 7	New York	radio (The Telephone Hour)
December 8	Philadelphia	Metropolitan
January 4	Miami	recital
January 6	Havana	recital
January 11	Florence, Ala.	recital
January 15	Lexington	recital
January 17	Indianapolis	recital
January 19	Kansas city	recital
January 21	Rockford	recital
January 24	Washington, D. C.	recital
January 31	New York	Carnegie Hall recital
February 1	New York	radio (The Telephone Hour)
March 4	Portland	recital
March 12	Williamsport	recital
March 15	Nashville	recital
March 18	Charleston, S. C.	recital
March 20	Atlanta	recital
March 22	Savannah	recital
March 24	New York	radio (broadcast of seventy-fifth anniversary celebration of Metropolitan Life Insurance Company)
March 26	Birmingham	recital
March 28	Little Rock	recital
March 31	Chicago	Metropolitan Opera
April 5	El Paso	recital
April 11	San Diego	recital
April 16	Los Angeles	recital
April 20	San Francisco	recital
April 26	Los Angeles	recital
April 28	Phoenix	recital
April 30	Tucson	recital
May 6	Spokane	recital

DATE	CITY	TYPE OF ENGAGEMENT
May 10	Butte, Mont.	recital
May 17	New York	radio (The Telephone Hour)

Season 1943–44

DATE	CITY	TYPE OF ENGAGEMENT
June 14	New York	radio (The Telephone Hour)
July 20 to		
September 5	Buenos Aires	Opera Teatro Colón
September 27	New York	radio (The Telephone Hour)
October 8	Beloit	recital
October 11	Denver	recital
October 13	Lincoln	recital
October 15	Fort Wayne	recital
October 18	Wilkes-Barre	recital
October 21	Philadelphia	recital
October 26	Buffalo	recital
October 29	Montclair	recital
November 2	Akron	recital
November 4, 6	Cleveland	soloist with Cleveland Orchestra
November 9	Chicago	soloist with Cleveland Orchestra
November 11	Urbana	recital
November 15	New York	radio (The Telephone Hour)
December 5	New York	recital, Carnegie Hall
December 20	New York	radio (The Telephone Hour)
December 31,		
January 1, 3	Philadelphia	soloist with Philadelphia Orchestra
January 4	New York	soloist with Philadelphia Orchestra
January 10	Richmond	recital
January 15	New York	radio (What's New)
January 21	Minneapolis	soloist with Minneapolis Symphony
January 24	Lebanon	recital
January 26	Baltimore	soloist with Baltimore Symphony
January 28	Baltimore	recital
February 2	Greenville	recital
February 4	Chattanooga	recital
February 9	Charlotte	recital
February 11	Columbia, S. C.	recital
February 21	New York	radio (The Telephone Hour)
March 2	Rochester	soloist with orchestra
March 6	Jamestown, N. Y.	recital
March 8	Toledo	recital
March 11, 12	Indianapolis	soloist with Indianapolis Symphony Orchestra
March 14	Dallas	recital
March 15	Denton	recital
March 17	Austin	recital

DATE	CITY	TYPE OF ENGAGEMENT
March 20	Houston	soloist with Houston Symphony orchestra
March 21	Shreveport	recital
March 27	Worcester	recital
March 29	London, Ontario	recital
April 3	New York	radio (The Telephone Hour)
April 13	Redlands	recital
April 16	San Francisco	recital
April 19	Fresno	recital
April 22	Oakland	recital
April 25	Los Angeles	recital
April 26	Bakersfield	recital
April 28	Salem, Ore.	recital
April 29	Corvallis	recital
May 1	Portland	recital
May 3	Aberdeen	recital
May 5	Seattle	recital
May 8	Great Falls	recital
May 22	Hollywood	recital

Season 1944–45

August 28	Hollywood	radio (The Telephone Hour)
October 1	New York	soloist with Philharmonic
October 3	Saratoga Springs	recital
October 6	Flint	recital
October 10	Louisville	recital
October 12	Dayton	recital
October 14	Lafayette	recital
October 17, 18	Kansas City	soloist with Kansas City Philharmonic
October 21, 30	Chicago	Chicago Opera Company
October 23	Winnetka	recital
October 26, 28	Cleveland	soloist with Cleveland Orchestra
November 2	Detroit	soloist with Detroit Symphony
November 4	Ann Arbor	recital
November 7	Buffalo	recital
November 9	Bridgeport	recital
November 13	Hollywood	radio (The Telephone Hour)
November 16	Elmira	recital
November 18	Ithaca	recital
November 26	Washington, D. C.	soloist with National Symphony
December 13	Boston	recital
December 25	Hollywood	radio (The Telephone Hour)
January 3	Havana	recital
January 11	Orlando	recital
January 13	Tallahassee	recital

DATE	CITY	TYPE OF ENGAGEMENT
January 15	New Orleans	recital
January 17	Edinburg	recital
January 20	San Antonio	soloist with San Antonio Symphony
January 27	High Point, N. C.	recital
February 15	Atlanta	soloist with Philadelphia Orchestra
February 16	Birmingham	soloist with Philadelphia Orchestra
February 26	Harrisburg	recital
March 1, 2	Chicago	soloist with Chicago Symphony
March 6	St. Louis	recital
March 8	Rochester	soloist with orchestra
March 11	New Brunswick	recital
March 19	Newark	recital
March 26	Hollywood	radio (The Telephone Hour)
April 1	New York	radio broadcast

April 3 through May 1, road tour with Metropolitan Opera. Five performances: Baltimore, Boston, Minneapolis, Milwaukee, Chicago

April 17	Colorado Springs	soloist with Colorado Springs Symphony
April 19	Hutchinson	recital
May 3	Syracuse	recital
May 7	Rock Hill	recital
May 21	New York	radio (The Telephone Hour)

Season 1945–46

June 12 to June 23	Mexico City	soloist with Opera Nacional
July 15	San Rafael	recital
October 1	San Jose	recital
October 16	Chico	recital
October 18	Longview	recital
October 20	Portland	recital
October 22	Seattle	recital
October 24	Vancouver	recital
October 5 to November 3	San Francisco	soloist with San Francisco Opera
November 1	Ontario	recital
November 5	Provo	recital
November 8	Denver	recital
November 12	Ottumwa	recital
November 14	Columbia	recital
November 22, 23, 25	New York	soloist with Philharmonic Symphony
December 2	Detroit	radio (Ford Sunday Evening Hour)
December 4, 5	Madison	recital
December 24	New York	radio (The Telephone Hour)
December 28	Minneapolis	soloist with Minneapolis Symphony
January 3	San Francisco	soloist with San Francisco Opera

DATE	CITY	TYPE OF ENGAGEMENT
January 5	San Diego	recital
January 8	Los Angeles	recital
January 11	Ogden	recital
January 16	Baltimore	soloist with Baltimore Symphony
January 17	Washington, D. C.	soloist with Baltimore Symphony
January 19	Winston-Salem	recital
January 24	Philadelphia	recital
January 28	New York	radio (The Telephone Hour)
February 5	Philadelphia	Metropolitan Opera
February 18	Jackson	recital
February 21	Springfield	recital
February 23, 24	St. Louis	soloist with St. Louis Symphony
February 26	Alexandria	recital
March 1	Fort Worth	recital
March 4	Houston	soloist with Houston Symphony
March 7	Bloomington	recital
March 9	Chicago	recital
March 11	Bloomington	recital
April 4	Boston	Metropolitan Opera
April 8	New York	radio (The Telephone Hour)
April 10	Trenton	recital
April 12	Boston	Metropolitan Opera
April 23	Cleveland	Metropolitan Opera
April 24	Columbus	recital
April 26	Reading	recital
April 29	Bloomington	Metropolitan Opera
May 2	Minneapolis	Metropolitan Opera
May 5	Detroit	radio (Ford Sunday Evening Hour)
May 6	Chicago	Metropolitan Opera
May 9	Cincinnati	recital
May 10	Chicago	Metropolitan Opera
May 13	St. Louis	Metropolitan Opera
May 20	York	recital
May 23	Haddonfield	recital
May 27	New York	radio (The Telephone Hour)
May 30	South Bend	recital

Season 1946–47

August 17, 18	Chicago	soloist with orchestra
October 1	Detroit	Philadelphia La Scala Opera Company
October 5, 6	Chicago	Chicago Opera Company
October 7	Winnipeg	recital
October 9	Fargo	recital
October 19	Battle Creek	recital

DATE	CITY	TYPE OF ENGAGEMENT
October 21	New York	radio (The Telephone Hour)
October 25	Portsmouth, Va.	recital
October 28	Lynchburg	recital
October 31 } November 2	Toronto	recital
November 24	Atlanta	recital
December 8	Oxford, Ohio	recital
December 10	Buffalo	recital
December 23	New York	radio (The Telephone Hour)
February 11, 12	Fort Wayne	soloist with orchestra
February 17	Oberlin	recital
February 21	Rochester	recital
February 23	New York	radio (We the People)
March 4	Philadelphia	Metropolitan Opera
March 6	New York	radio (The Telephone Hour)
March 26	Boston	Metropolitan Opera
April 8	Cleveland	Metropolitan Opera
April 13	Oklahoma City	soloist with Oklahoma State Symphony
April 18	Minneapolis	Metropolitan Opera
April 24	Tuscaloosa	recital
April 28	New Orleans	recital
April 30	Port Arthur, Tex.	recital
May 2	Dallas	Metropolitan Opera
May 4	New York	radio (Prudential Family Hour)
May 5	Lawrence	recital
May 8	Ann Arbor	recital
May 14	St. Louis	Metropolitan Opera
May 21, 22	Billings	recital
May 24	Bozeman	recital
May 27	Yakima	recital
May 29	Salem	recital

Season 1947–48

June 20	Hollywood	radio (Arthur's Place)
July 8	Hollywood	soloist with orchestra, Hollywood Bowl
July 13	Salt Lake City	soloist with Tabernacle Choir
July 21	Philadelphia	soloist with orchestra, Robin Hood Dell
July 24	New York	soloist with orchestra, Lewisohn Stadium
July 30	Milwaukee	soloist with orchestra
September 26 } October 2, 9, 13	San Francisco	San Francisco Opera
October 17	Eugene	recital
October 22	Hollywood	radio (Duffy's Tavern)

APPENDIX

DATE	CITY	TYPE OF ENGAGEMENT
October 23	Los Angeles	San Francisco Opera
October 27	Albuquerque	recital
October 29	El Paso	recital
November 2	Los Angeles	San Francisco Opera
November 5	Denver	recital
November 7	Kansas City	recital
November 10	El Dorado	recital
November 12	Sherman	recital
March 8	Savannah	recital
March 10	Montgomery	recital
March 17	Hanover	recital
March 22, 23	Louisville	soloist with Louisville Philharmonic
March 25	Jackson	recital
March 30	Bowling Green	recital
April 1	Peoria	recital
April 3	Chicago	recital
April 5	St. Paul	recital
April 7	Winnipeg	recital
April 27, 29	East Lansing	recital
May 3	Columbus, Ga.	recital
May 5	Knoxville	recital
May 7	Notre Dame	recital and soloist with orchestra
May 10	Lima, Ohio	recital
May 13	Birmingham	recital
May 17, 19	Havana	recital

Season 1948–49

August 13	Denver	soloist with Denver Symphony Orchestra
August 26	Hollywood	soloist with orchestra (Hollywood Bowl) joint with Melchior
August 30	New York	radio (Voice of Firestone)
October 5	Buffalo	recital
October 9	Cleveland	recital
October 14	Detroit	recital
October 15	Toledo	recital
October 17	Memphis	recital
October 19	Carbondale	recital
October 21	Lexington	recital
October 24	Washington, D. C.	soloist with National Symphony Orchestra
October 26	New Haven	recital
November 14	New York	radio (Fred Allen Show)
February 21	Richmond	recital
February 28	State College, Pa.	recital

DATE	CITY	TYPE OF ENGAGEMENT
March 7	Northfield	recital
March 8	St. Peter	recital
March 11	Minneapolis	soloist with orchestra
March 14, 15	Omaha	soloist with orchestra
March 17	New Castle	recital
March 25, 26, 28	Philadelphia	soloist with Philadelphia orchestra
March 29	New York	soloist with Philadelphia orchestra
April 5, 6	Erie	soloist with Erie Philharmonic Society
April 9 and 10	Cincinnati	soloist with Cincinnati Symphony
April 19	Moscow, Idaho	recital
April 21	Walla Walla	recital
April 23	Portland	recital
April 25	Seattle	recital
April 27	Klamath Falls	recital
May 3	San Francisco	recital
May 6	Pasadena	recital

Season 1949–50

Kansas City
Ontario
Denver
San Antonio
Beaumont
Oxford, Ohio
San Francisco, two Standard Hour Broadcasts
Charlottesville
Cincinnati
University of Miami
Puerto Rico, radio (Duffy's Tavern)
New York, Carnegie Hall American Oil Broadcast
Washington, D. C.
Tampa
Daytona Beach
Syracuse
Toronto, two concerts

Season 1950–51

DATE	CITY	TYPE OF ENGAGEMENT
June 27	Aspen	soloist with orchestra
July 2	Aspen	soloist with orchestra
July 7	Red Rocks	soloist with orchestra
August 3	Hollywood	soloist with orchestra (Hollywood Bowl)
August 20	New York	radio (NBC Summer Symphony)

Date	City	Type of Engagement
September 4	Boston	recital
October 5	Ann Arbor	recital
October 11	Wellesley	recital
October 16	Durham	recital
October 18	Houston	recital
October 20	Oklahoma City	recital
October 23	El Paso	soloist with El Paso Symphony Orchestra
October 29	Sioux City	soloist with Sioux City Symphony Orchestra
November 1	Amarillo	recital
November 4	Salt Lake City	soloist with Utah Symphony Orchestra
November 7, 8	Kansas City	soloist with Kansas City Philharmonic
November 10	Atlanta	recital
November 11	Athens	recital
November 15, 16	Louisville	soloist with Louisville Philharmonic
November 29	New York	TV (Jimmy Durante Show)
January 21	Jersey City	recital
January 24	New York	TV (Jimmy Durante Show)
February 13, 14	Toronto	soloist with Toronto Symphony Orchestra
February 20	Washington, D. C.	recital
February 23	St. Petersburg	recital
February 26	Jackson	recital
March 3	New York	radio (soloist with NBC Orchestra)
April 10	Akron	recital
April 13-14	Cincinnati	soloist with Cincinnati Symphony Orchestra
April 17	Huntington, W. Va.	recital
April 22	Richmond, Cal.	radio (The Standard Hour)
April 25	Pasadena	recital
April 28	Hollywood	recital
May 1	San Francisco	recital

Season 1951–52

June 17	San Rafael	recital
August 19	New York	radio (NBC Symphony Broadcast)
October 6	New York	TV (Jimmy Durante Show)
October 7	New York	TV (Celebrity Time)
October 27	Helena	recital
October 29	Portland	soloist with Portland Symphony Orchestra
November 11	Lexington	soloist with Cleveland Symphony
November 14	Hamilton, Ont.	recital
November 19	Larchmont-Mamaroneck	recital

DATE	CITY	TYPE OF ENGAGEMENT
November 27	Buffalo	recital
December 29	Los Angeles	TV (Jimmy Durante Show)
January 9	Springfield	recital
January 30	Gainesville	soloist with Symphony Society of Central Florida
January 31	Greenville	soloist with Symphony Society of Central Florida
February 1	Spartanburg	soloist with Symphony Society of Central Florida
February 2	High Point	soloist with Symphony Society of Central Florida
February 15	Albuquerque	recital
February 18	Lubbock	recital
February 20	Topeka	recital
February 24	Memphis	recital
February 25	Highland Park	recital
February 28	Wilmington, N. C.	recital
March 3	Orlando	soloist with Symphony Orchestra of Central Florida
March 20	New York	recital and joint appearance with William Primrose, Waldorf-Astoria Ballroom
April 15	Honolulu	recital

Season 1952–53

April 22 to June 28	tour of Japan and Far East	concerts
August 28	Hollywood	soloist with orchestra (Hollywood Bowl)
September 30	Claremont	recital
October 2	Modesto	recital
October 6	Seattle	recital
October 8	Spokane	recital
October 22	Norfolk	recital
October 24	Roanoke	recital
October 29	Birmingham	soloist with Birmingham Civic Symphony
November 9	Davenport	soloist with Tri-City Symphony
November 11	Denver	soloist with Denver Symphony
November 17	Ottawa	recital
November 23, 24	Miami Beach	soloist with Miami Symphony
December 1	Evansville	recital
December 3	Nashville	recital
December 6	Cape Girardeau	recital
December 9	Honolulu	recital
February 24	Brooklyn	recital

DATE	CITY	TYPE OF ENGAGEMENT
February 26	Haddonfield	recital
February 27	Westfield	recital
March 1	Elmhurst	recital
March 5	Waterloo	recital
March 11, 21	New York	Metropolitan Opera
March 23	Sarasota	recital
April 7	Los Angeles	recital
April 11	Beverly Hills	TV (All Star Revue—Jimmy Durante)
April 13	Los Angeles	recital
April 16, 17	Tucson	recital

Season 1953–54

July 24	Red Rocks	soloist with Denver Symphony
July 31	Ravinia Park	soloist with orchestra
August 4	Wheeling	recital
August 6	Ravinia Park	soloist with orchestra
October 19	Eureka	recital
October 20	Coos Bay	recital
October 22	Albany, Ga.	recital
October 24	Beverly Hills, Ill.	recital
October 26	La Crosse	soloist with La Crosse Symphony
October 31 ⎫ November 1 ⎭	Davenport	soloist with Tri-City Symphony
November 3	Fort Wayne	soloist with orchestra
November 5	Midland	recital
November 9	Knoxville	recital
November 12	Belleville	recital
November 15	Des Moines	soloist with orchestra
November 18, 19	Salt Lake City, Ogden	soloist with Utah Symphony of Salt Lake
November 23	Missoula	recital
November 25	Richland	recital
March 20	San Antonio	soloist with San Antonio Symphony
March 23	Hattiesburg	recital
March 25	Dallas	recital
March 30	Danville	recital
April 5	Grand Forks	recital
April 7	Casper	recital
April 9	Burlington, Cal.	recital
April 10	Carmel	recital
April 12	Riverside	recital
April 13	Monrovia	recital